NEW YORK TIM[...]

Featu[...]

60 MINUTES, ANDERSON COOPER 360, CBS THIS MORNING, FOX & FRIENDS, FOX BUSINESS CHANNEL, FOX NEWS

PRAISE FOR
EXTORTION

"We recommend [Schweizer's] book to you highly—a terrific book."
— **Lou Dobbs, Fox Business Channel**

"A great book—well researched." — **Sean Hannity, Fox News**

"Rich in detail." — **Norah O'Donnell,** *CBS This Morning*

"The truth eventually comes out . . . through the work of individuals like Mr. Schweizer . . . If ever there were an issue on which left and right could come together, it's this one." — *New York Times*

"Schweizer names guilty parties and specific cases committed by politicians from both sides of the aisle . . . He exposes powerful figures in politics, law firms and corporations." — *Forbes*

"The missing link that helps you understand what's going on in Washington these days . . . With example after example, Schweizer describes how the money flows into Washington and how the politicians control those flows . . . [*Extortion* is] well worth your time."
— *Washington Times*

Also by Peter Schweizer

Throw Them All Out:
How Politicians and Their Friends
Get Rich Off Insider Stock Tips, Land Deals,
and Cronyism That Would Send the Rest of Us to Prison

Architects of Ruin:
How a Gang of Radical Activists and Liberal Politicians Destroyed
Trillions of Dollars in Wealth in the Pursuit of Social Justice

Makers and Takers:
Why Conservatives Work Harder, Feel Happier, Have Closer
Families, Take Fewer Drugs, Give More Generously,
Value Honesty More, Are Less Materialistic and Envious, Whine
Less . . . and Even Hug Their Children More Than Liberals

Do as I Say (Not as I Do):
Profiles in Liberal Hypocrisy

Reagan's War:
The Epic Story of His Forty-Year Struggle and
Final Triumph over Communism

Victory:
The Reagan Administration's Secret Strategy
That Hastened the Collapse of the Soviet Union

Peter Schweizer

EXTORTION

How Politicians Extract Your Money, Buy Votes, and Line Their Own Pockets

Mariner Books
Houghton Mifflin Harcourt
BOSTON • NEW YORK

To
Bernadette Casey Smith and Owen Smith
with humble thanks for their friendship, support, encouragement,
and wisdom over the years

First Mariner Books edition 2014

Copyright © 2013 by Peter Schweizer

Library of Congress Cataloging-in-Publication Data
Schweizer, Peter, date.
Extortion : how politicians extract your money, buy votes,
and line their own pockets / Peter Schweizer.
pages cm
ISBN 978-0-544-10334-4   ISBN 978-0-544-33455-7 (pbk.)
1. Political corruption — United States. I. Title.
JK2249.S34 2013
320.973 — dc23
2013026342

5 2021

Printed in the United States of America
5 2021

4500821736

CONTENTS

INTRODUCTION

"Throw Fear"

You're only as good as your last envelope.

— SILVIO DANTE, *THE SOPRANOS*, 1999

THE POTOMAC RIVER that snakes by Washington, D.C., was given its name by the local native Americans centuries ago. Potomac was the name of a local tribe. According to some accounts, the word means "the place where goods are off-loaded," or "the place where tribute is paid." As journalists say, that latter meaning is a fact too good to check.

It is often said that "money is corrupting politics." And as ever, this is true. Outside interests, from labor unions to large corporations, are influencing and distorting our government in the search for favorable policies. And these interests are well prepared to push money and special favors into Washington, D.C., in order to get them.

But a deeper, more sinister problem that has been overlooked better explains the dismal state of our national government: *politics is corrupting money*. While we have focused on the power that contributors have over officials, we have largely ignored the power that officials have over contributors. We have focused on the *buyers* of influence (those outside special interests), but paid little heed to the *sellers* of influence — bureaucrats and politicians.

In short, we have come to believe the problem in Washington is a sort of legalized bribery. If outside interests can only be held at bay, we can and will get better leadership.

But what if we are wrong? What if the problem is not bribery . . . but extortion? What if the Permanent Political Class in Washington, made up of individuals from both political parties, is using its coercive *public* power to not only stay in office but to threaten others and to extract wealth, and in the bargain pick up *private* benefits for themselves, their friends, and their families?

What we often think of as the bribery of our national leaders by powerful special interests in Washington may actually make more sense understood as extortion by government officials — elected and unelected. Far from being passive recipients of money and favors, they make it happen. They leverage their positions to shake the money tree for themselves and their political allies. And as we will see, they do so using a variety of methods, many of which you probably have never heard of before.

The assumption is that we need to protect politicians from outside influences. But how about protecting ourselves from the politicians?

Journalists and academics look at politics through a mythical lens that harkens back to Aristotle and Plato: politics is the business of producing correct policies. We may dispute what is correct, but in the traditional view, that is the goal of the process. Media reports on government actions, whether debates, legislation, or regulation, almost always present them in terms of pure policy. New laws are for a specific purpose, perhaps even a noble one.

But what if that isn't the real point of the exercise? What if politics is really largely about fund-raising and making money? The commercial motives of the Permanent Political Class in acting or not acting are rarely questioned and virtually never fully understood.

Popular culture takes the same naive approach. We all love the image of Jimmy Stewart in *Mr. Smith Goes to Washington*—the idealistic new senator seduced and targeted by powerful outside interests. "Lost causes are the only ones worth fighting for," Stewart's character says as he fights the lobbyists and the political machine. Virtually every new candidate for office runs as an outsider, vowing to take on special interests. If only he can resist those outside forces, everything will be okay. When bad things happen in Washington, we assume the problem is that our national leaders have given in to seductive outside forces, the "special interests." From time to time we erect laws and rules to protect politicians from these temptations.

But what if we have it backwards? What if the greater culprits are *inside* the halls of power in Washington rather than on the outside?

Some at the heart of Washington power have hinted at this cold, hard reality. As Edward Kangas, former global chairman of Deloitte Touche, put it: "What has been called legalized bribery looks like extortion to us. . . . I know from personal experience and from other executives that it's not easy saying no to appeals for cash from powerful members of Congress or their operatives. Congress can have a major impact on business. . . . The threat may be veiled, but the message is clear: failing to donate could hurt your company."[1]

Former Microsoft chief operating officer Robert Herbold told me, "You're crazy if you don't play along. They will go after you." Ray Plank, the founder and former chairman of Apache Corporation, has seen his company cough up to both parties for fifty years.[2] He told me that campaign money and lobbying contracts are "protection money. It's what you expect from the mafia."[3]

Former politicians who once played the game now admit the same thing. As former senator David Boren puts it, "Donors . . . feel victimized. Now that I've left office, I sometimes hear from large donors that they feel 'shaken down.'"[4] Former senator Russ Feingold admits, "It's not like businesses and business leaders call up politicians and beg them, could I please give you some money? It goes the other way, which is that people are called constantly by politicians when you have a system like this, or their representatives, or their allegedly independent agents. And it's more like extortion than it's like bribery."[5] One survey of corporate executives conducted by the Committee for Economic Development found that half gave to political candidates because they "fear adverse consequences for themselves or their industry if they turn down requests."[6]

Politics in modern America has become a lucrative business, an industry that has less to do with policy and a lot more to do with accessing money and favors. As we will see, bills and regulations are often introduced not to effect policy change, but as vehicles for shaking down people for those money and favors. Indeed, the motive on both sides often has nothing to do with creating a "correct" policy, but instead is often about maximizing profits.

Raising campaign money is not just about winning elections and staying in power. As we will see, the Permanent Political Class has come up with all sorts of creative ways to transfer those funds into other pockets, which can be accessed to enhance their own wealth and lifestyle. And they have carved out convenient loopholes in the law that allow lawmakers to legally convert votes into cash.

The same goes for lobbying. Hiring a lobbyist aligned with a powerful politician is more important than hiring a lobbyist with a certain expertise or experience. Hiring a former staff member or family member is better still. It's the favor that matters. Sometimes such favors are requested by politicians. Other times they don't need to ask out loud. Several powerful politicians have multiple members of their immediate family (spouses and children) who make big money from lobbying.[7]

Over the course of American history there have been repeated attempts to restrict the flow of money going into political parties and campaigns. Contrary to what you might have been told in school or by the media, the advocates of these efforts have not just been good-government, public-spirited citizens. They have also been corporations and individuals tired of being shaken down.

At the turn of the twentieth century, extortion was a widespread problem in Washington. The method was perfected by Mark Hanna, who served as President William McKinley's chief fund-raiser. (Hanna once famously said, "There are two things that are important in politics. The first is money and I can't remember what the second one is.") Issuing a blunt warning to large businesses, Hanna gave them an "assessment," an "invoice" of sorts, that they were expected to give to the Republican Party. If they failed to pay it, they would face big trouble. Standard Oil was assessed a $250,000 fee. Banks were expected to pay a fee of 1 percent of their capital.[8] By 1900, when McKinley was up for reelection, the White House was able to shake down the business community for $2.5 million (over $67 million in 2012 dollars). It sounds relatively small by today's hyperbloated standards, but at the time it was huge.

By 1904, the problem had become exponentially worse after the political class systematized the extortion technique: Teddy Roosevelt appointed George Cortelyou, who was the U.S. secretary of commerce and labor, to head up the Republican National Committee. In his cabinet capacity, Cortelyou had oversight of the Bureau of Corporations, which was responsible for investigating any corporations whose business crosses state lines. As the *New York Times* put it at the time, "the chief of the Department which has become the custodian of corporation secrets [was] put at the head of the partisan committee whose principal function [was] to collect campaign contributions which come chiefly from great corporations."[9] In one instance, several Chicago packing companies under investigation by the government's Bureau of Corporations were hit up for $50,000 in campaign donations.[10]

Cortelyou's demands became so great that companies decided to do something about it, in the form of the Tillman Act of 1907 (named for its champion, Senator Benjamin "Pitchfork Ben" Tillman, now mostly remembered for his racist, segregationist beliefs). The Tillman Act made it illegal for businesses to give campaign contributions to federal candidates. Many corporations were tired of being extorted, and they enthusiastically supported the bill. As one Republican official noted after the law passed, corporate leaders were "entranced with happiness. . . . [T]hey are now in a position to throw us unceremoniously out of the door if we ask them for a penny. . . . They mean to take advantage of the laws forbidding them to give money for political purposes." (In the 1940s, the act was amended to apply to unions.[11]) A *New York Times* editorial entitled "Happy Corporations" at the time quoted a "great financial authority": "'[We] welcome . . . this legislation with very much the same emotions with which a serf would his liberation from a tyrannous autocrat.'" The *Times* went on: "[The act] will lessen a very mean and sordid practice of blackmail. The beneficiaries of [regulation] will still find methods of furnishing the sinews of war to the party that controls their favors, but the great number of corporations that have suffered extortion through weakness and cowardice will have their backbones stiffened, and parties will be put to it to fill their coffers by really voluntary contributions."[12]

More recently, reforms that ended the practice of "soft money" contributions came as a result of increasingly extortive demands by both parties for large donations from outside companies. (Ray Plank was one of those who fought successfully to shut off the soft money spigot.) For the Republicans, the master of this sort of fund-raising was House Majority Leader Tom DeLay of Texas. DeLay created a corporate enemies list, telling companies that if they failed to make large enough donations, there would be legislative repercussions. For the Democrats, the equally heavy hand was Terry McAuliffe, who organized elaborate fund-raisers for President Bill Clinton, including barbecues where corporations were expected to cough up $500,000 to "honor" the president. Charles Kolb, president of the Committee of Economic Development, expressed the attitude of many corporate leaders pushing for a ban on soft money donations when he said, "We're tired of being hit up and shaken down."[13]

Washington, D.C., is beset by gridlock and partisan fighting. Few substantive issues seem to get settled. Popular explanations for the gridlock focus on the increased polarization of congressional districts, and therefore of members of the House, with too few deal-making moderates in the middle. This explanation is accurate — but not the whole story.

Reams of legislation are introduced every year that have little to do with the politician's constituents. Why are our representatives spending so much time on bills that have very little to do with their own voters?

In recent years, despite thousands of bills introduced into Congress every year, only a small percentage (approximately 5 percent) become law.[14]

Of course, what matters for laws is quality, not quantity. But why would legislators bother to introduce so many hopeless bills? What if they are not even designed to pass? What if they are instead designed to make money? The cold harsh reality in Washington is this: the very conditions that are so maddening for most Americans—gridlock, problems being ignored, hyperpartisanship—are the very conditions that are most lucrative for the Permanent Political Class.

Washington may not be working for citizens, but it's working quite well for members of the Permanent Political Class who profit handsomely.

While the rest of the country looks on in frustration and anger, gridlock and a handful of massively complex laws are actually evidence that Washington *is* working, at least for those in power. The system is functioning precisely how they want it to function. Gridlock, complex laws, highly technical bills, and regulations that target specific groups have a *commercial* purpose for the Permanent Political Class.

Ray Plank, whose company has given to both parties over the decades, believes that gridlock exists because that's where the money is.[15] "There's no money to be made by fixing problems," Plank told me. "So why are they going to fix them?"[16] In many cases "gridlock" really means "lobbyist-lock" or "donor-lock," which pits several sides against each other. It's an arms race between two or more sides, and the Permanent Political Class is the ultimate winner.

What goes on in Washington's halls of power has less to do with lawmaking than with moneymaking. Far from being about policy, much of what happens in Washington is about extorting money. This isn't to say there are not people in leadership positions with deeply held convictions. But from a commercial standpoint, there is money to be made by passing, or threatening to pass, certain laws. And the two political parties, far from being mortal enemies, as often depicted, desperately need each other for these same commercial reasons. Indeed, party and ideological differences matter less than you think.

Politics in Washington is a lot like professional wrestling. What seems like vicious combat to the uninitiated is actually choreo-graphed acting. Professional wrestlers face off in the ring, shout-ing and pointing fingers and appearing to hate each other. But in fact, they are partners in a commercial enterprise to entertain and extract money from an audience. No matter who wins the match, everyone gets paid.

John Hofmeister, who served as the president of Shell Oil Com-pany, recounted for me how it works. In his appearance before a congressional committee in 2008, politicians from both parties grilled him about the oil industry and high oil prices. Congress-woman Maxine Waters even threatened to nationalize the oil indus-try.[17] Ignore for a minute the question of who is responsible for high oil prices and consider what happened after those lively hearings according to Hofmeister. "After the hearings, a lot of those who had been attacking Shell asked me to donate to their campaigns or help to organize a fund-raiser for them."[18]

From a commercial standpoint, conflict, division, and calam-ity are good for business in Washington too. To be sure, both sides have their true believers, but the Permanent Political Class is also filled with entrepreneurs looking to maximize the opportunity to make money and increase their power base. It's not uncommon for the same lobbying firm to be advising both sides in a political race or both sides on an important bill.

Microsoft's Bob Herbold put it simply: "They are only interested in themselves." Herbold has done considerable business in Asia, which has a reputation for payoffs and bribes. "There is corruption everywhere," he told me. "But we are masters over those countries at legalizing corruption."[19]

Consider, for example, one particular highly confrontational bill. Democrats have threatened to impose a tax on Internet sales in the form of a bill that would allow states to tax online purchases, whether or not the retailer has a physical presence in the state. Each time it comes up, there are financial opportunities for both Democrats and Republicans. Democratic lobbyists could be hired by large firms that want to "talk down" the bill's sponsors from proceeding. Those Democrats who sponsor the bill can solicit campaign donations from Internet retailers who hope their donation might convince the sponsors to kill the bill. Republicans, on the other side, might denounce the bill as a terrible idea that is destructive to the economy, but the threat of its passage is a moneymaking opportunity for them too. Stopping the tax comes with a price: campaign donations and lobbying arrangements for their friends. After all, they are the only thing standing between the retailers and financial Armageddon. John Hofmeister calls this practice "legalized corruption where the corrupters (elected members) have assumed the legal authority to set in motion the policies and practices that manipulate the corruptees (vulnerable donors)."[20]

The bill might go away; the executioner might take away the guillotine for a time. But it will return. The bill will reemerge, and the money will be extorted again by both sides. Sometimes bills only finally pass after the donors have been wrung dry.

Solving problems and settling issues is good lawmaking, but it's not lucrative. It is gridlock, confusion, and rehashing fights that create streams of income — like an annuity — for the Permanent Political Class.

This sort of extortion is illegal if we practice it in our private lives. Threatening to harm someone if he or she refuses to fork over cash is classic extortion. Twenty years ago, several American cities were plagued by stoplight windshield washers called "squeegee men." Their approach was simple: They would approach your car at a stoplight with a washcloth or a squeegee in one hand, then begin wiping the windshield, expecting payment from you. And if you refused? The threat went unstated: Would the squeegee man run a key along your exterior to ruin your paint job? Smash your window? Needless to say, the squeegee men usually got paid.

This sort of street-level extortion was not tolerated. New York City and other municipalities cracked down. Squeegee men were arrested for jaywalking or other crimes. New York mayor Rudy Giuliani argued that this sort of behavior created a hostile environment. (Studies at the time showed that women drivers felt particularly threatened.) Even in Canada, the city of Toronto outlawed the practice under a "safe streets law."

But as we will see, for government officials, this sort of extortive behavior is okay. Instead of standing on a street corner with a squeegee and a scowl, these extorters wear nice suits, speak eloquently, and know how to present themselves in front of a television camera. They dismiss their extortion as "just politics," similar to how some defenders of the squeegee men argued that they were just trying to make a living. But in Washington the extortionists do considerably more damage and make far more from their extortion racket than the squeegee men ever could.

The Permanent Political Class operates far less like Jimmy Stewart in *Mr. Smith Goes to Washington* than like the organized crime lords in *The Sopranos* or *The Godfather*. I'm not arguing that politicians are criminals (however tempting that argument might be for some people). Indeed, I'm going to argue that they practice an effective and lucrative form of "legal extortion." But don't try this at home. Because of the ways in which American laws are written, politicians and bureaucrats are able to employ extortion techniques that would send the rest of us to prison. Likewise, lawmakers have written the laws in such a way that they can sell their votes — and can do so legally.

In the classic mob film *The Godfather*, Michael Corleone, the Godfather's son who becomes the Boss, recalls a disputed agreement. "Luca Brasi held a gun to his head—and my father assured him that either his brains or his signature would be on the contract." Members of the Permanent Political Class, of course, don't threaten physical violence. But they do extract their money by threatening a sort of "financial violence" to those they extort.

The Chicago Mob (often called "the Outfit") believed that the best way to extort people was to "throw fear" at them.[21] In Washington, politicians can throw fear at individuals in a lot of different ways.

If you are a politician, the key is linking what you do in your official duties to a sophisticated fund-raising apparatus. Washington politicians have direct, detailed, and regular communication between their congressional staffers—who write, analyze, and assess bills, as well as perform constituent services—and their congressional fund-raising teams. This allows politicians and their fundraisers to target those who might be vulnerable to political extortion. Sometimes you have to wonder: who is more important, the chief of staff or the chief fund-raiser?

Even a minor request can become an opportunity to extort. In August 2012, for example, Congressman Tim Bishop of New York squeezed a donation out of a constituent who needed help getting a permit. Eric Semler wanted to celebrate his son's bar mitzvah with a fireworks display near his house, but he ran into local resistance. Semler contacted Bishop's office. But before anyone did anything to help him, Semler received a request from the congressman's campaign staff seeking $10,000 in campaign contributions. The congressman's daughter wrote to Semler, "Our Finance Chair, Bob Sillerman suggested to my dad that you were interested in contributing to his campaign and that I should be in touch directly with you." The request came three days before the party.[22] Semler ended up donating $5,000 and said the congressman's staff solicited him. Bishop said Semler "volunteered the money as a show of thanks."

This is just a minor and inartful form of extortion. But as we will see, far more significant opportunities can be pursued, whether artfully or not. Studies demonstrate that beyond those who have an interest in politics, "many donors are reluctant to give contributions and only do so when asked."[23]

There's a lexicon for modern political extortion. Politicians from some parts of the country refer to "milker bills," which are intended to "milk" companies and individuals to pass or stop legislation that will benefit or hurt them. Others call them "juicer bills" because they are introduced largely for the purpose of squeezing money out of the target. Some call them "fetcher bills" because they are drafted and introduced to "fetch" lavish and lucrative attention from lobbyists and powerful interests. Whatever you call them, these bills are designed not to make good law, but rather to raise money. The politicians are not necessarily interested in having the bill pass. Often these bills are very narrow in focus and would do little to benefit their constituents.

Indeed, politicians often don't want these bills to pass because if they do, the opportunity for future extortion is removed. A good milker bill can be introduced repeatedly, milking donors year after year. Laws that do pass, particularly narrowly focused ones, are purposely designed to expire every few years so politicians can then revisit the issue and "juice" the same people. The best kind of all is the "double-milker," or "double-juicer," which is designed to play two deep-pocketed industries against one another, setting off a lucrative arms race. Members of Congress can milk each bill multiple times. In addition to their regular campaign committees, they also have leadership political action committees (PACs) and joint fundraising committees — all of which can grab a teat and squeeze. This money can be funneled to other politicians to buy votes or converted into accounts that enhance a politician's lifestyle.

Milker bills have a long history in some of our most corrupt cities. The muckraker journalist Lincoln Steffens first wrote about them in his 1904 classic *The Shame of the Cities*. He described a state of corruption whereby politicians introduced "strike bills" that would affect certain businesses. The bill would be so detrimental to a group of businesses that they would be driven to pay large sums of money to "put the strike bill to sleep."[24] That was politics on a local level, where corruption could more easily remain hidden. Today it happens on an even larger, national scale in Washington, D.C.

The practice is the same, but the payments have become much bigger. The extortion process with a milker bill occurs in steps. A congressman or a senator announces that he is gathering data on a certain subject and doing "prep work" on a particular piece of threatening legislation. He and his cosponsors consult with the Office of Legislative Counsel in the Capitol Building on how the bill should be drafted and reach out to fellow legislators to gather support. So far, so good. They also reach out to lobbyists, most especially former staffers who are now lobbyists, and let them know what is planned. Next, a call is placed to their fund-raisers so they can zero in on lucrative targets.

Then the politicians hold committee hearings and hand out draft versions of the legislation. Along the way, their personal staffs communicate with fund-raising aides, who begin soliciting the targeted companies who stand to win or lose with the bill's passage. If they play it right, they can extract money and favors from both sides. (Presidents do this too, but instead of using legislation, they announce that the federal bureaucracy is looking at a new regulation.) The point of the exercise is not necessarily to pass the bill or regulation, but to exert threats of impending legislation to extort benefits.

No explicit verbal threats, or quid pro quo, need be made. The "squeegee men" in New York City would not utter a word about extortion when they began "cleaning" windshields. They didn't have to. It's the same in Washington. Politicians and their fund-raisers usually don't call a donor and state outright that the donor has to give money or do a favor. Politicians and their fund-raisers have plenty of ways to signal their intentions loud and clear. The Permanent Political Class is well aware of the power it possesses. Its members don't need to shout. As John Hofmeister told me, "These engagements themselves take place with carefully orchestrated behaviors, such that a distant observer would never know what is actually taking place."[25]

So what you find is that corporations and wealthy individuals often have to "walk both sides of the street" by giving to both candidates in a congressional race. Or they feel they must give generously to a powerful congressman who faces no challenger. As we will see, members of Congress often have very successful campaign fund-raisers immediately *after* an election. Conversely, giving to the wrong candidate in a tight race can make a donor a target. One lobbyist recounts how his firm gave money to the loser of an election (a Democrat). After the election, the winner (a Republican) called the lobbyist and asked for a donation that was much larger than the check the lobbyist had cut to the Democrat. Why the difference in amount? "The late train is a hell of a lot more expensive than the early train," he was told.[26]

Companies know how the game gets played. When a small defense firm was invited to a congressional wine-tasting fund-raising event for Congressman Jim Moran a couple of years ago, senior executives tried to figure out who had the time to attend. The one executive who could make it was a nondrinker. When he protested, the company's chief technology officer emailed him: "You don't have to drink. You just have to give."[27]

Timing is everything in comedy—and in extortion.

Americans write checks to politicians for a host of reasons. Sometimes it is out of admiration. Sometimes it is out of fear. To extract the maximum amount of revenues in the shortest period of time, politicians from both sides have discovered the importance of asking for money at just the right time. Along with milker bills, another popular method of extraction used by a congressman in a position of leadership or the chair of a powerful committee is the "tollbooth." The Speaker of the House or a powerful chairman will erect one on the eve of an important vote. Donations are solicited days before a vote is scheduled to take place. If the tribute offered by those who want the bill to pass is not large enough, the vote will be delayed. Tom DeLay made an art of this practice. As we will see, Speaker of the House John Boehner has perfected it.

Presidents operate in a similar manner. The vast machinery of the executive branch affects every sector of the economy and can be leveraged for donations. President Richard Nixon was a master at this. He regularly mixed the regulatory powers under his control with his fund-raising needs. Dairy farmers who made up the Associated Milk Producers accused the Nixon White House of extorting money from them by threatening antitrust action by the Department of Justice unless they coughed up hundreds of thousands of dollars. Likewise, American Airlines was reportedly shaken down for campaign donations to avoid retaliation by the Civil Aeronautics Board.[28]

As we will see, the Obama administration is using a similar approach when it comes to extorting and threatening large companies, using legal ambiguities and threats of criminal action to extort campaign contributions or to attempt to intimidate those who are donating to their opponents. It's an exercise in power that also enriches the political and business allies of senior administration officials at the Department of Justice.

Even bureaucrats can get in this game, though they don't need campaign funds. Indeed, extortion is a regular part of bureaucratic behavior. Many of the complex rules and regulations that we have to comply with are written by unelected bureaucrats deep in the bowels of government. There are about 170 federal entities that issue regulations. There are about 60 federal departments, agencies, and commissions, with about 240,000 full-time employees who make and enforce them. Americans are awash in regulations that are increasingly complex and difficult for the average person to understand.[29]

Simple rules are easy to follow. Complex rules require an interpreter. The Depression-era Glass-Steagall Act, which reformed the entire U.S. banking system, was thirty-five pages long. The recent Dodd-Frank financial reform bill is *twenty-three times* longer — and many of the new rules have not even been written yet. Even savvy Wall Street attorneys say they are befuddled in their efforts to understand what major portions of the law actually mean.

Famed criminal defense attorney and civil libertarian Harvey Silverglate and Harvard law professor Alan Dershowitz believe that many professionals in America — particularly lawyers, accountants, bankers, and doctors — commit on average three felonies a day *without knowing it.*[30]

Why is this happening? Because of liberals running rampant? Bureaucrats with bad grammar? Lobbyists in control? The deeper answer can be found by the traditional route: follow the money. The commercial possibilities for bureaucrats explain what's really happening. There is money to be made in creating complex rules and laws that nobody can understand. Those who write these laws and regulations can leave their posts and charge companies large fees to decipher the very regulations they wrote. This has become a common practice, a form of indirect extortion. *You might be breaking a law and not know it,* the pitch goes. *Pay me money and I will tell you if you are or not.* We will see this in the case of Dodd-Frank. And elsewhere: the author of complex Medicare reforms in the Bush

White House was able to cash out and charge health care companies $1,000 an hour to interpret the convoluted regulations he wrote.

The United States has relied on English common law to guide our thinking on extortion. *Blackstone's Law Dictionary* defines extortion as "an abuse of public justice, which consists in any officer's unlawfully taking, by colour of his office, from any man, any money or thing of value, that is not due to him, or more than is due, or before it is due."[31] What we often see as bribery is often actually a form of extortion. The two, of course, overlap. If you give money to a politician, it can both (a) get you unfairly *favorable* treatment and (b) protect you from unfairly *negative* treatment. Donating to campaigns and hiring lobbyists are essentially forms of paying insurance money. In the annals of case law, courts have conceded that "the line is a fine one" between "an altogether 'voluntary' payment" and those who are giving money or favors "in fear of retaliation."[32]

Or, as one professor puts it, "the difference between legalized extortion and illegal corruption is largely definitional, the incentives are virtually the same except that the cost of corruption might be punishment or jail." The simple fact is that bribery and extortion are "not distinctly different." The same transaction might be both. In fact, corrupt officials who take bribes are often prosecuted under statutes forbidding extortion. As federal judge Richard Posner has put it, the difference between extortion and bribery is difficult to determine because in either case the politician or bureaucrat is *active*. They are not the passive recipients of money or favors. Cows don't milk themselves. And oranges don't juice themselves.[33]

Because of the way our laws are written, this political extortion is extralegal rather than illegal.[34] So long as politicians and bureaucrats don't explicitly demand a quid pro quo, their actions are not illegal. As long as they don't spell out precisely what they are selling and demanding what they will get in return, they are fine.

But it's different for the rest of us. By Congress's standard, the squeegee men in New York City weren't committing extortion either. And the Mafia street thug who offers a business "protection" from violent criminals on the street would also not be guilty of extortion by this definition — so long as there is no explicit quid pro quo. If a threat is only implied, and the mafiosi are subject to Congress's rules, they can extort to their heart's content. In the real underworld, there was reportedly a mobster named William "Butch" Petrocelli who was so intimidating that he simply stared at the target. He didn't need to utter a word. The target knew what he meant — and gave him the extortion money. Perhaps he missed a lucrative calling in politics, where such a skill would not have landed him in jail.[35]

The great thing for the Permanent Political Class is that they get paid either way. They can get paid for doing something, or they can get paid for not doing something. As they propose legislation that will harm or help certain companies and industries, they are simultaneously calling those affected and soliciting donations, on both sides of the issue. This is a wealth strategy that is unavailable to anyone in America today outside of politics.

At least in one respect, dealing with the Mafia is easier. With the Mafia, businesses can feel confident that if they pay the fee, no harm will come. Mobsters don't like other mobsters extorting on their turf. But in Washington paying for protection only buys that peace for a little while, and only from certain politicians. A competing politician can always step up and demand more.

And like the Mafia, political extortion can often involve a web of family members, who extract from the target on several levels: campaign contributions and favors for the politicians, jobs for the politicians' children, and lobbying contracts for their spouses.

The rampant extortion in Washington explains why government continues to grow, regardless of who is in power. And it also explains why government is getting meaner. It's more lucrative for the Permanent Political Class that way. Just as the Mafia likes to expand its turf to seek more targets for extortion, an expanding government increases the number of targets for a shakedown. And the meaner government gets, the more often threats of extortion are successful. No wonder that now a large portion of the American people distrust the federal government, regardless of who is in power. According to Pew Research, only 30 percent of the American people trust the federal government. This also explains why Transparency International, an international organization that tracks "perceptions of corruption" in countries around the world, has the United States well below Singapore and Barbados on its "corruption perception index."[36] Meanwhile, Washington, D.C., and the Permanent Political Class prosper.

The numbers are startling. The World Bank scores what it calls "worldwide governance indicators" and measures each country's "control of corruption." In recent years, the United States has continued to slip in the rankings.[37] Since 2009, the United States has dropped to the very bottom of developed countries in that category. The World Economic Forum has created a similar scale as part of its *Global Competitiveness Report*. Here, too, the United States scores below most other developed countries when it comes to dealing with corruption.[38]

What happens in Washington doesn't stay in Washington. It undermines the entire country.

Is it any wonder that the Italian Mafia was initially developed in Sicily — by politicians?[39]

2

AMERICA'S MOST EXPENSIVE TOLLBOOTH

Politics is the art of putting people under obligation to you.
— JACOB ARVEY, ILLINOIS PARTY BOSS (1990)

THEY CALLED IT THE "MOB TAX."

If you are in the New York City construction business, you need permits from a myriad of government agencies to get your construction project approved. For quite a while, the mob controlled everything — not just unions but also the city employees who approved the permits. So you had to pay a fee, or a "tax," to the mob to make the normal permitting process work for you. Paying the mob to get institutions to function the way they were supposed to was just the regular cost of doing business in the New York City construction industry.

If a policeman expected extra payment for performing his duties, or an IRS employee demanded some personal benefit for doing what he was hired to do, either one would end up in trouble with the law. Each could be charged with extortion. But the rules are different for the Permanent Political Class in Washington. Politicians are paid salaries to make their judgments on bills and to represent the interests of their constituents. But all too often, when they are put in leadership positions with real authority and power, politicians institute the equivalent of a "mob tax." They expect — they require — payments to perform such regular duties as holding hearings, voting, and passing legislation. Or they sell their votes to other members for money.

When we pay public officials to do their jobs, we expect them to do it and not to try to leverage their position for additional benefits or favors.

Politicians often complain that they don't get paid enough. But compared to a one-star U.S. Army general, who faces the prospect of an overseas deployment, they do quite well. A one-star Army general with forty years of service can earn up to $143,000 per year in basic pay. A freshman congressman starts out at $174,000. If he becomes Speaker of the House, he can pull down $223,500.[1] Bureaucrats' salaries can be even higher: hundreds of employees at the Treasury Department earn more than a congressman.[2]

If an Army general were to ask for favors in return for performing his duties, he would be drummed out of the military and might even go to jail. But if you are lucky enough to climb the ranks of the Permanent Political Class and become a powerful committee chairman, or even Speaker of the House or Senate majority leader, you have a unique tool to extract money and favors from companies and individuals. I call it the "tollbooth." And it's completely legal.

You pay money at a tollbooth in order to use a road or bridge. The methodology in Washington is similar: if someone wants a bill passed, charge them money to allow the bill to move down the legislative highway.

Of course, politicians don't explicitly say this. An explicit quid pro quo, getting favors in exchange for holding a vote, would violate federal law. But as an unspoken tool of extraction, the toll-booth method is very powerful. Everyone on the inside pretty much knows what is going on. Tollbooths are especially powerful when the stakes are high for a wealthy and successful industry. Imagine for a minute that an important bill has passed out of committee, but not yet been scheduled for a vote on the House floor. You wait and wait. Then suddenly you and your colleagues are solicited for donations by a fund-raiser who works for the politician who gets to decide whether a vote will be held. What will you do?

Congressional staff and the fund-raising staff are in regular contact with each other in every congressional office, particularly those of more senior politicians or politicians in leadership positions. With seniority comes responsibility. And with that increased responsibility comes the opportunity to use leverage to generate cash.

In 2011, two politicians who didn't have a great deal in common cosponsored a bill called the Wireless Tax Fairness Act of 2011 (H.R. 1002).[3] Zoe Lofgren is a liberal from California who represents a district including San Jose. Trent Franks is a conservative from Arizona whose district covers an expanse of northwest Phoenix. They have political differences, but on this bill they agreed. So did 230 colleagues who would eventually join them as cosponsors. The bill prevented state and local governments from levying new taxes on cell-phone users' bills for at least five years. With local government budgets tight, the fear was that city, county, and state governments would see cell-phone taxes as a source of revenue. Cell-phone users were already paying 16 percent in federal taxes and fees on their phone bills. Of course the bill was popular with the public: one survey revealed that 67 percent of consumers favored the bill.[4]

Within the House of Representatives, there was widespread bipartisan support. Cosponsors included conservatives such as Michele Bachmann of Minnesota and liberal stalwarts such as Gary Ackerman of New York. Obviously, the bill was important to cell-phone companies as well, particularly large operators like AT&T and Verizon. Imagine the nightmare of having to add different state and local taxes to every individual phone bill, depending on the jurisdiction. And imagine what higher cell-phone taxes might do to the type of phones and cellular plans people chose. Local taxes could deeply affect their bottom line.

Given the bill's widespread support in the House, it looked like smooth sailing. The legislation was introduced in March 2011 and sailed through the House Judiciary Committee in July on a voice vote with little opposition. But once a bill clears a committee, it is then up to the Speaker of the House to schedule a floor vote for the full House to consider it. If the Speaker doesn't want to hold a vote, he or she doesn't have to.

John Boehner represents a quintessentially American district in Ohio, west of Columbus and on the border with Indiana. First elected in 1990, Boehner is famous for both wearing his emotions on his sleeve and his skill as a deal-maker. But he isn't just skilled at negotiation. He is also extremely effective as a fund-raiser.

Now he had leverage. Why schedule a vote for free? AT&T has a long history as a Washington player and is well aware of the power that resides in the one who holds the Gavel — namely, the Speaker of the House. AT&T executives know how the game is played and understand the necessity of being generous with the powers that be. When Boehner was the minority leader in the House (he became Speaker in January 2011), AT&T employees gave him few contributions. In 2009 they had given his campaign a total of $5,000 in a single PAC contribution. But in 2010, when it became clear that Republicans were going to regain control of the House, AT&T execs saw the need to offer their tithes to the likely new speaker. AT&T, like most large corporations, tends to give more money to the party in power, which has ultimate control of their regulatory and financial life. So AT&T employees sent him twelve donations on a single day, November 2, 2010 — election day.[5]

By the fall of 2011, as AT&T was awaiting the fate of the Wireless Fair Tax Act, the company was also locked in a battle with the Department of Justice over a proposed $39 billion merger with another cell company, T-Mobile. The Obama Justice Department was suing in federal court to block the merger. AT&T was looking for help from members of Congress, but it would only come with a price. On September 15, fifteen Democrats in the House signed a letter asking President Obama to drop the case or at least settle it.[6]

House Republicans had a letter of their own, signed by one hundred members, including a man who had the power to move Washington, Speaker John Boehner. Saying that blocking the merger would "thwart job creation and economic growth," the Republican signatories also asked the Obama administration to settle with AT&T over the merger.[7] Days later, Speaker Boehner received a flood of cash from AT&T executives. On September 30, forty-seven donations arrived from AT&T executives in Texas, Georgia, New Jersey, Illinois, Virginia, and Washington State. It was a $54,550 haul in cash, from a single company in a single day.[8]

Meanwhile, the Wireless Tax Fairness Act lingered, waiting for a floor vote. Everyone expected Boehner, given his general aversion to raising taxes, to support the bill and hold a vote. But as the months went by and mid-October arrived, it was unclear whether the vote would ever come.

Members of Congress from both parties had their hands out. Employees of Verizon and AT&T wrote over two hundred checks totaling over $180,000 to the campaign committees of members of Congress during September and October of 2011.[9] But with his unique leverage, John Boehner was the toll collector. Finally, he declared a vote for the bill on November 1, 2011, and on the *day before*

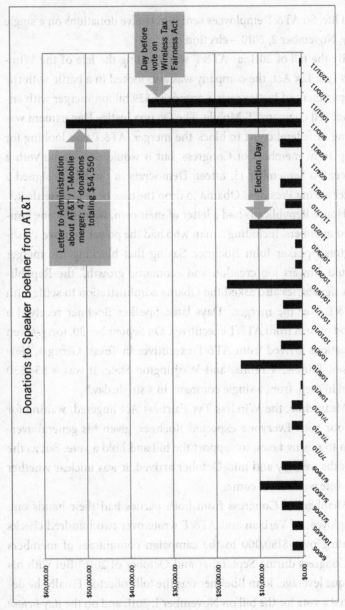

TOLL COLLECTOR OF THE HOUSE[11]

Donations to Speaker Boehner from AT&T

Day before vote on Wireless Tax Fairness Act

Letter to Administration about AT&T / T-Mobile merger; 47 donations totaling $54,550

Election Day

Total amount donated

$60,000.00
$50,000.00
$40,000.00
$30,000.00
$20,000.00
$10,000.00
$0.00

6/8/05
10/14/05
5/2/06
5/16/06
6/18/07
6/19/09
1/7/10
1/14/10
1/15/10
4/1/10
4/4/10
4/10/10
5/3/10
5/9/10
6/9/10
10/10/10
10/17/10
10/9/10
10/25/10
10/25/10
11/5/10
11/17/10
1/28/11
5/4/11
6/24/11
8/26/11
9/30/11
10/3/11
11/30/11
11/31/11

Source: John Boehner, financial disclosure documents, 2005–2011 (MapLight.org)

the vote, Boehner's campaign collected the toll: thirty-three checks from wireless industry executives, totaling almost $40,000. Twenty-eight of those checks came, again, from executives with AT&T.[10]

The day of the vote, employees of Verizon, another company with a lot at stake in the bill, sent twenty-eight checks to members of Congress — with, for example, $1,000 going to Republican Harold Rogers of Kentucky and $2,000 to Democrat John Dingell of Michigan, both senior members in the House.[12]

The tribute had been paid. The vote was held. The Wireless Tax Fairness Act passed the House easily on a voice vote.

Checks don't just magically appear. And they don't arrive by chance. Someone writing a $25 check to a candidate may be sending it because he or she believes in the candidate. But when corporate executives make donations on the same day at the same time, especially when a large group of them do so, it is likely there has been an organized solicitation. The timing explains how the two events are related.

AT&T, with its long Washington experience, knew the angles. It pays to bestow largesse on those in powerful positions in Washington. In 2005, AT&T faced a myriad of issues related to its Cingular cell-phone subsidiary, so it had been suggested that the company hire a new lobbyist. The one they selected was Joshua Hastert.[13] It's not that Hastert was an expert in the cellular industry. Sporting a pierced tongue and goatee, he also didn't fit the part of a traditional power-lobbyist. His previous work experience included owning a record store in Illinois and a small music label called Seven Dead Arson. He also happened to be the son of the then–Speaker of the House, Dennis Hastert.[14]

For the Wireless Tax Fairness Act in 2011, AT&T hired a team of lobbyists that included William Clyburn Jr., the cousin of the Democratic whip, Congressman James Clyburn of South Carolina. Clyburn was the third most powerful Democrat in the House. AT&T

paid his cousin $30,000 over a three-month period to, among other things, "monitor" the status of the bill. Clyburn's other clients included the U.S. Telecom Association (USTA), which favored the bill. USTA paid him $60,000.[15] Hiring Clyburn as a lobbyist had an added benefit for AT&T and USTA: Congressman Clyburn's daughter, Mignon, was a sitting member of the powerful Federal Communications Commission.[16] The FCC, of course, has regulatory power over AT&T and the telecom industry. Did Congressman Clyburn specifically ask that his cousin land these contracts? We cannot know unless someone talks. But he probably didn't have to. As with the Mafia, demands can be unspoken and still remain clear.

The Wireless Act vote had been a lucrative toll, but Boehner was not done collecting cash. As on any toll road, you don't just charge one car. In late September, he also scheduled votes on two other bills that had passed out of committee. For each bill, wealthy industries were eager to see a vote on the House floor.

The Access to Capital for Job Creators Act (H.R. 2940) would make it easier for smaller companies to get access to capital by loosening regulations surrounding stock offerings.[17] Another bill, the Small Company Capital Formation Act (H.R. 1070), would do something similar.[18] Both had passed out of committee months earlier (the Small Company Act back in June), with widespread support. And who wanted these bills to pass? Investment firms, brokers, and venture capitalists — all vigorously supported the bills because they would reduce regulations and encourage the free flow of capital (or so they argued).

Boehner scheduled a vote on both bills for November 2 and 3.[19] In the days before the vote on both bills, a flood of donations came into Boehner's fund-raising office from — who else? — investment bankers, brokers, and venture capitalists around the country.[20] This was not a spontaneous act of charity. Individuals from California to New York, Tulsa to Vero Beach, all made contributions on the same day.[21] The toll must be paid. Credit Suisse Securities contributed $5,000, and the head of global investment banking with Barclays contributed $2,000.[22] UBS and JP Morgan also sent money.[23] The Speaker of the House took in $91,000 in the forty-eight hours of October 30 and 31 from investment banks and private equity firms, two days before the vote. But Boehner wasn't done. During the same time period, he took in $46,500 from self-described "investors" and another $32,450 from bank holding companies.[24]

With the tolls paid, the votes took place on the full House floor. Both passed easily.

Boehner has always been famous in Washington for his lavish fund-raising parties, including the notorious "Boehner Beach Party." "We've never had any speaker in the Republican Party who has been as integrated into the fundraising needs as John Boehner," said Republican congressman Pete Sessions of Texas, then chairman of the National Republican Congressional Committee.[25] The tollbooth method provides leverage to extract money — without the beach sand or the bikinis.

Boehner knows well the capacity of Washington to extort favors and to strike fear in the hearts of powerful corporations, a necessity for extortion. In 2010, when he was still the minority leader in the House, he saw that bankers and other financial executives were reluctant to fight the Democratic-controlled Congress on certain regulatory matters. At one point he encouraged executives at a conference organized by the American Bankers Association to stand up to "little punk staffers" on Capitol Hill.[26] But he knew they would rather pay their protection money than risk provoking a fight with the powers that be.

The relationship between powerful corporations and the government is a mix of persuasion and fear. Corporations try to influence legislation they don't like by hiring lobbyists and making contributions. But the relationship works both ways. Politicians want corporations involved in the process on their terms: it allows for maximum extraction.

Taking tolls didn't start with Boehner. The toll collectors come and go depending on which party is in power. The only thing that may change is the price of the toll.

Leaders of powerful committees have a similar, if perhaps smaller, capacity to extort money and favors from those with money who expect the wheels of government to turn yet find them frozen. In both the House and the Senate, legislation largely emanates from powerful committees under the effective control of a senior experienced politician. (The U.S. Senate is not quite as tightly controlled as the House, as it allows any senator to introduce a bill on the full floor, whereas House members must introduce their bills through committee.) The key component for the Permanent Political Class is creating the conditions under which paying a toll becomes a necessity and there is no other way around the toll road. One of the most effective methods is what is called a "tax extender."

Tax extenders temporarily reauthorize tax breaks that have not been made permanent law. They are extended every couple of years by Congress — sometimes every year. For example, beginning in 1981, Congress enacted a special tax credit for companies that spend money on research and development (R&D). The credit allows for specific tax deductions that are extremely helpful for innovative companies that are constantly investing in new technologies. For the high-tech sector, the tax break is huge. "It's a key factor in America's innovative economy," former Microsoft COO Bob Herbold told me.

The R&D tax credit, which many experts consider critical for America's economic success, has never been made permanent. Instead, it has been renewed again and again since 1981. And there are more and more such highly specialized tax credits (some beneficial to the overall economy, some not so much) that are similarly renewed. In 1998 there were forty-two such "tax extenders." By 2011 that number had grown to 154.[27]

Why doesn't Congress just make these tax deductions permanent? Why go through the process of renewing them year after year?

If you are sincere in asking those questions, you are not thinking like the Permanent Political Class. Making them permanent would take away the ability of the Permanent Political Class to return again and again to wealthy industries for the largesse to keep the credits on the books. "They trot out the R&D tax credit every few years, and it's always with their hands open, looking for money," says Herbold. "It's like an annuity for them. They won't make it permanent because it doesn't make sense for *them* to make it permanent."

Dealing with blackmail in the criminal world is never easy. The problem with blackmailers is that once you pay them money, they might come back again and again asking for more. At some point, you just have to stop paying the blackmailer. You run out of either money or patience. But Washington has been using tax extenders to extort donations for more than thirty years.

Lobbyists have likened the tax extenders ploy to Lucy pulling the football away from poor Charlie Brown in the last second.

In the House of Representatives, much of the work on tax extenders is done by the powerful House Ways and Means Committee and its current chairman, Congressman Dave Camp of Michigan. In the Senate, tax extenders are under the control of the powerful Senate Finance Committee, under the chairmanship of Senator Max Baucus of Montana.

December 2011 was unusually warm in Washington. Perhaps that stemmed in part from the enormous heat being generated on Capitol Hill over the federal budget and tax policy. President Obama and Senate Democrats were locked in a battle with congressional

Republicans about the tax code and the federal budget. And tax extenders were at the heart of the battle.

It had become standard practice for more than a decade: create regular uncertainty for companies large and small over whether certain tax credits would be renewed. Five times over the past ten years it had been necessary to act on extenders retroactively.[28]

In December 2011, dozens of important tax extenders were set to expire at the end of the month. One was the R&D tax credit. Another was a special fifteen-year depreciation for construction improvements by restaurant leaseholders. There was also section 179 expensing, which encourages small businesses to invest in new equipment by expensing much of the cost up front instead of over time. In 2012 this provision allowed businesses to deduct up to $139,000 for the cost of new equipment. If not renewed, the deduction would drop to only $25,000.[29]

Many companies had a lot to lose and were panicked. These tax extenders affected such industries as real estate, housing, energy, and automobiles. "I'm working on several tax extenders, and we're working our butts off," said lobbyist Rich Gold.[30]

So, of course, those in a position to extract a toll did. Senator Max Baucus, as the chairman of the Senate Finance Committee, generally did not attract many contributions from the energy industry. (Those firms spent more money on members of the Energy Committee.) But several of the tax deductions scheduled to expire would have a huge effect on energy companies, especially smaller independent producers who lacked the capital of the global multinationals. On December 14, 2011, the Senate Finance Committee held hearings on complex tax issues related to energy and changes that the White House had proposed making it more difficult for fossil fuel and natural gas producers to log drilling expenses. If these tax extenders expired, it would cost the independent energy industry $3.5 billion in new taxes.[31] According to Baucus's campaign finance records, he had not received a check from the energy industry since May 2011, more than six months earlier. But with the future of energy industry tax extenders in doubt, dozens of small companies from Kansas, Oklahoma, Texas, and Illinois wrote checks totaling $46,100.[32] In December, Baucus pocketed checks from the Domestic Energy Producers Alliance and $5,000 from the National Stripper Well Association and $2,000 from the American Independent Energy PAC. On December 21 alone, nineteen checks from independent energy companies were deposited by his campaign, totaling $28,000.[33] These were smaller companies like Cobra Oil and Gas in Wichita Falls, Texas, and Vess Oil in Wichita, Kansas. Why did all these smaller companies write checks during the same time period (most of them on the same day) and after so long a period of not donating to Baucus's campaign? Did they organize themselves to coordinate their donations, or were they solicited by Baucus's office to ensure the tax extenders would go through? We have no way of knowing.

Money also flowed to Baucus's leadership PAC. His former political adviser Shannon Finley was now a lobbyist registered to work for the American Petroleum Institute. She sent a $5,000 check in December.[34]

During the 112th Congress, a senator needed to raise an average of $10,476,451 and a representative $1,689,580 to clinch the coming election.[35] But for those who sit on a powerful committee like the House Ways and Means Committee, raising money is not difficult. These committee assignments bring greater opportunities for leverage, which encourages — perhaps even compels — people to make donations. Analysis of contribution data from the 103rd Congress shows that a member of the Ways and Means Committee raises on average a quarter of a million dollars more than colleagues on other committees.[36] Tax extenders are a big reason.

The chairman of that powerful committee in December 2011,

Dave Camp, has represented a rural district north of Lansing, Michigan, on the Lower Peninsula since 1991. Camp regularly wins reelection with approximately two-thirds of the vote. Generally low-key, he told the *Wall Street Journal,* "I don't think you need to bang the gavel, pound your fists or shout to be effective."[37] Yet even with a safe seat, he works to raise funds, not a difficult task given his power over tax policy. In 2012 he raised almost $4.4 million to keep his seat safe.[38] Much of it comes from milking those looking to extend tax credits or deductions.

In December 2011, Camp kept it open whether tax extenders would be, well, extended. More than sixty tax extenders were set to expire within weeks.[39] Meanwhile, his fund-raisers took in a massive number of checks from those who were jostling most over the extenders — corporate PACs and lobbyists. Camp received PAC checks from the Redding Rancheria Indian Tribe in California (concerned about expiring tax credits for companies establishing businesses on Indian reservations) as well as the Association of Home Appliance Manufacturers, Blue Cross, the Real Estate Roundtable, and others. In all, in December 2011 he collected twenty-four checks from corporate PACs, fifteen checks from lobbyists, and only seven from individuals.[40]

And he was only getting started. Congress recessed for Christmas, and Camp went home to Michigan for the holiday. When Congress returned to Washington in January, the tax extenders were still in limbo. It was a catastrophe for certain companies and industries — but a boom time in Washington. Extraction of money was intensifying. Camp and his committee outlined their plans to have lengthy discussions on which extenders should stay and which should go. They were scheduled to be held on April 26, 2012, by the House Subcommittee on Select Revenue Measures. The subcommittee planned to look at seventy-five tax extenders that had expired or were expected to expire, everything from deductions for oil and natural gas and alternative fuels deductions to special tax breaks for TV and movie producers, railroads, mining companies, rum, and investment companies.[41] It was what a fighter pilot might call a "target-rich environment" for exploitation.

In announcing the hearings, subcommittee chairman Pat Tiberi of Ohio declared, "As Chairman Camp and I stated last month, the Ways and Means Committee is engaged in a process to review dozens of tax provisions that either expired last year or expire this year. This hearing provides a formal opportunity for the Subcommittee to hear from our House colleagues about the merits of extending — or not extending — many of these tax policies." It was a chance for members of Congress to make a pitch for the tax extenders they had introduced in legislation in Congress.[42] And of course, it meant the tollbooth was still open for a few more months.

In Connecticut, ten nervous senior executives at General Electric made donations to Camp on March 19 totaling $16,000. Those executives included the chief operating officer, chief financial officer, and vice chairman of the company.[43] General Electric had an enormous amount of money at stake in the tax extenders drama. They had become masters of sorts over the years in turning profits but largely avoiding taxes, thanks to a favorable and complicated tax code.

But Camp's most lucrative play was targeting corporate PACs. From the beginning of March to the date of the hearings to vet which extenders might stay and which might go, he collected 120 checks totaling over $230,000 from corporate or trade association PACs, the vast majority of which had money at stake in the tax extender debate. The money came from the National Federation of Independent Business, the National Association of Home Builders, Walmart, General Motors, General Electric, Associated Builders and Contractors, Johnson & Johnson, and more.[44]

Pat Tiberi, who was in charge of those subcommittee hearings, was milking hard too, and his bucket almost overflowed. In the six weeks between the announcement of the hearings and the end of April when they were held, Tiberi collected 128 checks totaling over $210,000 from PACs, including hospitals, the Teamsters Union, Comcast, the American Meat Institute, and McDonald's — in other words, virtually anyone anxious about the fate of those tax extenders.[45]

Tax extenders cause chaos for companies that constantly need to decide whether certain tax deductions will still be available to them the following year. But for the Permanent Political Class, tax extenders function perfectly.

Congressman Bill Young grew up outside of Pittsburgh in a small coal town. He spent his early years in a shotgun shack before his family moved to Florida. First elected to Congress in 1971, he comes across as courtly and genial. But he can be tough as steel. In a 1999 *New York Times* interview, Young said, "In my life I've been shot, I've been hit by a truck, survived an airplane crash, I've had my chest opened and my heart rebuilt. And it's sort of hard to get me flustered after all that."[46]

Bill Young is the chairman of a very powerful and important subcommittee, the House Appropriations Committee's Subcommittee on Defense. Members of Congress who sit on the appropriations committees have extraordinary power. Those who are subcommittee chairmen, like Young, are sometimes called "Cardinals" because they wield so much power. Politicians love committees like Appropriations. As then-Congressman Ray LaHood indelicately told the *Peoria Journal Star,* "The reason I went on the Appropriations Committee, the reason other people go on the Appropriations Committee, is they know that it puts them in a position to know where the money is at, to know the people who are doling the money out, and to be in the room when the money is being doled out."[47]

All defense spending essentially goes through Young's subcommittee. In the early months of 2012, Young's subcommittee was piecing together its report on defense spending for fiscal year 2013. The pie they were preparing to cut up and divide among programs and contracts: how to spend approximately $519 billion in non-war-related defense spending. The committee would essentially establish the foundation for where defense dollars would be spent.[48]

This is the sort of document that can make or break the programs of defense contractors, both large and small. Writing checks when asked during these critical early months can be particularly important. The document was set to be released on May 7 by Young's subcommittee.[49] So, as the document was being hammered together, Young's fund-raisers went to work (as can be seen by his campaign's hefty dinner tabs for the time period).[50] On March 30, Young collected thirty-seven checks totaling over $30,000, mostly from defense contractors, employees of defense contractors, and lobbyists who worked for defense contractors.[51] During the two weeks preceding that date, he had already collected another fifty-two checks totaling over $58,000 from a similar group.[52] For Young, the tollbooth is an important component in the extraction of contributions. In those first three months of 2012, he collected $181,452 in donations.[53] In the final nine months of the year, he collected only $72,850.[54]

But paying a "toll" to Young doesn't just mean writing checks. It can also mean hiring former staffers who became lobbyists and now represent defense contractors before their former boss. Many of them gather and work at a lobbying outfit called Van Scoyoc Associates. Young's former chief of staff Doug Gregory, former legislative aide Bryan Blom, and former district director David Jolly have all been employed there.[55] The firm represents large firms like Lockheed Martin, but also a large number of smaller defense-related firms you have never heard of: DRS Technologies, SGT, Inc., and AeroVironment, Inc., to name just a few.[56]

Young's daughter-in-law, Cindy Young, is also a lobbyist, who has represented (what else?) defense contractors large and small. Miss Young has represented half a dozen defense contractors.[57]

Defense contractors know the power of Young's purse. Having received $45 million in earmarks from Representative Young since 2004, top-ten defense contractor Science Applications International Corporation (SAIC) had a vested interest in staying in the congressman's good graces.[58] When his twenty-year-old son received his GED and started working in the defense contracting business, SAIC made sure to offer him a plum job. The National Forensic Technology Center probably had a similar idea when it hired Young's other son. Congressman Young had steered $28.6 million to the nonprofit over the previous decade.[59]

Tax extenders are essentially the Washington, D.C., version of the "mob tax": paying members of Congress to do something that they are supposed to be doing in the first place. Those who wonder why the American tax code is so complex, convoluted, and constantly changing fail to appreciate what a wonderful tool it is for extortion. When you start seeing it as a source of enrichment for the Permanent Political Class, you will realize why we have the tax system we have.

3

PROTECTION: FOR A PRICE

I have built my organization on fear.

— AL CAPONE

IT'S ONE OF THE OLDEST and most effective forms of extortion: the protection racket. Pay me money and I will promise to not make your life miserable. Fail to pay and bad things will happen to you.

Protection money has been the Mafia's bread and butter for centuries. In the city of Palermo on the island of Sicily, 80 percent of the businesses pay protection money (*pizzo*) to the Mafia.[1] If you fail to pay, you will be harassed, you might have your business burned down, and you might even lose your life.

In one famous case, a Palermo businessman named Libero Grassi refused to pay protection money and wrote an open letter to the mob in the local newspaper, *Giornale di Sicilia.* He addressed the letter "Dear Extortionist." Nine months later, in August 1991, he was killed by the Mafia.[2]

The Permanent Political Class in Washington plays the protection racket too. Failure to pay will not get you killed — but it could kill your business. It might even make a difference in whether you will end up in jail. If protection money paid to the mob keeps them from literally burning down your business, protection money paid to the Permanent Political Class prevents them from figuratively burning down your business.

Current CEOs are loath to talk about it. They face regulatory and legal jeopardy and don't want to make themselves a target for retribution. But former executives who are freer to speak out say it happens much more often than you might think. John Hofmeister, former president of Shell Oil, told me that while it didn't happen to him during his tenure, he is familiar with the practice. "Anytime you are vulnerable to legal or regulatory compliance you can expect them to come after you with requests for money," he said. "It's like clockwork."

Ray Plank, the founder and longtime CEO and chairman of Apache Corporation, is even blunter. "They basically come to you and say, 'We are going to shove this bat up your ass and give you an enema. You better play ball.' We saw a great deal of it. It's an insidious blight."

Companies large and small, as well as professionals like doctors, accountants, and lawyers, face a myriad of rules and laws that they are required to comply with every day. Undoubtedly, some of these laws are good. But many of them are complex and difficult to understand. Professor Alan Dershowitz estimates that today the average professional commits three felonies a day without realizing it, thanks to the complex layers of regulation and legal requirements that have been built up over time.[3] And then there are the subjective legal actions that the federal government can take that might put you or your company in real legal jeopardy. This is precisely what happened when the Justice Department went after Microsoft in the 1990s on the grounds that it was engaged in anticompetitive activities. More recently, the Justice Department went after Apple and five book publishers over ebook pricing decisions. Fighting these cases costs tens and even hundreds of millions of dollars.

When Microsoft and other wealthy companies experience legal action that involves the threat of large fines (or perhaps even jail time for executives, depending on the charge), that makes them a prime target for financial shakedowns. Politicians and members of the Permanent Political Class are all too willing to offer some form of "protection" for the right price.

Indeed, consider the realities and the decisions that businesses must make when they are being investigated for possible criminal conduct by the Justice Department and then the president's staff solicits them for donations. Or consider a lucrative industry under heavy political attack that is then asked to donate or hire individuals as consultants to make the problem go away.

As we saw earlier, Richard Nixon famously tied the actions of the Department of Justice (DOJ) and other regulatory agencies to his campaign fund-raising activities. Since then, the practice has become more subtle and less explicit. Being politically active and giving to candidates, as well as hiring the right lobbyists, does offer some protection. And the merging of law enforcement and political fund-raising has grown even closer in recent years. Indeed, when President Obama established his Justice Department staff after the 2008 election, something unprecedented happened. For the first time, at least half a dozen senior positions were occupied by individuals who had been campaign bundlers (fund-raisers) for a presidential candidate, including not only Attorney General Eric Holder but also senior officials who dealt with criminal and civil prosecutions: Associate Attorney General Thomas Perrelli, Deputy Associate Attorney General Karol Mason, and Associate Attorney

General Tony West.[4] Presidents have always selected Justice Department officials who share their views on legal issues. But seeking out individuals who actively raised large sums of money for the presidential campaign and then putting them into law enforcement positions — that is new in American politics. If an attorney general and his top lieutenants raised large sums of money from certain companies and industries, can we trust that they will judge those firms and industries impartially? If senior law enforcement officials are motivated enough to raise $500,000 for a candidate, can we be certain that politics won't be part of their legal decision-making?

OBAMA CAMPAIGN BUNDLERS INSIDE THE DEPARTMENT OF JUSTICE[5]			
Name	Department of Justice Position	Amount Bundled	Election
Eric Holder[a]	Attorney General	$50,000– $100,000	2008
Thomas Perrelli	Associate Attorney General	Over $500,000	2008
Karol Mason	Deputy Associate Attorney General	Over $1 million	2008, 2012
Spencer Overton	Principal Deputy Assistant Attorney General for the Office of Legal Policy	Over $1 million	2008, 2012

a. Attorney General Holder was a campaign co-chairman for the Obama campaign.

William Orrick	Counselor to Assistant Attorney General of the Civil Rights Division	$200,000–$500,000	2008
A. Marisa Chun[b]	Deputy Associate Attorney General	$200,000–$500,000	2008

b. Deputy Associate Attorney General Chun advised Tom Perrelli.

In recent years few industries have been as under the gun as Wall Street and the financial industry. With the 2008 financial crisis, fraudulent mortgages, complaints of excessive compensation, large profits, and taxpayer bailouts, it is hard to have any sympathy for Wall Street. Yet the Obama administration has not filed any criminal charges against any major Wall Street investment banks or their officers. Could there be a simple reason? Could the Washington discussion about whether or not to investigate, whether or not to bring charges, be a cover for something else? Is it possible that Nixon's methods are being replayed again in a new form?

While the Permanent Political Class debates how to deal with the problems in America's financial sector, they are distinctly bipartisan about one thing: extracting as much money out of Wall Street as possible for their own benefit. Politicians on both sides have played the extraction process perfectly. President Obama raised record sums from Wall Street in 2008 and then declared on *60 Minutes*, "I did not run for office to be helping out a bunch of fat cat bankers on Wall Street."[6] On the other hand, Obama privately positioned himself as the one politician who could protect the "fat cats" from the mob. Conversely, Republican congressional leaders publicly decried the verbal and regulatory attacks on capitalism, but privately relished the opportunity to seek out and receive "protection money." They knew they could use the Democrats' threats to raise money for themselves.

In early 2009, there were cries for aggressive legal actions against Wall Street firms. CNN predicted that some bankers could very well end up in jail.[7] Commentators like Tom Gardner of The Motley Fool financial news service declared that "hundreds [of bankers] should go to jail."[8] It was amid that public clamor that President Obama, in April 2009, gathered twenty-five finance executives to the White House for a frank discussion. As ABC News reported, the president told them: "My administration is the only thing between you and the pitchforks."[9] One individual who attended the meeting told *Politico*, "The signal from Obama's body language and demeanor was 'I'm the president, and you're not.'"[10]

To play this game best, an extortionist needs to sound convincingly threatening. Attorney General Eric Holder, despite having come from a law firm that represented many of the largest Wall Street firms, talked about criminal charges against individual Wall Street executives. And as the so-called Occupy Wall Street movement arose and occupied a park next to Wall Street, President Obama sounded supportive. According to the president, the protests and the civil disobedience reflected a "broad-based frustration about how our financial system works."[11] Democratic House leader Nancy Pelosi explained, "I support the message to the establishment, whether it's Wall Street or the political establishment and the rest, that change has to happen."[12] Congresswoman Debbie Wasserman Schultz, head of the Democratic National Committee, added, "We understand their [Occupy Wall Street's] frustration, we applaud their activism."[13]

But time dragged on, without any criminal charges being brought. Soon the midterm election cycle loomed, and a major piece of financial regulation — the Dodd-Frank Wall Street Reform and Consumer Protection Act—moved toward passage. Wall Street money flowed to some of its fiercest critics in the 2010 election. That year, seven out of the ten top recipients of Goldman Sachs contributions, for example, were Democrats. Former Clinton secretary of labor Robert Reich declared that this was evidence that Wall Street was "bribing elected officials with their donations."[14] I would argue that Reich had the power equation wrong. It was the Permanent Political Class that threatened to cause severe damage to the financiers—not the other way around. As the late economics professor Peter H. Aranson puts it, "The real market for contributions is one of 'extortion' by those who hold a monopoly on the use of coercion—the officeholders."[15]

The midterm election passed, and so did Dodd-Frank. But the extortion market continued. In mid-April 2011, executives at Goldman Sachs were worried. On April 13, the Senate Permanent Committee on Investigations released a scathing report on alleged criminal conduct by Goldman and other firms during the financial crisis.[16] The 635-page report created a panic. *Forbes* was soon reporting that Goldman executives were hiring white-collar defense attorneys.[17] The Department of Justice was reportedly looking at possible criminal indictments.

In the weeks leading up to and following the report, a handful of Goldman executives poured more than $200,000 into the coffers of the Obama campaign and the Democratic National Committee. Three of those executives had never given to Obama before and had never even written large political checks.[18] But now, in a non-election year, they were donating to the campaign. Goldman would learn that the Department of Justice had dropped its criminal investigation.[19] Obama campaign advisers would also say publicly that their 2012 campaign strategy would involve "channeling anti–Wall Street anger" to their advantage.[20]

The message could not be more clear. The Democratic National

Committee organized and promoted a March 7 White House dinner in the Blue Room for twenty "top Wall Street donors who could be key fundraisers" for Obama's reelection bid, as *Politico* put it. They discussed policies that would affect the financial industry.[21]

"This was not a fund-raiser," insisted Press Secretary Jay Carney. And indeed, it would have been inappropriate to host an explicit fund-raiser at the White House. But it was scheduled to "solicit ideas about how to improve the economy," according to *Politico*, and the line between explicit and implicit fund-raising can be awfully hard to draw.

A *Bloomberg* survey found that fully 77 percent of Wall Street executives believed Obama was "anti-business."[22] Many of his supporters on Wall Street were frustrated by his anti–Wall Street rhetoric and were vowing not to support him this time around. But what choice did they have? The money continued to flow. By July 2011, just as Goldman executives were making their donations, cash from Wall Street made up fully one-third of President Obama's campaign money raised by bundlers.[23] As CNBC put it at the time, "Obama is relying more on Wall Street to fund his re-election this year than he did in 2008."

By January 2012, Wall Street bundlers had already raised $2 million more than they had raised for Obama in 2008. They made up the largest bloc of bundled contributors to his campaign.[24]

Many on Wall Street were furious with the rhetoric. Paul Levy of JLL Partners voted for Obama in 2008 but had become frustrated by the rhetoric. "If he's busy attacking people with wealth, why does he want to go to fancy restaurants and fancy homes to have these events? If he wants to go where the people go, I'm happy to go where the people go." Levy suggested a fund-raiser at McDonald's.[25]

Robert Wolf had been a supporter of President Obama's since 2007, when he had first met him as a candidate. Wolf had bundled for Obama in 2008 and now served as an informal adviser to the president during the first term. Some considered him a "First Friend" to the president. Wolf ran the U.S. banking operations of the giant Swiss Bank UBS, which was under investigation by the federal government on several fronts. The Internal Revenue Service was looking into allegations that the firm was helping U.S. citizens evade U.S. taxes. During a 2009 hearing, Senator Carl Levin claimed: "Swiss bankers aided and abetted violations of U.S. tax law by traveling to this country, with client code names, encrypted computers, countersurveillance training, and all the rest of it, to enable U.S. residents to hide assets and money in Swiss bank accounts."[26] At the same time the Department of Justice was investigating other financial matters that involved the conduct of certain UBS executives. The Securities and Exchange Commission also had several other probes of UBS underway.[27]

Through it all, Wolf continued raising money for President Obama. In February 2009, UBS entered into a deferred prosecution agreement with the DOJ relating to charges that it impeded the IRS by hiding taxpayer identities. Although UBS did pay some fines, they were largely seen as slaps on the wrist considering the legal charges the firm and its executives might have faced. The DOJ dropped the charges against UBS eighteen months later, after the firm provided identities and account information for about 4,450 of their U.S. customers.[28] Other bundlers came from JP Morgan Chase, JP Morgan, Goldman Sachs, and Bank of America, all of which were under SEC investigation and possibly under Department of Justice investigation as well.[29]

Extortion usually implies that the victims are innocent. Blackmail is the term used when they are guilty. I am not suggesting that UBS was innocent of wrongdoing, or that the other Wall Street firms had nothing to answer for. But the government should regulate or prosecute wrongdoing — not turn it into an opportunity to make money. Consider the case of another Obama bundler, Jim Chanos of Kynikos Associates. Chanos had not bundled for Obama in 2008. But in 2011 the hedge-fund titan signed up to raise money for the president's reelection. The SEC was investigating Kynikos because of a civil complaint filed against the firm in 2006 by the insurance and financial services firm Fairfax. Chanos bundled between $200,000 and $500,000 for the president's 2012 reelection.[30] In November 2012, the SEC closed its investigation of Kynikos.[31]

Pfizer vice president for policy Sally Susman was another Obama bundler for the 2012 election. In July 2011, Pfizer headquarters was scheduled to be the site of a fund-raiser for the campaign. Only after the *Boston Globe* asked campaign officials about the propriety of holding the event at a pharmaceutical company regulated by the government was it moved to the University Club.[32] But Pfizer remained a cornerstone of the campaign's bundling operations. All this took place as the drug giant was facing criminal investigation by the Justice Department over alleged violations of the Foreign Corrupt Practices Act going back some ten years. Susman, who is also Pfizer's lead lobbyist, bundled more than $500,000 for the 2012 campaign.[33] In August 2012, the drug giant was able to settle the criminal case with DOJ officials.[34] History shows that making donations lessens the possibility that the SEC will ding you for a financial crime.[35] How can we be sure that senior Justice Department officials, who raised money for the presidential campaign, won't be influenced by the same thing?

There is no explicit quid pro quo here. It is all unspoken. Friends help friends get elected by raising money. And friends who get elected don't like friends who helped them raise money going to jail.

Both political parties were trying to grab the public high ground while in the background extracting what they could. Senator Harry Reid criticized Republican senators for holding "backroom negotiations" with Wall Street executives over the Dodd-Frank financial reform bill. But when he made the charge, Reid had only recently himself held a fund-raiser in New York City organized by Goldman Sachs president Gary Cohn.[36] Republicans, on the other hand, criticized Democrats for extorting Wall Street, while playing a similar game themselves.

Leading the tightrope walk with Wall Street for Obama was Broderick Johnson, who joined the Obama campaign as a senior adviser in the fall of 2011.[37] Johnson had worked for Obama in 2008 and was tied in with Wall Street, for whom he had lobbied since 2007. During the 2008 financial crisis, Johnson had lobbied for the bailout of the Financial Services Forum, an industry association comprising the twenty biggest financial CEOs in the United States. He also lobbied directly for JP Morgan, Bank of America, Fannie Mae, and the investment firm J. C. Flowers & Company.[38]

Johnson's role in the campaign was to be its "representative in meetings with key leaders" and to help "ensure that there is constant, open communication," according to Obama 2012 officials.[39] He was part of the campaign's senior staff, helping to provide "an ear to the ground."

In addition to representing financial industry and Wall Street firms, Johnson is an attorney. He was a perfect liaison between Wall Street firms facing government investigations and the campaign. As Johnson's current consulting website explains, "From one end of Pennsylvania Avenue to the other, we communicate with key policy and decision makers on an ongoing basis to secure useful intelligence in support of our clients' overall business strategies. As relevant government decisions are being made, our outreach efforts yield sharper insights as to what may be happening or what has to happen to ensure successful client driven outcomes."[40] Such is the language of the sophisticated Washington player. He works for Obama, he works for Wall Street, and somehow, the latter ends up giving a lot of money to the former.

But the extortion was a bipartisan endeavor. The heated anti–Wall Street rhetoric and the threats to tax financial services into oblivion were good for Republicans too. The GOP message: we will protect you from those madmen . . . for a price.

When John Boehner became Speaker of the House in January 2011, he was already an effective and efficient fund-raiser. Much of the money came from his district and from businessmen around the country. Wall Street money had been part of the mix but not in any sizable quantities. But 2011 would turn out to be a banner year for him, precisely because Wall Street was under fire and feeling the heat. And precisely because he was implicitly offering them protection, Boehner was able to raise large sums of money.

One of the most contentious issues in 2011 was over taxes paid by Wall Street investors. America's tax code had always been straightforward about one thing: income should be taxed differently than interest and capital gains made off of investments. But that distinction was now under fire as "unfair" because investors were paying a lower percentage on their capital gains than middle-class Americans were on income from their jobs. The *New York Times* called it the "Most Unconscionable Tax Loophole" in America.[41] President Obama, along with many Democrats in Congress, was threatening to change it. Particular attention was focused on one of the biggest winners in 2010, hedge-fund titan John Paulson, who pulled in $4.9 billion. Forget for a minute the policy question of whether a change in the capital gains rate is good or bad. Instead, see it for what it largely created: an opportunity for extraction by both sides who were offering "protection."

Boehner was generally opposed to large tax increases. But in the spring of 2011, he indicated that he *might* be open to considering a change in the capital gains rate.

Boehner then went to Wall Street looking for money. Over a two-day period, June 8–9, he deposited 144 checks worth $274,800 in contributions from hedge-fund and finance executives.[42] Thirty-five of those checks, totaling over $56,000, came from employees of a single hedge-fund group, Paulson & Company.[43] Paulson execs had never given to Boehner before. Cantor Fitzgerald executives were also quite generous—and also had no prior history of supporting Boehner. But now they needed his "protection." Would they have done so without this threat?

In 2011 Boehner raised six times what he had raised in 2010 when he had merely been minority leader. But it's not just politicians who extort. Well-connected members of the Permanent Political Class also got in on the Wall Street game. Anita Dunn joined the Obama campaign in 2008 and served as director of communications. When President Obama was elected, she moved to the West Wing, where she served as communications director. Her husband, Robert Bauer, became President Obama's White House counsel. They were lauded as one of Washington's "Power Couples" by *Newsweek* magazine.[44]

During her tenure in the White House, Dunn was part of a vocal group of political activists who tilted to the left. She became a staunch critic of the hedge-fund industry and of Wall Street for their excessive compensation.[45] Shortly after leaving the White House, she became a director at the consulting firm SKDKnickerbocker. The firm specializes in corporate communications, crisis communications, and public relations. Dunn's contributions at the firm included providing "strategic communications" advice to clients.[46] Immediately upon joining the firm, she peddled some very expensive advice to those she had so aggressively criticized.

Dunn helped craft an SKDKnickerbocker proposal that went out to hedge funds, in late 2011, ostensibly to boost their image. The idea was simple: Dunn and her partners were offering to develop a national "paid media" pro–hedge-fund campaign as well as a "comprehensive public affairs operation" to "raise awareness about the positive role hedge funds play in the American economy" and to "eliminate the need for politicians to take aim at hedge funds."[47]

The proclaimed goal of the campaign, to be done in conjunction with the PR firm McLean/Clark LLC, was to get politicians to "think twice" about attacking hedge funds and give them "political cover" to defend the hedge-fund industry.

The reaction from those in the hedge-fund industry was one of astonishment. As one executive who didn't want to be named (because of the possibility of retribution) put it, "First we see Dunn attack us on television, and then she tells us to hire her to head off the exact attacks that she herself is hurling at us. The entire thing begins to stink like a protection racket."

The proposal warned that hedge funds needed to do something to respond to the attacks Dunn herself had helped to fuel. As the packet noted, "Both the leftist Occupy Wall Street activists and the right-wing Tea Party movement herald a new era of populist peril for anyone associated with finance. Given current U.S. volatility, various measures of a similarly reactionary nature might very well attract strong political support. . . . Hedge funds make inviting targets." As if to add fuel to the fire, Dunn's fellow managing director at Knickerbocker is Hilary Rosen, who sits on the board of the Center for American Progress Action Fund, which was engaged at that very time in a campaign attacking the hedge-fund industry.[48] The game is simple: make threatening noises, while offering services to protect against those threats. Dunn has become a go-to person for corporations under pressure from the Obama administration. With easy access to the White House, and as a senior campaign official, she is a logical source of protection. When AT&T was facing both Department of Justice and Federal Trade Commission litigation over a proposed merger with T-Mobile, it hired Dunn's firm to provide strategic advice.[49]

The Permanent Political Class regularly solicits donations from firms and individuals concerned that they might be in legal jeopardy or face serious costs. It's easy to see the opportunities for extracting donations.

Consider this dilemma. On June 18, 2012, President Obama was scheduled to appear at a New York City campaign fund-raiser hosted by members of the publishing industry. But two months earlier, the Obama administration had filed antitrust cases against five leading publishers, claiming they were fixing prices on the sale of electronic books. The Obama Justice Department was also suing Apple, as the prices in question came about at Apple's encouragement. These were the five largest publishers: HarperCollins, Hachette, Simon & Schuster, The Penguin Group, and Macmillan.[50] By August, many of them had settled the suit. Granted, the publishing industry tends to be liberal and would be expected to support a candidate like President Obama. But does the legal threat create further motivation to donate? It caught the attention of seasoned reporters like John Aloysius Farrell of the *National Journal*. "In any other field of business, the timing would suggest a classic political shakedown — Nice little literary business you got here. It would be a shame if anything were to happen to it — or an attempt by a shady commercial interest to grease its way in Washington."[51]

We've come to accept this as routine: companies facing legal action from the federal government being solicited at the same time for campaign donations. On the street, this would be considered de facto extortion.

Consider the challenges faced by the telecom industry in the spring of 2012. The cherry blossoms had already turned on the Washington Mall, and America was increasingly preoccupied by a presidential election, but what worried the telecom industry was the possibility of being sued for doing something the federal government told them to do. Telecom companies had been advised to cooperate with federal law enforcement and U.S. intelligence agencies that were monitoring criminal or terrorist activity over the Internet or telephone lines. The problem? They might be sued in civil court by customers on the grounds that they had violated the privacy rights of people using their services. A bill pending in Congress, called the Cyber Information Sharing and Protection Act (CISPA), would allow telecom companies to share information with U.S. government law enforcement and intelligence agencies dealing with a possible cyber or terrorist threat, while also granting them legal immunity from lawsuits.[52] The telecom companies had been granted immunity previously, but that was set to expire. And now there was a strong push by some in Washington to repeal the immunity. President Obama was hinting at it, as were a number of members of Congress. This would be a disaster for these industries: in effect, they would be forced to share information with government agencies while being left open to lawsuits for doing so. Again, forget for a minute the policy implications of this bill and consider the extortion opportunities.

The bill had been introduced in the House almost six months earlier. Because of some heated opposition, it was possibly stalling. One of the key votes on the issue was Congressman James Clyburn of South Carolina. A member of the powerful House Committee on Appropriations, Clyburn was the third-ranking Democrat in the House, behind Nancy Pelosi and Steny Hoyer. Owing to his seniority, Clyburn was well respected by his colleagues. Democrats in Congress were heavily set against extending the immunity, while Republicans were generally in favor. Clyburn was open to extending it, but he was also well positioned to extract money. The vote was scheduled for April 26. In the weeks before the vote, he kept coy about what his position might be. Meanwhile, he collected checks from AT&T, Verizon, and the National Telephone Cooperative Association in late March, for a total of more than $10,000. As the vote came closer, Clyburn saw the arrival of more checks. T-Mobile and the Cellular Telecom and Internet Association each sent him money, as did Time Warner Cable and the Echostar Dish Network.[53] Funds also arrived from a lobbyist for the Cellular Telephone and Internet Association, and Telecom Industry Association.[54]

In the end, only 42 Democrats would vote in favor of the bill, and 140 against, granting the telecom companies immunity. But Clyburn voted in favor of immunity.[55]

The power of federal government officials to control or threaten large corporations is immense, even beyond legitimate law enforcement functions. In 2011 the Department of Health and Human Services (HHS) declared that the federal government would not work with the pharmaceutical company Forest Labs unless it replaced its CEO.[56] HHS claimed that the longtime chief executive, Howard Solomon, had engaged in "marketing violations." But Forest Labs had committed no real legal or regulatory violations. "The action against the CEO of Forest Labs is a game changer," Richard Westling, a corporate defense attorney, told the *Wall Street Journal*. "It would be a mistake to see this as solely a health-care industry issue. The use of sanctions, such as exclusion and debarment to punish individuals where the government is unable to prove a direct legal or regulatory violation, could have wide-ranging impact."

In 2009, during the height of the debate over health care reform, the company Humana found itself subject to investigation because it had communicated with its customers and expressed concerns that the proposed reform bill would increase health care costs and hurt benefits to seniors. Senator Max Baucus, the chairman of the powerful Senate Finance Committee and a supporter of the bill, contacted a former aide who was then at the Centers for Medicare and Medicaid Services (CMS), which oversees federal dollar spending on those programs, and asked him to investigate the communication. Needless to say, Humana wants to be on good terms with CMS. If they get on the agency's bad side, they risk being excluded from Medicare and Medicaid programs. CMS promptly launched an investigation of the company for expressing its opinions and sent a warning letter telling it not to do the same in the future.[57]

The power of the purse is enormous in Washington. But where does all the money go? Is it mainly just for individual politicians' campaign funds? Or are there more nefarious ebbs and flows? You would be amazed at the complex rivers of cash, and where they flow.

4

THE UNDERGROUND WASHINGTON ECONOMY

Government is supposed to exist for the good of the people,
not the other way around, and clearly not for the
personal enrichment of those who hold public office.

— ROD BLAGOJEVICH, FORMER GOVERNOR OF ILLINOIS, APRIL 17, 2006

I N THE CLASSIC FILM *The Godfather,* the Mafia boss Don Vito
Corleone (played by Marlon Brando) is visited by Johnny For-
tane (Al Martino), a famous singer who also happens to be his
godson. Johnny's career is fading, and he's been turned down for a
role in a movie by some sleazy Hollywood studio boss. He's come
to ask Corleone for help. His godfather is all too glad to help. "I'm
going to make him an offer he can't refuse," he tells Johnny.

Later we see the studio boss waking up to find a severed horse
head in his bed. Johnny, needless to say, gets the part.

The Mafia economy is simple. Mobsters run legitimate businesses alongside illegal ones, and they use muscle and force to protect those businesses and to extort cash. As we will see throughout
this book, political fund-raising can be remarkably similar. According to Clyde Wilcox, a Georgetown University professor who studies political giving psychology, "You start your fundraising network

by thinking of people ... who can't say no."[1] But how, exactly, do they do it? The other chapters of this book reveal the opportunities and the results. This chapter is about methods.

Campaign fund-raising generates the headwaters of the political economy in Washington. We know that it is used for winning elections. But once money has been raised by politicians, it can be moved, redirected, and shifted to other tributaries apart from campaigns. The money can be shifted into politicians' own personal pockets, or those of their family members. And it can be transferred to the pockets of other politicians — perhaps in exchange for a vote on a particular bill.

For regulators, the river of campaign money is a challenge, since it is visible only part of the time. It flows underground at critical junctures where it is not easily visible to the general public or to journalists. Indeed, there is an Underground Economy of politicians' money that flows through the nation's capital that is much wider and deeper than the nearby Potomac.

Politicians spend an extraordinary amount of time raising money. By some estimates, it takes up between 30 and 70 percent of their day. Some of that effort is retail: sending out fund-raising letters and collecting small checks sent through the mail, online, or at a local county political event. But the heavy lifting is often done in Washington, D.C., in the shadow of the Capitol dome, while Congress is in session. This is wholesale fund-raising. Federal laws don't allow lawmakers to collect checks in congressional buildings or in the Capitol Building (with one critical exception we discuss later). So politicians typically walk to a nearby location to either make phone calls or attend private fund-raising events. The number of events that take place is enormous. For well-positioned bars and restaurants, these events create a constant flow of business. Even in an off-election year, fund-raising remains constant (in 2011 congressional representatives and senators had more than 2,841 fund-raisers in the nation's capital), and they often list their committee assignments on the invitations so that invitees know how they can do invitees favors, or cause them harm.[2]

Former Senate majority leader George Mitchell recalls being flooded with calls from colleagues asking that he not schedule legislative business at certain times because of fund-raising obligations. In fact, there were so many of these requests that he had to ignore them: "If I put all the requests together, the Senate would never vote. I once had my staff keep a list of such requests on one day . . . and had I honored all of the requests, there could not have been a vote that day." The requests spanned from 9:00 a.m. in the morning until midnight.[3]

Politicians report making hundreds of phone calls between legislative votes, committee hearings, and nightly fund-raising receptions (sometimes multiple receptions in the same night). Closed-door fund-raisers in Washington are ritualistic events with their own set of unwritten rules. The media and the general public are not invited in. And an "invitation" to one of these events is a little like the studio boss being "invited" to reconsider his decision not to include Johnny in his movie. You can choose not to attend the event, or choose not to donate, but you may very well suffer the consequences.

In the days leading up to the contentious Dodd-Frank financial reform bill vote, Congressman Joseph Crowley, a member of the powerful House Ways and Means Committee, held four fund-raising events targeting financial institutions that stood to gain or lose from the vote. The day before the final vote, Crowley held two fund-raising events, including a cocktail hour hosted at a lobbyist's home. Of the forty-two guests who showed up, thirty-one were lobbyists for the financial reform bill or their coworkers. After cocktails, Crowley then went to a dinner with thirteen other lobbyists who were working on the financial reform bill. The cost to attend was $2,500 for PACs or $1,000 for individuals. Emails from his campaign show that he specifically targeted financial industry lobbyists for donations. Crowley raised $90,000 in one night.[4]

The day before the final vote on Dodd-Frank, Congressman Tom Price of Georgia, a member of the Financial Services Committee, solicited donations at a "Financial Services Industry Luncheon." It was organized with the input of Bank of America employees, who helped to write the invitation list. All but three of the individuals who attended Price's luncheon were lobbyists for the bill.[5]

Congressman John Campbell of California, also a member of the House Financial Services Committee, asked representatives of several large financial institutions — Bank of America, Chubb Corporation, MasterCard, and New York Life — if they wanted one-on-one meetings about the bill. Campbell also held a "Financial Services Dinner" in October 2009, one day before the markup of the bill in committee. Like Price and Crowley, Campbell also held multiple fund-raising events in the days before the final vote.[6]

John Hofmeister, the former president of Shell Oil, recalls, "If you are invited, you are expected to be there. There is an implicit aspect of the request that makes that clear. And when you get there, you better show up with a check."

Hofmeister's description of these events resembles a shakedown. Not much needs to be said, unless you fail to comply. "You are standing in the room, and there is a glass bowl in the center. You are supposed to place your check in that bowl. Someone who works for the politician is watching from the corner to make sure everyone puts their check in the bowl. It's public. If you don't — they are going to come and ask you why. That is the expectation."

And if you fail to pay your tithe? Politicians will be very blunt, says Hofmeister. "'Why am I meeting with you?' they will ask. 'What have you done for me?'"

Many executives and corporate PACs do what Hofmeister did — they purposely give to both sides. It's kind of like paying protection money to two rival gangs. "I made it a practice to give to each side equally," he told me. "If you want access or to raise something with them that concerns you, they check to see if you are a donor before they meet with you."

Politicians spend so much time raising money because that is how you win elections. Outspending your opponent is no guarantee, of course. American politics is full of examples of wealthy candidates going down in flames. But the evidence is pretty overwhelming that money matters. Nine out of ten times in the House of Representatives, and eight out of ten times in the Senate, the candidate who spends the most money wins.[7]

Campaigning has always required money to reach voters. Back in 1757, a young fresh-faced former Army lieutenant named George Washington ran for a seat in Virginia's House of Burgesses. He "provided his friends with the customary means of winning votes" by delivering a quart and a half of cider, wine, and beer to each of the 391 voters in his district.[8]

Today you can substitute media advertising and data sets for wine and beer as the best way to reach voters.

Most politicians absolutely hate raising money. Many will echo the words of former congressman Walter Minnick of Idaho, who said, "It's absolutely the most distasteful thing to do as a congressman, or a senator, or a candidate."[9] Connecticut's Senator Chris Murphy laments having to squeeze fund-raising events between floor votes and says, "The conditions under which we labor are pretty depressing."[10]

This very fact, that politicians generally hate raising money, is a good reason to keep the current system. Having to raise money is one of the few things that keeps these people humble. As former senator Slade Gorton recalls, "I felt that for all of us who were senators, and who were being treated as minor nobility, that the fact that we had to go ask people for money was very healthy and that it gave you at least a slight degree of humility."[11]

The problem is not that politicians need to raise money; the problem is in how they do it, and in how they can redirect funds once they have them. Reformers want to restrict fund-raising (some even call for taxpayer-funded elections) because they believe that fund-raising is ultimately about "buying votes." But the reality is that there is little evidence that vote-buying actually goes on in the way most people think it does. Three political scientists compared more than forty studies on the links between PAC donations and votes and found that, "in three out of four instances, campaign contributions had no statistically significant effects on legislation or had the 'wrong' sign — suggesting that more contributions lead to less support."[12]

Two other scholars looked at a large amount of academic data on campaign contributions and congressional voting and concluded that, with the preexisting views of politicians factored in, there is very little evidence that campaign contributions directly influence voting.[13] So why give money? If you are a CEO and you are spending millions of dollars on lobbying, without any statistically significant result, you are letting down your shareholders. Why do it?

Because you think you have no choice. Campaign contributions are not about buying votes, they are often about extortion. Legislators have the bargaining power, and they largely initiate solicitations of money. It isn't a bribe. In white-collar crime, the distinction between bribery and extortion is often based on the determination of "which party initiates the exchange."[14] This also explains why many corporate executives and PACs largely give to incumbents regardless of party. A challenger can't do very much to them. But if they fund only the losing candidate, there might be hell to pay from the winner. If it's a close election, execs might hedge their bets and give to both candidates to secure protection from both sides.[15] Of course, once an election is over, there is only one extortionist left. Corporate PACs send money "disproportionately to incumbents, majority party members, and those serving in leadership positions, especially those on the most powerful committees."[16]

Committee chairs and ranking party officers (leader, whip, etc.) face their own pressure to extort. The underground money economy of the Permanent Political Class works in hidden ways. When newly elected members of Congress come to Washington, D.C., they often find that they—much to their surprise—are already in debt. And we aren't talking about the national debt.

Both Democrats and Republicans in the House of Representatives have created a largely hidden system of "party dues" that requires members to extract money beyond their own campaign donations to fund their respective parties.

These party dues are not voluntary. Members are not asked to pay—they are required to pay. And paying those dues greatly influences which committee or subcommittee assignment they get.

We want to believe that committee assignments are based on knowledge, expertise, and background. But a member of Congress will end up on a powerful committee like the House Ways and Means Committee or Financial Services Committee only if he or she can raise money. The more powerful their committee assignments, the more money members are expected to extract from the industries they have oversight over or regulate. For a newly elected member of Congress on a weak committee—for example, the Ethics Committee, which is considered the least attractive committee for a variety of reasons — the annual party dues can run around $150,000. And for those on a powerful committee? The sky is the limit. Those in leadership positions or on powerful committees can be expected to raise $600,000 or more as part of the system.

The Democratic and Republican Parties both have internal party dues lists in the House of Representatives that make it very clear that leadership positions and committee assignments come with a price tag.

For the Democrats, being the ranking member on an exclusive committee like Ways and Means or House Financial Services will run you $500,000 in the 2013–2014 election cycle, according to internal party documents. Being the ranking member of a less powerful committee means giving the party $250,000. If you're happy being a rank-and-file member, you only need to raise $125,000.[17]

The Republicans have a similar system. At the National Republican Congressional Committee, they actually post the price list for each Republican member of Congress on the wall. If you are behind in what you need to pay, it is marked in red for everyone to see. The list is broken down into sixths for any calendar year. So Congressman Fred Upton, chairman of the powerful Energy and Commerce Committee, is required to raise $990,000 for this election cycle for the party.[18] Congressman David Camp, chairman of the powerful Ways and Means Committee, is expected to do the same.[19] Congressman Lamar Smith, chairman of the less prestigious House Judiciary Committee, is expected to kick in $405,000, according to party documents.[20]

Democrats have a "members points system" that rewards congresspersons for collecting cash and attending party fund-raisers. The amount of money raised is extraordinary and separate from the fund-raising they do for their own campaign committees. Congresswoman Nancy Pelosi, according to internal Democratic

Congressional Campaign Committee (DCCC) documents, raised a stunning $52.9 million for the party in 2011–2012. Speaker of the House John Boehner raised even more.

Raising money is what helps an ambitious member of the House rise in the ranks far more than ideas or competence. For example, according to DCCC documents for the 2011–2012 election cycle, Congressman Joe Crowley of New York was a vice chairman of the DCCC in that election cycle and raised over $8 million. As a result, he is now the Democratic Caucus vice chairman.[21] Congresswoman Alyson Schwartz also raised millions and in early 2013 was reappointed to the powerful House Ways and Means Committee, after being removed the cycle before.[22] On the other hand, the failure to raise funds means the possibility of being cut loose. Congressman Gary Miller of California, according to internal Republican Party documents, was more than $359,000 behind in his 2012 dues and was not going to receive support through the party's "Patriot Program," a "goal-oriented program" that offers extensive support and assistance for those seeking reelection, even though Miller is in what some analysts have said is the most vulnerable district in the country.[23] (Internal party dues documents from both parties are reprinted in Appendix 1.)

But you get what you pay for. Built into these valuations is the implicit extortion value of the seat. Sitting on the House Financial Services Committee means you can extract lots of money from wealthy financial institutions. But a slot on the Ethics Committee gives you little opportunity for extortion — except perhaps from your fellow members of Congress who are facing ethics investigations. Members of the Ethics Committee can and do receive donations from their colleagues and party leadership! The modern congressional-assignment pricing system is very much like the old Tammany Hall machine in New York City. At its height, Tammany could charge a candidate a fee to allow him to run for office (which meant winning that office, since New York City was a one-party town). If you wanted to be a senator, you paid. Once you were in office, you could earn back your investment through graft.

Today's Congress is similar. It's a largely pay-to-play system. Politicians who get on a powerful committee but refuse to pay their dues will get yanked from the committee no matter how knowledgeable they might be on the relevant issues. House Minority Whip Steny Hoyer suggested such a thing might happen when several members on powerful committees weren't raising enough money. He threatened them with a "separate vote on their panel [committee] assignments if they fail to pay their party dues," reported the *National Journal Daily*. One of Hoyer's top aides told the magazine, "You sit on an exclusive committee and you have a responsibility to do more." It was a thinly veiled reference to extracting more money.[24]

What this system does, of course, is encourage members of Congress from both parties to amass more power for their committees. If you have more industries and companies under your purview, it will be easier for you to pay your party dues, not to mention easier to raise your campaign funds. Reducing the power of committees makes both tasks more difficult.

Current members of Congress acknowledge the existence of these "dues" in private conversations but don't want to talk about them publicly, for fear of retribution from party and congressional leaders uneager to see the pay-to-play system exposed. Those who have recently left Congress are more willing to speak openly. Former Democratic congressman Jim Cooper of Tennessee has spoken about the clear link between paying your dues and getting on key party committees.[25] Former Republican congressman Thaddeus McCotter from Michigan denounced the practice while in leadership as akin to a "pay-to-play."[26]

Lawmakers who have trouble raising money to pay off their

yearly debt can wipe out portions of it by performing certain tasks. The National Republican Congressional Committee will give members of Congress "credits," such as $5,000 for attending a congressional fund-raising dinner or making a certain number of fund-raising calls.

Apart from the hidden dues system, there is another major — but also hidden — source of politicians' funds: each other. Federal laws are very clear: a politician can't solicit or receive campaign contributions in congressional buildings or in the U.S. Capitol. But there is a little-talked-about exemption to that rule. It's an exemption that doesn't get talked about, but is a major tributary in the flow of money into the hands of the Permanent Political Class. The exemption states that "the rules and standards of conduct enforced by the Standards Committee do **not** prohibit **Members** from soliciting (or receiving) campaign or political contributions **from other Members** in the House buildings" (emphasis in the original). It's a huge loophole that makes it possible for members to link their votes to cash.[27] This can involve large sums of money. Members of Congress receiving these funds can even convert them into personal cash in their own pockets!

The Federal Election Campaign Act of 1971 allows for the transfer of unlimited campaign funds from campaign committees to any national, state, or local committee of any party.[28] Politicians can also transfer money to another candidate, with certain limitations. Leadership PACs are not just about electing fellow party members to office. They also play a key role in determining how much time you get on the House floor or whether your bills get voted on. One academic study found that politicians who transfer funds to their colleagues "enjoy more success in getting their bills scheduled for legislative action."[29]

Raising money is far easier for a powerful member of Congress than for a junior member. If you are the Speaker of the House, you have maximum power to move or halt bills. So you can amass large sums of money and then transfer those funds to junior colleagues in exchange for favors and votes. Suppose you are the Speaker of the House and in your leadership PAC you currently have $2 million. You are trying to push some recalcitrant members from your party to join you on a vote for something. It is perfectly legal for you to meet with those members in your office and offer to transfer cash from your PAC to their campaign funds.

Both parties use donations to buy votes. In 2009, when the American Clean Energy and Security Act was up for a vote, the outcome was in doubt. During the week of June 23, 2009, right before the vote, four Democratic leadership PACs gave out $130,000 in donations to forty-one Democrats who were on the fence. Congressman Jim Clyburn's Friends of Jim Clyburn PAC handed out $60,000 to undecided members two days before the vote.[30] The bill did pass the House, by a scarce seven votes.[31]

It's mind-boggling to look at all the tributaries of cash that flow underground and aboveground in Washington. Consider the 2012 elections and Speaker of the House John Boehner's fund-raising machine. Boehner has a personal campaign committee, a leadership PAC, and a so-called joint fund-raising committee. He can tap wealthy donors for all three committees, and indeed, he often does. Boehner's campaign committees transferred $22.4 million to the National Republican Congressional Committee for the 2012 election, according to FEC records. Over $11 million of that came from his campaign committee, Friends of John Boehner, and more than $10 million came from his joint fund-raising committee. Meanwhile, his leadership PAC, the Freedom Project, together with his campaign account, gave a total of $2.4 million directly to 2012 congressional candidates.[32]

With a so-called leadership PAC, Boehner can transfer money to his colleagues' campaign committees ($10,000 a year per colleague) and donate another $10,000 to the same colleagues' own PACs. He can also transfer unlimited amounts of money to the National Republican Congressional Committee, which can then turn around and spend unlimited funds supporting those candidates' reelection bids. Alabama recently barred transfers of money between political action committees in the wake of a fund-raising scandal in that state. But even though it's illegal in Alabama, it's perfectly legal in Washington.

Leadership PACs are often larded with donations from corporate and/or labor union PACs, as well as from PACs controlled by lobbyists. House Minority Leader Nancy Pelosi's leadership PAC, PAC to the Future, took in $457,895 in 2012 from individuals as well as $645,000 from other PACs. She transferred $854,500 to other Democrats running for office, many of them incumbents.[33] Leadership PACs can raise money more quickly than regular campaign committees because while individual donations to campaigns are limited to $2,600, leadership PAC donations are capped at $5,000 (as of 2013). Pelosi and Boehner run their PACs in a similar manner. In 2012 Pelosi moved $187,700 from the Nancy Pelosi Victory Fund (a so-called affiliated committee) to her leadership PAC. "The reason you form a leadership PAC is you want to help your colleagues, because the more you help your colleagues, the more influence you have," Congressman Rob Andrews of New Jersey told the Office of Congressional Ethics Board. "The more influence you have, the more you can get done."[34]

Boehner and Pelosi can give money to candidates to help them win, but they can also give donations in exchange for votes or in exchange for support when they seek a leadership position. In 2009, for example, FEC records show that Pelosi's leadership PAC made a series of donations to so-called Blue Dog Democrats. These were centrists who were concerned about some aspects of the health care reform bill. They ended up voting for the bill. How crucial were

Pelosi's donations to getting their support? They will never answer this question. FEC records indicate that Speaker of the House John Boehner, facing a challenge for his position in early 2013, likewise used the transfer of campaign donations to certain members of Congress to shore up support from those who might be inclined to vote against him. Perhaps we should take some vicarious pleasure in the fact that our politicians are willing to extort one another, not just us.

Politicians say that the purpose of a leadership PAC is to help elect their colleagues. But because politicians are able to discuss votes and transfer money between themselves, it is easy to see how the buying and selling of votes might very well be occurring more frequently than we think. Money often flows to incumbent members of Congress in safe seats, raising the question: why exactly is money going to incumbents virtually certain to get reelected, particularly on the eve or day of a critical vote?

Because the political class has created this exemption for themselves, they take full advantage of the opportunity to leverage their position and extract donations from others. In short, they can't legally sell their votes to us. But they can sell them to their colleagues.

In recent years, big fights over the federal budget and the debt ceiling have erupted against a backdrop of money transfers between politicians. How are these transfers connected to those fights? And what about the cash transfers we don't know about? Congressional leaders can direct money flows from party committees that don't always show up right away on disclosures.

Consider what happened in 2011, when Capitol Hill was in full gridlock mode over the federal budget. On September 20, Speaker of the House John Boehner scheduled a floor vote on a stopgap spending bill. It included spending for the victims of a series of recent natural disasters—most notably those who suffered massive hurricane damage in New Jersey and New York — but the bill also included spending increases in other areas. The bill went down to defeat, but in a very unexpected way. Fiscally conservative Republicans joined with an overwhelmingly large group of Democrats to oppose the bill. The two groups opposed it for different reasons, but together their opposition sent the bill crashing to defeat on a 230–195 vote.[35]

It was a stinging rebuke to GOP Speaker John Boehner. As the *New York Times* put it, the vote "showed the Republican leadership's continuing struggle to corral the most conservative members of the caucus, as more than 40 Republicans rejected the measure because they did not believe it cut spending enough."[36] For Democrats, it was a huge victory. Even though they were in the minority, they had managed to throw a wrench into GOP plans. Republicans knew that they would need some Democrats to cross the aisle to make up for the Republican freshmen in revolt. However, only six Democrats supported the bill in the end. "The most important part of the vote was Democratic unity," as one senior House Democratic aide told the *National Journal*.[37]

When a contentious vote on another budget bill came up in December, events played out differently this time. An infusion of money helped. Under fire from Senate Republicans, the House leadership prepared for another critical vote to determine the fate of an important budget bill (H.R. 3630: Middle Class Tax Relief and Job Creation Act of 2012). The bill included the extension of a payroll tax cut and unemployment benefits. The night before the vote it was still open as to whether House Republicans had the votes. On December 20, John Boehner's leadership PAC sent out a whopping $420,000 in contributions to his Republican colleagues.[38] The bill was referred to the conference committee on a narrow vote of 229–193, the same day, a huge win for Boehner.[39]

Many of these donations went to incumbent Republicans who were in safe seats. For example, $5,000 went to Congresswoman Diane Black, who would win reelection less than a year later by over fifty-three percentage points.[40] Scores of other colleagues in safe seats who won reelection by twenty percentage points or more received contributions as well. These individuals ended up voting in favor of the bill, helping to quell what the *New York Times* called a "revolt" against Boehner.[41] Likewise, Republican whip Kevin McCarthy used his leadership PAC to send donations around the same time to safe incumbents, including those in safe seats who won by margins of 20 percent or more.[42] Why give campaign cash on the day of a vote or near a vote to incumbents in safe seats?

Democrats do the same thing, particularly when they are in the majority. As we saw earlier, this happened during the 2009 vote over the Clean Energy Act. The vote came down to a handful of members. Democratic Majority Leader Steny Hoyer pumped cash to Congressmen Gregory Meeks, Ed Markey, and Jan Schakowsky, all of whom won reelection by more than thirty percentage points.[43] And all voted in favor of the energy bill.[44]

But leadership PACs are not only helpful in buying votes. They are also key in getting a member's own bills through a committee and voted on by the full House. One key determining factor in who politicians donate to is whether they serve on the same committee.[45] It helps smooth the way for their bills.

Academic studies show that giving money to your colleagues is helpful if you want to get your bill voted on. Because the House leadership sets the legislative agenda and creates the calendar, you have to go through them to get your bill to a vote. And one of the best ways you can accomplish that is by donating to colleagues through your leadership PAC. One scholar scrutinized every piece of legislation, "including bills, resolutions, and amendments," that was presented in the House between 1987 and 2002.[46] She then cor-related that data with all contributions from members of Congress to each other. She found that increasingly raising money and giving it to colleagues significantly boosted your chances of getting your bill to a vote on the House floor.[47] The problem has become even worse since then as more and more members have created leader-ship PACs.

The simple fact is that members of Congress build alliances to pass legislation, and the currency they often use is money.[48] As one member bluntly put it, "Having a leadership PAC helps me tremen-dously with my colleagues, whether it's getting legislation through, getting their support for it . . . or if I ever get in trouble, they will be more willing to help me."[49]

Leadership PACs also allow yet another way around fund-rais-ing restrictions, a little-known technique called "conduit contribu-tions." These are contributions that a politician solicits for a col-league but funnels through his or her own leadership PAC before transferring it to the colleague's campaign coffers. There is no cap on the amount of money that can flow. Obviously, this can be a key method for getting colleagues to support a bill or something else you might want. During the 2010 election cycle, for example, Con-gressman Nick Rahall from West Virginia received over $82,000 in "conduit contributions" funneled through West Virginia senator Jay Rockefeller's leadership PAC, Mountaineer PAC. Another col-league, Congressman Alan Mollohan, received over $77,000.[50] The most adept at this method during the 2010 cycle was Democratic whip Steny Hoyer's Ameripac, which funneled over $2 million to his colleagues and to party committees.[51]

Politicians are not allowed to use campaign cash for their own personal use, but they have managed to find a way around even this restriction. And the tributaries of the Underground Economy in

Washington allow for the creative transfer of campaign money into the private pockets of politicians and their families. Water always flows downhill, but this is a real low point.

Many Americans struggle to decide how to invest their money. From year to year, the stock market, the bond market, and money market accounts have all featured inconsistent and unpredictable returns. But for members of Congress there is a unique "investment" that can guarantee them essentially any rate of return they think they can get away with.

Back in 1998, a member of the California State Assembly, Grace Napolitano, loaned her congressional campaign committee $150,000. She won the election and has served in the U.S. Congress ever since. She never asked for the money back. Instead, she charged her campaign an eye-popping 18 percent interest for almost twenty years, never paying off the loan. She pocketed more than $200,000 in interest payments during the first decade of the loan.[52] In 2006 she dropped the interest rate to 10 percent, but kept paying herself interest.[53] During the 2008 and 2010 election cycles, she pocketed another $94,245 in interest.[54] Napolitano is a longtime member of the House Committee on Natural Resources and the House Transportation Committee, which means that donations from industries in those areas were not only donating to her campaign but also putting money in her pocket.

Napolitano is not alone in using this technique to convert campaign donations into cash lining her own pocket. At least fourteen other members of Congress do the same thing. They are supposed to charge a "commercially reasonable" rate on loans to campaign committees, but that number is never defined, nor is the provision enforced. Congresswoman Colleen Hanabusa of Hawaii loaned her campaign $125,000 and pocketed more than $31,000 in interest payments during the 2008 and 2010 election cycles. (Hanabusa sits on the powerful House Armed Services Committee.) Congressman Paul Broun of Georgia loaned his campaign $309,000 and collected nearly $29,000 in interest during the 2010 election cycle. (Broun originally told the Federal Election Commission that he wouldn't charge any interest at all.)[55]

Like many things related to politicians, there are no strict rules here — or no rules that cannot be skirted. A politician can carry a loan like Napolitano's on the books for years and generate considerable cash flow by doing so. The FEC doesn't enforce requirements about interest rates or put caps on how long loans can be kept in place. Candidates carry these loans even though they often have the cash to pay them off. Why would they ever pay them off? Who wouldn't want to be able to loan money to themselves and get a guaranteed double-digit interest rate in return? It provides a hidden way to convert campaign donations into personal cash.

Though it is actually legal for politicians to pay themselves a salary when they are running for office (few do in fear of negative publicity), nothing stops them from paying their family members and family businesses for ill-defined services or undefined purposes. During the 2008 and 2010 election cycles, eighty-two members of Congress had their family members on the campaign payroll or hired them as "consultants."[56] Here is a sample:

- Congressman Alcee Hastings paid his girlfriend $622,747 over a four-year period.
- Congressman Jerry Lewis paid his wife $512,293.
- Congresswoman Maxine Waters paid her daughter and grandson a total of $495,650.
- Congressman Ron Paul might be a libertarian, but he's no penny-pincher when it comes to putting family members on the payroll. He had *six different relatives* on his campaign pay-

roll, for a total of $304,599: his daughter, his grandson, his daughter's mother-in-law, his granddaughter, his grandson-in-law, and another relative.

Members of Congress also hire family businesses for services:

• Congressman Tim Bishop paid his daughter's company $250,000 in consulting fees.

Often campaigns with little or no opposition are prime locations for family members pulling down salaries.

• Congressman Rodney Alexander hired his daughter to run his campaign in 2008. He paid her a $65,299 salary. Did I mention that he was unopposed that year? In 2010 he hired her again and raised her salary to $82,702. No Democrats filed to oppose him that year, although he did face a campaign by an unknown "independent." He won again with 79 percent of the vote.[57]

• Congressman Bobby Rush paid his wife, son, and sister for campaign work. His wife, Carolyn, was paid $116,500 during the 2010 campaign. Rush received 80 percent of the vote and coasted to victory.[58]

• Congressman Buck McKeon of California made his wife the campaign's treasurer and also the highest-paid employee on the campaign's payroll. For the 2010 election, her salary was $118,764.

• Congressman Collin Peterson of Minnesota decided that the best person to serve as the treasurer of Peterson for Congress was a music director for a church in Tennessee. That person happened to be his son, who was paid $54,421 in salary during the 2010 election.[59]

- Congressman Ralph Hall of Texas put his daughter-in-law on the campaign payroll and paid her $77,232. Congressman Hall regularly wins his district with approximately 70 percent of the vote.[60] He also paid his son's law office thousands in rent.
- Congressman Joe Barton (also of Texas) has had his daughter on the campaign payroll. His daughter received $79,285 in salary and $11,080 in bonuses in 2008 and 2010. In those years, Barton won with 62 and 66 percent of the vote, respectively, in what were not really competitive races.[61] Barton also set up a charity called the Joe Barton Family Foundation, which has received donations from companies that also donate to his campaigns. His daughter-in-law is the executive director and made $48,000 in salary in 2010.
- Congresswoman Sue Myrick paid her stepdaughter's company Myrick/Gunter Advertising $230,497 for television and radio advertisements during the 2008 campaign. "Myrick" appears in the company's name because the stepdaughter bought the business from the congresswoman after she was elected to office. In 2010 Myrick paid her stepdaughter's firm $178,321. Myrick regularly wins reelection with 70 percent of the vote.[62]

There are some other ways in which campaign dollars can be used to benefit politicians and their families. Like many members of Congress, Congressman Randy Forbes of Virginia pays rent to himself. During the 2010 election cycle, his campaign paid $35,400 to rent a building that he owns in Chesapeake, Virginia.[63] Congressman Gary Miller is the founder and president of G. Miller Development Company, a California-based construction company. You might think that a construction company can't do much for a campaign. You would be wrong. In 2010 Miller's campaign committee paid his construction firm $61,975 for "fund-raising."[64]

Congressman Robert Andrews of New Jersey might get the

award for creativity and artistic ability: He funneled campaign money to several theaters that would engage his daughter (an actress and singer) to perform. His campaign donated money to the Rock School of Dance, where his daughter trained, and then paid the Prince Music Theater and the Walnut Street Theater, both in Philadelphia, tens of thousands of dollars in donations for events and "expenses." His campaign also bought tickets for school groups to attend performances. His campaign committee donated to the Broadway Theater in Pittman, New Jersey, where his daughter performed. And when she performed at Six Flags Great Adventure Theme Park in New Jersey, his campaign picked up meal expenses.[65]

Congressman Silvestre Reyes of Texas must eat a lot of food and travel in high style. During the 2010 election cycle, his campaign committee reimbursed him $144,115 for travel, office supplies, and food. His campaign also reimbursed his niece for $90,905 worth of "office supplies, travel expenses, campaign gifts, and charitable donations." Congressman Aaron Schock of Illinois used campaign funds to reimburse stays at five-star resorts in Miami and in Athens, Greece. No word if there are any Illinois district voters in those locales.

So much for our partial tour of the hidden rivers of cash in Washington. They flow in many directions, and via some very clever culverts and springs. But now it is time to go back to the headwaters. With so many uses and recipients, the system needs a lot of cash at the start. Aside from milker bills, what else can the Permanent Political Class deploy?

5

THE DOUBLE-MILKER

You May Not Be Interested in Washington, but Washington Is Interested in You

Heck, what's a little extortion among friends?

— *CALVIN AND HOBBES* (BILL WATTERSON)

O N APRIL 13, 2011, VICE PRESIDENT Joe Biden picked up his first Grammy Award. About four hundred people were packed into the Liaison Capitol Hill Hotel, including musicians Don Henley and Bruce Hornsby and the jazz great David Koz. Presenting the award to Biden was music legend Stevie Wonder.

Biden was not picking up the award because he had a side career as a soloist or had joined an indie rock band. Instead, the National Academy of Recording Arts and Sciences was giving the award to the vice president for a political performance. He was being recognized for his "commitment to intellectual property rights" and for "[leading] the effort" to fight online piracy.[1]

Sometimes politicians and the Permanent Political Class get paid out of love: people have a simple affection for a certain politician or they share a common political philosophy. But sometimes love is not enough and the Permanent Political Class needs to motivate through fear. If you are concerned that government action or inaction will severely damage you, you are much more likely to stroke the Permanent Political Class with a check. In Washington, it is far more important to be feared than loved.

A milker bill gives politicians the opportunity to "milk," or squeeze, an industry for money. Whether the bill passes or not, the politicians still cash in. The best milker bills are those that allow the Permanent Political Class to squeeze two cows at the same time, one on each side of an issue. Nothing beats a so-called double-milker.

Sometimes milker bills are effective for motivating existing allies. Enthusiasm and motivation matter a lot in political fund-raising. But even if certain industries like you, are they motivated to give as much as they possibly can? Politicians can use milker bills to remind even friends how much power they have and how much their friends need them. Such a drama played out in 2011 when President Barack Obama and members of Congress played two powerful and wealthy industries off against each other. It ended in a draw as far as the industries were concerned. But as far as the Permanent Political Class was concerned, it was a bonanza.

In American politics it is hard to find two bigger, fatter cash cows than Hollywood and Silicon Valley. Celebrities usually give out of passion for certain policies. But the "suits" — the executives at big Hollywood studios and recording companies — aren't just in it for love. Sometimes they need a nudge to give. They need to fear that something is going to happen or is not going to happen that will dramatically affect them. They care above all for their bottom line.

The same can be said for the high-tech industry, which for years (as we will see) has attempted to steer clear of Washington. Techies might like a candidate, but that doesn't mean they will give as much as they can. But make them fearful about a potential change in their business model and suddenly they will dig very deep into their wallets.

In 2011 members of the Permanent Political Class reminded both of these cash cows that they could dramatically help or hurt them. They did it with double-milkers — magnificent opportunities to milk both industries for large sums of money.

Film studios, TV networks, and recording labels have battled online pirating and bootlegging for years. Making and sharing illegal copies of songs and movies takes a big bite out of profits. Pirated digital content sites get huge traffic. In 2011, it is estimated, pirating websites got 53 billion hits.[2] Pirated Kanye West songs, Harry Potter movies, episodes of *The Office*, and many other stolen files were estimated to cost the U.S. economy more than $63 billion in 2011.[3] And it was not just the big entertainment conglomerates that were troubled. The AFL-CIO considered online piracy pure theft, just like "stealing goods off of a truck."[4]

Ever since the Internet exploded as a platform for pirating songs, movies, and television programming, the problem had festered. And Joe Biden, back when he was still in the Senate, had discovered that it was both an important issue *and* a lucrative tool for fundraising (which is not true of every important issue, to be sure). As chairman of the Senate Judiciary Committee, he had been considered a good friend of Hollywood. When he became vice president, he amped up his support. And why not? Piracy was unquestionably illegal, and Hollywood had contributed massive sums of money that had helped buoy the Obama-Biden ticket in 2008.

In December 2009, Biden convened a meeting in the White House Conference Center with twenty-five titans from the entertainment industry to make a serious push to combat online piracy. The high-wattage meeting included Edgar Bronfman of Warner Music Group, Michael Lynton of Sony Pictures, Warner Brothers'

Barry Meyer, and Jeff Zucker from NBC Universal. For good measure, Biden had Attorney General Eric Holder, Commerce Secretary Gary Locke, and the head of Homeland Security make appearances to lend their support. But this was Biden's show. He pledged that the Obama administration would be more aggressive on the issue. "It offends me that the international community has treated this as a mild irritant. It's flat unadulterated theft, and it must be dealt with," he said.[5]

The Obama administration installed lawyers in the Department of Justice who had litigated for the Recording Industry Association of America, and the president appointed a new and aggressive intellectual property enforcement coordinator to fight for Hollywood. Biden showed up regularly at board meetings of the Motion Picture Association of America (MPAA), the industry-lobbying group, something that had never previously been done by such a senior government official.[6] Online piracy, he told the MPAA, "is pure theft, stolen from the artists and quite frankly from the American people."[7]

Biden was not one to mince words. He declared that copyright theft was like "smashing the window at Tiffany's and reaching in and grabbing what's in the store."[8]

The VP took the same message overseas, pressing foreign governments to crack down on pirates. From Russia to China, he chided foreign leaders.[9] Back at home, on June 23, 2010, Biden announced an interagency strategy to protect intellectual property rights.[10]

The studio bosses and the Hollywood unions wanted more than talk. They wanted a federal law with teeth. Instead of trying to get the Chinese government to do something, they wanted to force U.S. search engines like Google and Yahoo to block access to websites that allowed illegal downloading of pirated materials. And they wanted Internet service providers to be responsible for doing the same. Legislation on the subject, introduced in 2009 and 2010, had gone nowhere. Now, working closely with Biden's office and politicians from both sides on Capitol Hill, the studios helped craft two bills—one introduced in the House on October 26, 2011, called the Stop Online Piracy Act (SOPA), and another introduced in the Senate on May 12, 2011, called the Preventing Real Online Threats to Economic Creativity and Theft of Intellectual Property Act of 2011 (PIPA)—and vowed to make a full-court press to pass them in 2011.[11] In February 2011, Biden invited industry leaders to the White House again to plot strategy.[12]

All of this took place as the Obama administration was gearing up for the 2012 election. And there were concerns that they might have trouble raising money. As the *Washington Post* put it in April 2011, "There were some signs that fervor for Obama in Hollywood and Silicon Valley has ebbed."[13] The *Hollywood Reporter* explained, "As the 2012 election fund-raising cycle heats up, the one-time darling [Obama] is finding far less enthusiasm from showbiz donors." The "disenchantment is incredibly palpable."[14]

The concern was less about Hollywood celebrities and performers—they tended to donate to candidates based on ideology or beliefs—than about the studio "suits" and their khaki-wearing, high-tech-firm counterparts who were troubled by the slow-growing economy. And enthusiasm had ebbed among the vast base of middle-class customers of these industries. There was a lot of concern within the campaign that smaller online donations might not match what had happened in 2008. The *New York Times* was reporting that many small Obama donors were "disgruntled."[15]

The campaign needed the "suits" and the "khakis" to step up. Wall Street firms had given generously in 2008, but they too were much less motivated to give for the 2012 election. In short, online piracy presented the perfect double-milker. Pitting the suits against the khakis meant that Team Obama could extract more money from both industries at a time when fund-raising was proving to be more difficult than expected.

The Obama campaign began in April 2011 by holding fund-raising events in California, targeting those who were on both sides of the online piracy bill.

The president boarded Air Force One and headed to San Francisco for a series of fund-raisers in the Bay Area with the khakis, who were opposed to the antipiracy legislation. Along with a visit to the Palo Alto headquarters of Facebook, where he cohosted a town-hall-style meeting with Facebook founder and CEO Mark Zuckerberg, the president attended two fund-raisers.[16]

The next day, the president held two events at Sony Pictures, where the chairman and CEO was an Obama supporter and a huge advocate of cracking down on Internet piracy. ("I'm a guy who doesn't see anything good having come from the Internet," he told one conference.[17]) The first event was a classic merging of Hollywood and politics. One thousand people crowded into Lot 30, where the studio had just finished filming *The Amazing Spider-Man* (the fourth installment in the successful franchise). Actor Jamie Foxx got up onstage to rev up the crowd.[18] When President Obama walked out, it was with U2's "City of Blinding Light" blasting out of the audio system. After a speech, the president slipped offstage for a small dinner at the Sony Commissary hosted by Michael and Jamie Lynton. Admission to the dinner cost $35,800 a pop.[19] Then it was off to another fund-raiser with Hollywood executives at the Tavern in nearby Brentwood. There film producer Jeffrey Katzenberg of DreamWorks introduced the president before he spoke.[20] White House officials were interspersed with the studio execs. White House senior adviser David Plouffe sat next to Katzenberg. White House press secretary Jay Carney broke bread with filmmaker Steven Spielberg. Actor and producer Tom Hanks was in attendance. "Hey, this is a private event," he quipped to the gathered media.

Thanks to that trip, April 2011 ended up being a very good month. The DNC bagged $12.4 million, largely from big checks donated to the Obama Victory Fund. It was twice what the Republicans raised.[21]

The timing of these April fund-raisers was perfect. PIPA, the Senate version of the online piracy bill, was being drafted in Washington at that very moment with the help of lobbyists from the MPAA. Just weeks later, on May 12, it was introduced in the Senate Judiciary Committee.[22] With key support from Senate Judiciary Committee chairman Patrick Leahy and ten others, the bill gained momentum quickly. By the end of the year, the bill would boast forty cosponsors. The suits in Hollywood were pleased.

PIPA had clear bipartisan support. Some of the cosponsors were obvious: Senator Al Franken had been in show business for decades, and Senators Dianne Feinstein and Barbara Boxer represented the state of California. Republican supporters included Senator Lamar Alexander from Tennessee (home of the country music industry) and Senator John McCain. It didn't take long for the bill to start moving. By May 26, the antipiracy bill had cleared the Senate Judiciary Committee with a unanimous vote.[23]

That's when the real battle began.

For online companies Google, Microsoft, eBay, Yahoo, and others, the Senate antipiracy bill and its House counterpart posed an enormous threat. Eric Schmidt, the executive chairman of Google, warned that antipiracy bills would "criminalize linking and the fundamental structure of the Internet itself."[24] Google's Policy Counsel told a congressional committee that the law would "undermine the legal, commercial, and cultural architecture" of the Internet.[25] The tech publication *CNet News* declared that the bills amounted to a "death penalty" for websites.[26]

Now the milking could begin in earnest. Hollywood had already been squeezed. When PIPA passed the Senate, two deep-pocketed cash cows found themselves in a kind of arms race that the Permanent Political Class could only have dreamed about until then. For the extraction industry in Washington, it was boom time.

Particularly exciting for the Permanent Political Class was the fact that Silicon Valley was suddenly fully engaged. Getting tech nerds to pay tribute to Washington had always been a difficult proposition. Many in the high-tech field tend to be libertarians— they just want to be left alone. And given the intensely competitive nature of the industry and the fast pace of innovation, politics is largely seen as a distraction. "They would rather be innovating," Bob Herbold, the former COO of Microsoft, told me. The Permanent Political Class was offended by this fact. "The [tech] industry had an attitude that government should do what it needs to do but leave us alone," one Hill staffer told *BusinessWeek*. "Their hands-off approach to Washington will come back to haunt them."[27]

When Microsoft emerged in the 1990s as one of America's richest companies, it embodied this tech-nerd attitude. It had only a small group of lobbyists who worked out of Microsoft's local sales office in Chevy Chase, Maryland, and campaign contributions from Microsoft execs were a rare occurrence. "Bill [Gates] was proud of both of these facts," Herbold, who was COO at the time, told me.

As far as the Permanent Political Class was concerned, that simply would not do. The tech nerds needed to be put in their place. One lobbyist at the time told author Gary Rivlin, "You look at a guy like [Bill] Gates, who's been arrogant and cheap and incredibly naïve about politics. He genuinely believed that because he was creating jobs or whatever, that'd be enough."[28] The company changed its tune when the Department of Justice brought an antitrust case against Microsoft. At the time, virtually all PC users relied on Microsoft's operating system, which gave the company the leverage of a platform. When they used that leverage to nudge users toward their own Internet browser and away from an initially popular competitor from Netscape, the government pounced. Microsoft soon had to ramp up its lobbying and donations. "We had to set up operations in Washington, and Bill hated that sort of thing," recalls Herbold. "So I had to do it." They were directed to hire certain well-connected advisers and lobbyists in Washington. "You hear about bribery in China," says Herbold. "They have nothing on us. We are just more sophisticated about it."

Campaign contributions started to flow. Microsoft even began hosting an annual "Capitol Hill Family Game Night" for politicians and their families.[29] With a fleet of Xbox 360s and a stack of the latest games, the event allowed lawmakers and staffers to learn about the latest game developments — for "educational purposes," of course. But the event also provided another small way to keep Washington entertained and off Microsoft's back. Not to be outdone in their attempts to entertain and influence the political class, the Motion Picture Association of America gives free screenings at its Washington headquarters for politicians and bureaucrats, arguing that these screenings were not social events but part of important intellectual endeavors for the Permanent Political Class. "The substantive content of the movie may be relevant, while to others it might be the opportunity to see in action the latest movie making techniques, or to put into context what they are learning regarding the challenges facing the industry."[30] Of course.

With the emergence of many other high-tech firms as fat cash cows waiting to be milked, politicians started advising the tech nerds to pay attention to Washington. Senator Orrin Hatch, who was then chairman of the powerful Senate Judiciary Committee, spoke for many in Washington, D.C., when he told tech company executives at a conference, "If you want to get involved in business, you should get involved in politics."[31] When Microsoft decided it didn't want to play the conventional Washington game, Hatch called the company "knuckle-headed and hard-nosed," according to *Wired* magazine. "I have given [Microsoft] advice and they don't pay any attention to it."[32]

Getting involved in politics includes, of course, making campaign contributions, as well as hiring family members and allies in the influence industry. It means doing favors for elected and unelected government officials. To make that happen here, Congress needed to put fear in the hearts of high-tech executives. "Members [of Congress] see a high-growth industry and they automatically think we have a lot more money to give," one lobbyist told *Roll Call*. "I think they are always surprised with how little money is out there for them. This is not the banks, or the pharmaceutical industry, or transportation, which are highly regulated. Tech is not highly regulated."[33]

Now, with the antipiracy fight in Washington, big firms such as Google were in play. Knowing the right people in power gives key Washington players a new sense of worth. The Permanent Political Class has always had such players. Attach yourself to someone with power and make your move at the right time and you too can become a player. Vice President Joe Biden was the point man for the administration, so his aides and former aides were suddenly players. Many became hired guns on both sides.

Leading the charge for the MPAA was Michael O'Leary, recently hired as vice president and counsel for the organization.[34] O'Leary had served as a counsel to Biden when he was on the Senate Judiciary Committee.[35] On the other side, Google, which was leading the opposition to the bill, made its own move. In early 2011, the technology giant hired an attorney named Katherine Oyama to be its policy counsel in Washington. Oyama came to Google from the White House, where she had served as the vice counsel to Vice President Biden.[36]

The battle pitted key Obama pillars of support against one another: Stephen Spielberg and Jeffrey Katzenberg versus Marissa Mayer — first at Google, then CEO of Yahoo — and Eric Schmidt of Google. Some of the media interpreted this as a problem, but they missed the point entirely. For the Permanent Political Class, this battle wasn't a problem, it was an opportunity. As at least the *Hollywood Reporter* recognized, "This is a great issue over which politicians can raise funds from donors on both sides."[37]

The number of companies with skin in the game was staggering. As *Politico* rightly observed, it was "a huge payday for lobbyists": 145 different companies lobbied for or against the bill in the House, and 157 for or against in the Senate.[38]

The stakes were high. For entertainment firms, this was "either make it or break it," said Bill Allison of the Sunlight Foundation. "It's not surprising that they're spending more to push these bills."[39] Cable giant Comcast alone hired nineteen different lobbying firms to fight for them. The National Cable and Telecommunications Association, in addition to its own army of in-house lobbyists, hired nine outside lobbying firms. Disney, TimeWarner, News Corporation, and others also hired their own well-connected firms.

Opponents like Google, Yahoo, and Microsoft armed themselves as well. In the fourth quarter of 2011, when the fight reached its zenith, the two sides together spent a whopping $104.6 million lobbying. In all, more than nine hundred lobbyists were paid big money.[40] It was a boon for the lobbying industry, which had been having a tough year.[41]

Those who had family members in office or were well connected did especially well. Former senator Gordon Smith represented the National Association of Broadcasters. He was a cousin to no less than three sitting U.S. senators: Mike Lee of Utah, Mark Udall of Colorado, and Tom Udall of New Mexico, a cosponsor of the bill. Senator Mark Pryor's brother, who lobbied for Microsoft, faced him from the other side. Senator Pryor conveniently sits on the powerful Commerce Committee.[42]

Dave Lugar, son of Indiana Republican senator Dick Lugar, also picked up Google as a high-paying client. (Senator Lugar was keeping quiet as to whether he supported or opposed the bill.) Dave Lugar pocketed $140,000 from Google in 2011.[43] He also helped his father raise funds. On December 13, he sent out a letter urging clients to attend a fund-raiser for the senator to the tune of $5,000 per person.[44]

Ex-politicians and their family members also had a nice payday. Google lapped up such ex-politicians as former majority leader Dick Gephardt and former congresswoman Susan Molinari, who would become the director of its Washington, D.C., office.[45] Molinari has had several interesting jobs since leaving Congress. At one point she was an anchor for *CBS News Saturday Morning*.[46] Along with her lobbying partner Rita Lewis (a former Tom Daschle aide), she also had helped to land a $4.6 billion appropriation for Hurricane Katrina relief for the state of Louisiana.[47] Her other clients have included the government of Panama. Her husband, former congressman Bill Paxon, is also a lobbyist.[48]

Comcast paid former congressman William Gray and his son Justin's boutique lobbying firm $440,000 throughout 2011.[49] Ex-congressman Vic Fazio represented AT&T.[50] A "government relations firm" named Madison Group netted a cool $140,000 from Google during 2011.[51] Michael Brown, the son of the late commerce secretary Ron Brown, worked on the Google account at Madison.[52] The firm Dutko Grayling landed a $320,000 lobbying contract from Google.[53] One of the managing principals at the firm is the brother of former Bush White House chief of staff Andy Card.[54]

Some powerful and well-connected lobbying firms even managed to walk both sides of the street — by representing both those for and against the bill. Super-lobbyist Tony Podesta, whose brother was White House chief of staff under President Clinton, was extremely well connected on both ends of Pennsylvania Avenue. A native of Chicago, Podesta was partners with Republican strategist Dan Mattoon.[55] When Dennis Hastert was Speaker of the House, Podesta and Mattoon had hired the Speaker's son to work for them.

Podesta was a frequent guest in the Obama White House.[56] Google paid his firm $350,000. Astonishingly, the National Association of Broadcasters also paid Podesta's firm $320,000.[57] The two clients had polar opposite views on the antipiracy bills. Google also hired firms like the FIRST Group, which featured recent chiefs of staffs of both Republican and Democratic senators.[58] Who says there is no bipartisanship in Washington?

Some congressional staffers smelled the cash and jumped into the money scrum after the ball was in play. Two of the Republican congressional staffers who helped write SOPA in the House and PIPA in the Senate quit their jobs — in order to become lobbyists for the MPAA and the National Music Publishers Association. One worked for House Judiciary Committee chairman Lamar Smith, and the other as a senior Republican aide on the Senate Judiciary Committee.[59]

The Obama campaign was hardly the only group extorting for campaign dollars. Congresswoman Debbie Wasserman Schultz was the Democratic whip in the House and head of the Democratic National Committee. When the Internet piracy bill passed the Senate, her fund-raisers put out the word that it was time to cough up cash. She had yet to take an official position on the bill. In less than a week — from April 27 to May 2 — an extraordinary wave of donations rolled in. A total of $63,500 flowed from the PACs of AT&T, Verizon, TimeWarner, Cox Enterprises, the Communication Workers of America, the Entertainment Software Industry Association, Microsoft, Disney, Viacom, Clear Channel Communications, Sony

Pictures, the Directors Guild of America, the National Football League, Yahoo, and GoDaddy.[60] During those same few days, checks also arrived for her leadership PAC from the chairman of 20th Century Fox, Microsoft, and executives from film companies like Fox Films, as well as from lobbyists at firms representing eBay, Time-Warner, the National Cable and Telecommunications Association, Google, and others. It was an extraordinary concentration of checks from parties that had a lot to win or lose from antipiracy legislation.

Congressman Lamar Smith, then-chairman of the House Judiciary Committee, continued his fund-raising as his staff was drafting the House bill.[61] Smith's former chief of staff, Joe Gibson, had gone into the lobbying business by forming the Gibson Group. He was working for broadcast giant Clear Channel, which supported the bill.[62] On March 25, he received twelve checks from company executives for more than $18,000.[63] "If you are a member of the Judiciary Committee, year after year after year, the content industry has been at your fund-raisers over and over," complained Computer and Communications Industry Association president Ed Black.[64] But despite grumbling, firms such as Google, GoDaddy, and Microsoft paid up.[65]

Smith also raked in donations through his Longhorn PAC, soliciting and receiving contributions from broadcasters, software groups, the recording industry, and lobbying firms involved on both sides of the antipiracy fight as the bill was being drafted.[66] In November, after hearings were held on the bill, Smith delayed moving it to the House floor. "Congress benefits from keeping us all in suspense," said Gabriella Schneider of the Sunlight Foundation. "Those special interests who have a stake in it are . . . contributing directly to campaigns and this gives them more time to do it."[67]

Lobbyists were expected to hold fund-raisers for senators and representatives if they wanted movement on the bill. Lobbyists hired by the MPAA organized a fund-raiser for Senator Orrin Hatch, who sat on the Senate Judiciary Committee and was a co-sponsor of the Senate bill.[68] Some politicians played coy by not taking a clear stand on the bill. House Oversight Committee member Ed Towns of New York lined up fund-raisers from both sides.[69] A lobbyist from the Podesta Group, which represented Google, Time-Warner, and the National Association of Broadcasters, hosted one, along with lobbyists representing Verizon, AT&T, Microsoft, and Comcast.[70]

In early December 2011, Hollywood executives came to Washington for another meeting with Biden to discuss a full-court press to support the bill. Jim Gianopulos of Fox, Barry Meyer of Warner Brothers, and Sony's Michael Lynton, along with entertainment industry union bosses, met behind closed doors with the vice president.[71] From Silicon Valley's perspective, this all looked like Armageddon. Piling on, Secretary of State Hillary Clinton wrote a letter to a cosponsor of SOPA to lend her support to the idea of aggressively dealing with online piracy saying the "the rule of law is essential to both Internet freedom and protection of intellectual property rights."[72]

But for his part, President Obama played it cool, in perfect double-milker fashion. He told the media he would "probably" sign the bill.[73] As *Mother Jones* reported, "The White House gave no indications that Obama had any problem with the legislation."[74] Yet Obama's position on the bill was out of character with his general attitude to the high-tech industry. Obama's stance on online piracy was particularly striking given what everyone regarded as his "deep ties to high tech."[75] And Silicon Valley had been "Obama's core . . . fundraising base."[76] He dined regularly with high-tech titans at the White House and in Silicon Valley.[77] Eric Schmidt of Google was an informal economic adviser of sorts.[78]

Obama rarely spoke of the antipiracy bill publicly, whether in

Hollywood or in Silicon Valley. Might his hints at support have been false?

Silicon Valley had been an early and eager backer of Obama in 2008, pouring money and expertise into his election.[79] But by 2011 there was considerable evidence that high tech was cooling to him. "I don't think they feel the love [for Obama]," said Gary Shapiro, head of the Consumer Electronics Association. "There's great disillusionment."[80] Rob Endere, a Silicon Valley tech veteran and Obama backer, told *Politico* on February 2011, "There has been growing disappointment with the President."[81]

In the first half of 2011, Silicon Valley had tipped in a paltry $1.7 million in campaign donations for Obama's reelection.[82]

Throughout the fall of 2011, the Obama administration continued to signal its support for antipiracy legislation, while it showed up for fund-raisers in high-tech communities. In late September, the president held a fund-raiser outside of Seattle at the 14,000-square-foot house of former Microsoft executive Jon Shirley. With a price tag of $35,800 per couple, the event drew fifty couples who showed up for a chance to question the president.[83] Then it was on to Silicon Valley for a visit to the home of Symantec CEO John Thompson and Facebook chief operating officer Sheryl Sandberg. The invitation read that this was an opportunity to "join President Obama in Silicon Valley." In a stately tent in the front yard of Sandberg's luxurious home, the price tag was again $35,800 per person. Lady Gaga performed, but as a paying guest.[84] For Silicon Valley execs concerned about antipiracy legislation, the high admission fee was a small price to pay.

Mimicking his April trip, Obama went directly to southern California for a $17,900-a-plate dinner with key Hollywood campaign financiers at the Fig and Olive Restaurant on Melrose. Not to be outdone by Silicon Valley, one hundred people showed up and paid full freight.[85] Between June and September, President Obama had more fund-raisers in California than in any other state.

The House version of the bill was introduced on October 26, 2011.[86] It was essentially a rewrite of the Senate version, which at that point had passed out of committee but had not yet passed the full Senate. Cosponsored by Judiciary Committee chairman Lamar Smith, the House version included dozens of cosponsors from both parties. The hearings held by the House Judiciary Committee in December of 2011 were stacked against high-tech. Of the six witnesses who appeared before the committee, only one was opposed to the bill.[87] Discussion was abruptly ended after little more than a day.[88] A committee vote was scheduled in January. It seemed certain to reach the House floor.

Panic now set in among tech nerds. There was real fear that the antipiracy bills would fundamentally change the nature of the Internet and create new liabilities for their companies.

In that atmosphere, Joe Biden showed up in Silicon Valley in January 2012 for a dinner with an A-list of high-tech executives at Zibibbo, a tony restaurant in downtown Palo Alto. They dined on baby arugula salad topped with dried apricot and goat's milk cheese and roasted portobello Wellington.[89] Among the diners were people on both sides of the antipiracy debate, including Jeffrey Katzenberg and Eric Schmidt. The dinner was the culmination of a day in which Biden held two fund-raisers, the first in the Bentley Reserve in San Francisco's financial district, and then a smaller fund-raiser at the same site. Days later he would be heading to Los Angeles to raise money from Hollywood.

The milking worked: the tech industry brought in more than $10 million over the second half of 2011, up from its $1.7 million in the first half. As the Permanent Political Class well knows, panic produces checks. Many in Silicon Valley had succumbed to the realities of the way in which the game was being played, with the rules established by the Permanent Political Class. "Many in our industry believe the way to tip the balance back our way is to simply play the same game, and out-donate the bastards," wrote John Battelle, a tech leader and cofounder of the Web 2 conferences. "(Lord knows we have the money. . . .)" This was, of course, music to the ears of the Permanent Political Class.[90]

Hollywood also poured in money. By January 2012, Hollywood had given more than $4.1 million to the Obama campaign, ahead of the $3.7 million it had contributed by the same point in 2008.[91]

Then suddenly, the Obama administration made a pivot. On January 14, 2012, the White House announced that it had problems with the antipiracy bills.[92] In a statement, the White House declared that the president "will not support legislation that reduces freedom of expression, increases cyber security risk, or undermines the dynamic, innovative global Internet." Members of Congress who had supported the bill initially also suddenly started to backtrack.[93] The fact that they had already collected large sums of money from both sides of the issue, and that friends and allies had been signed to lucrative consulting and lobbying arrangements already, made the timing near perfect. The House Judiciary Committee never brought its version to a vote.

Public stories about the two bills focused on grassroots Internet protests, including a blackout by such firms as Wikipedia on January 18. But both sides had passionate supporters.[94] Why did the White House flip?

Many in Hollywood, particularly the suits, were bitter at what they saw as a betrayal. "He [Obama] didn't just throw us under the bus . . . he ran us down, reversed and ran over us again," one film executive and longtime Obama supporter said to the *Financial Times*.[95] The White House "tried to play it both ways," said Marge Tabankin, who advised Hollywood clients on politics. "And this industry said that, for everything we've done, it would have been nice if they at least had tried to work out a compromise."[96] Tabankin was largely right, but for one thing: the Permanent Political Class *had* played it both ways successfully. President Obama had done so on the presidential level, but so had members of Congress on both sides of the aisle.

MPAA chairman Chris Dodd threatened that Hollywood might withhold campaign cash. "Don't make the false assumption here that because we did it in years past we're going to do it this year."[97] But the threat was pointless: the Hollywood suits had been outmaneuvered. "Most of us have maxed out [on fund-raising] already, unfortunately," one exec told the *Hollywood Reporter*. The Permanent Political Class had largely milked the Hollywood suits until they went dry. And now the suits had no leverage left.[98]

Not all was lost, particularly for President Obama's biggest Hollywood supporters. Jeffrey Katzenberg and Steven Spielberg had raised millions in donations for the Obama campaign and had given millions themselves to both the campaign and pro-Obama super PACs. Both were supporters of the antipiracy bills. So when China's Vice Premier Xi Jinping visited Los Angeles, Vice President Biden negotiated directly with Chinese officials to allow access to the Chinese market for American films. Up until this point, only twenty U.S.-made films could be distributed per year in the world's fastest-growing movie market.[99] Biden convinced Beijing to raise the limit to thirty-four, including those shot in 3-D or in IMAX format. Katzenberg was in close contact with Biden and White House officials during those negotiations. And Spielberg attended at least one private event with Jinping. At a public event with Jinping, Katzenberg announced his company's plans to establish Oriental DreamWorks, a $350 million production studio in Shanghai, a joint venture with Chinese companies. Since Oriental DreamWorks would be a local venture, the quota for American films wouldn't apply.[100]

The United States had many trade issues with China, but access for Hollywood films had moved to the top of the list. And with the sensitive joint-venture deal in place, Katzenberg and Spielberg were big winners.[101]

Still, the biggest victory was won by neither Katzenberg and Spielberg nor Google. By far the biggest winners in this saga were the members of the Permanent Political Class in Washington. After the fight, the high-tech community recognized the new reality in which it was operating. What Microsoft learned in the '90s, the rest of Silicon Valley had now learned too: they had to become Washington players.

"The high-tech industry moves incredibly fast," Bob Herbold told me. "Their hands are full just trying to compete. That should be their focus. There are some people in the industry that like this system — they don't want to see it exposed. But most are innovators and hate it. Problem is, they feel like they have no choice."[102]

In September 2012, tech firms formed the Internet Association, a new industry group that included Google, Amazon, and Facebook. The social media giant Facebook signed former Clinton, Bush, and Obama White House aides to lucrative contracts to keep the company out of Washington's crosshairs.[103] In 2012 large high-tech companies dumped record amounts of cash into lobbying.[104] Google lobbying spending soared to $16.48 million in 2012, and Facebook spent $3.99 million. The Permanent Political Class is pleased.[105]

"It's kind of like trying to get someone hooked on drugs," says former BB&T chairman John Allison. "It starts on one issue, protecting the company. But then when corporations can figure out what government can do for them, they get hooked."[106]

The milking, of course, continues. The piracy problem will be revisited, and the high-tech industry is facing the possibility of new regulations in the video game industry.[107] In the wake of the tragic shooting in Newtown, Connecticut, in December 2012, Vice

President Biden criticized the industry, arguing that video games contribute to a national culture of violence. (The Connecticut gunman, Adam Lanza, was apparently a fan of the online game World of Warcraft.) Members of Congress from both parties are now lining up. "Connecticut has changed things," said Virginia Republican representative Frank Wolf in an interview. "I don't know what we're going to do, but we're going to do something."[108]

What that "something" might be is open to question. But whatever it is, it creates fear in the gaming industry. President Obama has asked the Centers for Disease Control to study the causes of violent behavior, including any role that movies, television, and video games might play.[109] And "something" also includes soliciting campaign donations and other benefits from the video-game industry. The industry was already spending about $5 million a year lobbying in Washington to fend off legislation. Now the Entertainment Software Industry Association, made up of video-game companies like Sony, Nintendo, and Microsoft, is busy expanding its lobbying operations in Washington by hiring the family and friends of the Permanent Political Class.[110]

6

SLUSH FUNDS

Don't write anything you can phone. Don't phone anything you can talk.
Don't talk anything you can whisper. Don't whisper anything you can smile.
Don't smile anything you can nod. Don't nod anything you wink.

— EARL LONG, FORMER GOVERNOR OF LOUISIANA

THE MOB'S METHOD required brawn and brains. The brawn was needed to extort and "throw fear." But once the mob had the money flowing in, operations needed to be structured to move the money around, hide it, and funnel funds where needed. Often, the Mafia mingled the operation of legitimate businesses with its criminal activities.

In the history of the U.S. mob, no one did that better than mobster Meyer Lansky, who was known as the "mob's accountant." Gangster Al Capone was a master of building his Chicago-based gangland empire around a cluster of criminal "growth industries." The feds could never get him on his violent activities, so the Treasury Department meticulously investigated the cash flow behind his business and charged him in 1931 for evading taxes. Also indicted were his brother Ralph "Bottles" Capone, Jake "Greasy Thumb" Guzik, and Frank Nitti.

On October 18, 1931, Capone was found guilty of tax evasion and sentenced to eleven years in federal prison. He also paid $215,000 plus interest due on back taxes.[1]

Seeing what happened to Capone, Lansky set up a sophisticated operation with Lucky Luciano to transfer funds between their various operations. He even bought a bank in Switzerland to launder money through a network of companies.[2] When the federal government came after Lansky on tax evasion charges in 1971, it had trouble tracking his money and was forced to depend on the unreliable testimony of a loan shark named "Fat Vinnie" Teresa. Lansky was acquitted. He died in Miami Beach in 1983 of lung cancer.

Today's Permanent Political Class lacks the colorful nicknames the mob used, but they too have mastered the art of funneling funds. Extorting money in the form of campaign contributions is not simply about getting reelected. Many politicians aggressively fundraise even though they face little or no opposition for reelection. Politicians have discovered a creative way to transfer donations into subsidies designed to benefit their lifestyles. We have already seen some of the ways in which politicians can shift money around and give themselves sweetheart interest rates. A traditional campaign committee, the primary vehicle for reelection, can also provide a politician with a solid stream of cash. Those candidates who are not in particularly tight races can put family members on the payroll, and they can make unlimited transfers of cash from campaign committees to party organizations and channel donations to colleagues. But politicians will have trouble using their campaign fund for personal benefit apart from high-interest loans. It's not that they haven't tried. Congressman Gregory Meeks tried to use $6,230 in campaign funds to pay for a personal trainer. His staff argued that the expenditures were legitimate because they helped him deal with the stress of his "official duties." The Federal Election Commission didn't buy it.[3]

But a leadership PAC is different. Leadership PACs are ostensibly about raising money to help political colleagues hold and win seats. But the FEC has few restrictions on how these monies can be used and does not restrict the "personal use" of such funds. "Congress has never extended the personal-use restrictions to leadership PACs," says former FEC chairman Michael Toner. "The FEC has looked at this over the years and has determined they don't have the statutory ability to address this. It will take an act of Congress."[4]

How unregulated are these leadership PACs? Consider the case of Ohio Republican Paul Gillmor's leadership PAC. During a recent election, PAUL PAC spent almost $6,000 on personal expenses: fast food, doughnuts, bar tabs, and golf. The problem? Congressman Gillmor was dead. He had tragically fallen down the stairs months earlier. And yet PAUL PAC was picking up the cost for pizza deliveries, visits to Mexican restaurants, Dunkin' Donuts, and more. Intrepid *Wall Street Journal* reporters Brody Mullins and Brad Haynes uncovered the story and asked the PAC manager about the expenditures. He had a simple explanation: the expenditures were necessary because the PAC members had "gathered many times as we were all grieving to help each other with the job search process." There was apparently nothing illegal about using "grieving funds" to go golfing.[5]

Seemingly everyone in political office wants a leadership PAC. Joe Kennedy III, elected in 2012, started his leadership PAC three months after being sworn in.[6] Congressman Aaron Schock of Illinois, a rising Republican star, formed his leadership PAC before he was even elected to office in 2008.[7]

And who can blame them? While they are required to disclose how they spend the money, the disclosures are so cursory and nondescript that they can get away with a lot. They don't have to spell out who attended a lavish weekend trip at a golf resort. They can simply list, as one senator did:

"PAC EVENT/LODGING/BANQUET/GOLF"[8]

"For the most part, it's really kind of an incumbent racket," says former FEC commissioner Brad Smith, who usually opposes tighter campaign finance rules. Campaign contributions are supposed to be a way for donors to support candidates and ideas they believe in. To be sure, some leadership PACs do devote a substantial portion of their funds to helping elect members of Congress. Yet many of them spend most of their money on events in swanky five-star resorts, food, and entertainment.[9]

Here are some of the unwritten rules about how politicians use leadership PAC money. First, "retreats," "strategic planning sessions," and other events never occur at a Hampton Inn or a Holiday Inn. They are almost exclusively held at five-star resorts that feature golf and high-end spas. Second, these events are timed for peak tourism seasons. Politicians don't tend to travel to upstate New York in the winter (unless they are going skiing) or to south Florida in August. Like a family putting together a vacation, members of the Permanent Political Class time these lavish events to conveniently coincide with the best time to enjoy the location. What leadership PACs provide is essentially a second personal bank account, or a second pocket from which politicians can pull money.

There are even some administrative perks from regulated industries that want to stay on their good side. While most Americans grapple with busy airlines and airports, politicians line up special privileges that allow them to sidestep such headaches. For example, Capitol Hill schedulers make reservations on dedicated phone lines that Delta and other airlines have set up especially for them. Ever have trouble with canceling a flight and getting a refund? Airlines permit members of Congress to reserve seats on multiple flights but pay only for the trips they take. And they never have trouble getting a seat. "We get on every single flight," one congressional aide told *Roll Call*.[10] Why do airlines pamper them? Precisely because they know that getting on the wrong side of the Permanent Political Class can cause their industry serious problems.

When politicians leave Washington on a flight, whether they are going back to their district for meetings, going golfing in Florida, or heading overseas for vacation, the Metropolitan Washington Airports Authority provides free parking in a private lot. There are ninety-seven reserved spaces set aside for them at Dulles International Airport, and eighty-nine at Reagan National.[11]

Senator Saxby Chambliss of Georgia loves to play golf. Over the course of his career, his leadership PAC has helped him dramatically improve his game. The so-called Republican Majority Fund has picked up the tab for golf outings at the best and most expensive golf resorts in the country: Pebble Beach Resorts, the Inn at Spanish Bay, and others. One year almost one-third of Chambliss's entire leadership PAC expenditures went for golf, including transportation: limos and at least one private jet.[12] During the 2012 election cycle, Chambliss's PAC dropped a cool $107,752 at the Breakers in Palm Beach. That's three times what he gave to the National Republican Senatorial Committee to elect other Republicans. He also spent $26,814 at Ruth's Chris Steakhouse, and $10,344 at Pebble Beach. Who contributes funds to Chambliss's leadership PAC? The largest three groups are lobbyists, followed by the tobacco and insurance industries.[13] All three groups, of course, need protection. So all three groups subsidize the lifestyle of a United States senator.

Congressman John Conyers of Michigan isn't such a big golfer, but he loves his sports. His PAC is called America Forward, but what mostly advances is the congressman's lifestyle. During the 2012 election cycle, for example, he raised $99,300, which is a small total by leadership PAC standards. (In 2010 he did much better, raking in more than $200,000.) But of that nearly $100,000 he raised, Conyers gave only $1,430 to other candidates, which is the stated purpose of his PAC. Instead, he spent more than six times that amount on the National Football League ($6,595) and ESPN ($6,900) to attend award events. Conyers spent even more on limousine services for himself ($1,500) than he did on candidates. (At least he was using a car service called Limo 4 Less.) The congressman also dropped serious money at the Rock Bottom Brewery ($1,300).[14] Conyers is the ranking member of the House Judiciary Committee. The vast majority of the money he raised came from corporate PACs and lobbyists.

These are hardly exceptions to the rule. Senator Roy Blunt of Missouri runs a leadership PAC called the Rely on Your Beliefs Fund. Like other leadership PACs, the vast majority of its money comes from PACs and lobbyists. Blunt's biggest donor during the 2012 election was Goldman Sachs. (Blunt sits on the powerful Senate Appropriations Committee.) How does he spend their money? After the November 2012 election, Blunt retreated to the beautiful sanctuary at Kiawah Island on Johns Island, South Carolina. The PAC dropped $11,334 there on November 14 for "PAC LODGING & EVENT CATERING." Two months earlier, the PAC dropped $12,481 for "PAC EVENT CATERING & FACILITIES FEE." On December 7, 2012, there was another $1,584 expense for "LODGING" at the resort, and on December 13, 2012, the PAC spent $11,684 on yet another event. In all, the PAC spent over $65,000 at this location during the 2012 election cycle.[15] Indeed, Blunt spent more at the Kiawah resort through his leadership PAC than he transferred from that PAC to the National Republican Senatorial Committee to elect other Republicans. And while he gave other Senate candidates over $240,000, that was a small fraction of the $1.1 million he raised. Meanwhile, his political aide Keri Ann Hayes received $296,000 in salary and benefits from the leadership PAC during the 2012 election cycle, more than all the Republican candidates received.[16]

Frequently politicians will put family members in charge of running their PACs. Congressman Rob Andrews of New Jersey made his wife (a lawyer and an associate law dean at Rutgers School of Law–Camden) a PAC compliance officer. Mrs. Andrews has approved some interesting expenditures over the years. She approved the use of donation dollars to fly herself, her husband, and their two daughters to Edinburgh, Scotland, to stay at a five-star resort for a wedding.[17] His leadership PAC paid $16,575 in airfare (including some business-class travel). The rest of the tab, a little less than $14,000, was picked up by his campaign committee. Andrews's leadership PAC even picked up the tab for the wedding gift . . . china, from Bloomingdale's.

It was quite the trip. The family tapped Andrews's campaign committee for "petty cash" for Scotland in the form of two checks for at least $2,500. They stayed in two rooms at the luxury five-star Balmoral Hotel in Edinburgh. Campaign contributors also picked up the tab for dinners, the in-room bar, and other expenses.

The expenditure of these funds (particularly those from the more regulated traditional campaign committee) sparked an ethics investigation. In an email exchange, Andrews's campaign treasurer laid out the fuzzy rules pertaining to the leadership PAC. "Aside from personal and official expenses exception [which are House rules, not federal law], there is wide discretion as to what expenditures further the Leadership PAC's goals." The treasurer cited the examples of politicians using leadership PAC money to buy tickets to Yankees games, travel to resorts, and golf at Pebble Beach. "As you can see, so long as the expense furthers the Leadership PAC's goals, and is otherwise not prohibited, it appears to be permissible." Although the Andrewses refunded the cost of the vacation, they did so only after ethical questions were publicly raised, according to the *Philadelphia Inquirer*.[18]

On another occasion, the Andrewses decided it would be nice to merge a campaign event with their daughter's graduation. The invitation they sent out to donors and friends read: "We hope that you and your family will join us in celebrating Rob's 20 years of serving in the House of Representatives and [the daughter's] graduation from the Baldwin School." Both events were held at the same time at their house, which allowed them to blend the costs of the two events, though the PAC did not pay for the entire evening. The graduating daughter apparently received congratulatory checks from people who came, but Mrs. Andrews insisted that "every single check that was given to her at the party, we shredded."[19]

Congressman Ander Crenshaw of Florida spent 80 percent of his leadership PAC money on expenses during the 2012 cycle. Americans Nationwide Dedicated to Electing Republicans (ANDER PAC) spent more money on expenses than it did on contributions to Republican campaigns: $72,000 on travel, hotels, resort fees, and the like, and only $17,500 on other candidates. Much of the PAC's money went for a lavish trip through the wine country of Napa, California. Tens of thousands of dollars went for the AVIA Hotel, for a reception at the Caldwell Winery, another at the Joseph Phelps Vineyards, and still another at the Palmaz Vineyards, and for a meal at a restaurant in Napa called Tuscany. The PAC also spent money at the Caves Valley Golf Course outside of Washington (including $185 for caddy fees).[20] Who was in Napa with Crenshaw? It's unclear, but what is clear is that his donation records show that defense contractors from BAE Systems, Boeing, Northrop Grumman, and Nextera Energy gave to Crenshaw's leadership PAC on the same days he took these trips.[21] Did I mention that Crenshaw sits on the defense subcommittee of the powerful House Appropriations Committee?[22]

Newly elected congressman Joaquin Castro used his Toward Tomorrow PAC to pay $10,000 for what is listed as a "Visa business" credit card payment.[23] Senator Chuck Schumer used his leadership PAC (Impact) for limousine services and tens of thousands of dollars for exclusive tickets to New York Yankees games. There are also large reimbursements for non-itemized credit card payments.[24] Senator John Thune of South Dakota used his Heartland PAC for lavish events at Pebble Beach, the Greenbrier Resort ($84,197), and Kiawah Island.[25]

Congressman Charlie Rangel paid $64,500 from his leadership PAC funds to commission a painting of himself.[26] Rangel also paid one of his sons to develop a website. Steven Rangel's Edisonian Innovation Works received $79,560 to make a website for the National Leadership PAC. The website was not exactly a great investment. As reported in a story in *Politico*, it looked as if it had been slapped together in a couple of hours. It even included numerous spelling errors, such as "Give Contribuition." There was an apology that the site was not finished but undergoing "routine maintenace." One web designer said the website was so bad that the fee should not have been more than $100.[27]

Congresswoman Rosa DeLauro has represented Connecticut since 1991. Along with her husband, former Clinton pollster Stanley Greenberg, she has regularly used her leadership PAC like a Diners Club card over the years. Several times a month she has tapped her Democratic Future leadership PAC to cater wine and food events at her house, using top-drawer caterers and wine companies. Many of the expenditures during the 2010 election were made to Schneider's, an exclusive liquor store that boasts eight full-time wine consultants. The food comes from high-end caterer Federal City Caterers. In the 2010 election, only 25 percent of the money raised for her leadership PAC went to other candidates, which was the ostensible purpose of the PAC when she formed it in 2005. Instead, two-thirds of the money raised went to operating expenses and what she describes as elaborate "policy dinners." Former congressman Toby Moffett, who is now a Democratic consultant working in government affairs, has contributed to DeLauro's leadership PAC and has attended these catered events. He calls them "a little bastion of enlightenment and intellectual discourse."[28] No doubt policy ideas are discussed at times. But it's a really cushy way to advance an agenda.

What about members of Congress who retire with leadership PAC money? Amazingly, they can continue to spend as they see fit, or they can even convert the funds to personal funds (after paying taxes on them). In 2012 the Federal Election Commission called on Congress to expand the ban on the personal use of political committee funds. "The Commission has seen a substantial number of instances where individuals with access to the funds received by political committees have used such funds to make unauthorized disbursements to pay for their own personal expenses," the FEC's legislative recommendation said.[29]

Don't expect Congress to pass such a law anytime soon. It would mean less golf.

7

TRUST ME

You're Gonna Need to Pay Me

If we walk in the woods, we must feed the mosquitoes.

— RALPH WALDO EMERSON

THERE IS ONE BIG DIFFERENCE between the Permanent Political Class and the Mafia. In the world of organized crime, the bosses are permanently in opposition to law enforcement. They might use bribery or extortion to control judges, witnesses, and the police, but they are always on the side of crime. If a member of a Mafia family decides to cooperate with law enforcement and become an informant, the Mafia will do anything and everything to kill him. You cross the lines at your mortal peril.

For the Permanent Political Class, by contrast, line-crossing is an art form. The name of the game is to make money and to extract it from the private sector, but you can do that from both sides of the public-private divide. You don't have to be a member of Congress — you can be a lobbyist or a lawyer. Better yet, you can pass back and forth between political office and this private-public sector of Washington, always working to extract wealth from various industries that fear the laws and regulations you help create.

In 2010 Congress passed, and President Obama signed, the Dodd-Frank Wall Street Reform and Consumer Protection Act. It was allegedly designed to provide new safeguards for financial markets by further regulating investment banks and other financial market participants. The trouble? No one can actually understand it. As one banker, publicly supportive of the law, told *The Economist*, when asked about the "Volcker Rule," a centerpiece of Dodd-Frank, the rule is "unintelligible any way you read it."[1] Sheila Bair, the former head of the Federal Deposit Insurance Corporation (FDIC), has called the Volcker Rule "extraordinarily complex" and says, "Regulators should think hard about starting over again with a simple rule."[2]

But that won't happen for one simple reason: Dodd-Frank was *designed* to be indecipherable by mere mortals. For the Permanent Political Class, the regulatory minefield creates a lucrative opportunity for extortion.

Part of the problem is the law's massive size. At 2,319 pages, it is dramatically larger than previous financial reform laws and approaches the monstrous length of the Obamacare bill. By comparison, the Federal Reserve Act of 1913, which established the Federal Reserve banking system and the single national currency, was 31 pages long. The Glass-Steagall Banking Act of 1933, which overhauled the entire banking system in light of hundreds of bank failures, was 37 pages long.

Dodd-Frank is also remarkably complex. Even seemingly basic principles are expanded and twisted to make compliance with them nearly impossible. For example, the so-called Volcker Rule, which grew out of a three-page memo from former Fed chairman Paul Volcker to President Obama in 2009, morphed into a 298-page description with 383 questions that break down into 1,420 subquestions.[3]

The cost of filling out the complex paperwork is enormous. The forms required by sections 404 and 406 of the law (which require the collection of systemic risk data from private funds, including hedge funds) will cost hedge funds approximately $100,000 to $150,000 to complete the first time, and then $40,000 a year after.[4]

The law was written to create more rules. As Jonathan Macey of the Yale Law School puts it, "Laws classically provide people with rules. Dodd Frank is not directed at people. It is an outline directed at bureaucrats and it instructs them to make still more regulations and to create more bureaucracies."[5] For example, the law requires 243 rules and sixty-seven studies by eleven different agencies.[6] The law also requires the creation of multiple new government entities, including the Financial Stability Oversight Council (FSOC) and the Consumer Financial Protection Bureau (CFPB).[7]

It's not that government officials and bureaucrats can't make things simple. At the height of the financial crisis in 2008, government officials produced a simple two-page application for banks to use in applying for federal Troubled Asset Relief Program (TARP) money. It was "the model of simplicity," with only four clear, concise bullet points. Federal officials used this document to lend nearly $50 billion to the biggest banks.[8] When a true crisis arises and time is precious, Washington *can* cut to the chase.

Government bureaucrats and law-writers can make things simple, but apart from dire emergencies, they generally choose not to. Complexity is a useful and lucrative method of legal extortion for politicians because, as University of London economist Anthony G. Heyes puts it, "it is precisely the complex, opacity and user-unfriendliness which underpin the value of their expertise." And that translates into "selling advice to those they previously regulated."[9]

George LeMieux was appointed to the U.S. Senate to represent

Florida in 2009 after Senator Mel Martinez stepped down. LeMieux jumped in quickly and saw immediately the complexity of a lot of bills. "Complexity always creates opportunities for those who know the details," he told me. "I tried to read Dodd-Frank, and it was incomprehensible."[10]

Consider, for example, how lucrative the indecipherable Dodd-Frank law has become for the members of the Permanent Political Class who actually wrote it.

Amy Friend was a chief aide to Senator Chris Dodd in crafting the Dodd-Frank financial reform bill and served as the chief counsel to the Senate Banking Committee. After the bill passed and became law, she left Capitol Hill and became a managing director at Promontory Financial Group, which describes itself as "a premier global financial services consulting firm."[11] This Washington-based consulting firm is headed up by many people like Friend—people who were once responsible for erecting or interpreting arcane financial regulations in public service and then joined the group, where they can charge high fees to help firms interpret and comply with these befuddling regulations. The firm is a "major power broker in Washington," says the *New York Times*, "helping Wall Street navigate an onslaught of new rules and regulatory scrutiny" (many of those rules having been written, of course, by those now working at Promontory). Banks complain about Promontory's high fees, which can run $1,500 an hour. Eugene Ludwig, the former comptroller of the currency under Bill Clinton, reportedly makes $30 million a year running Promontory. He lives in one of the most expensive houses in Washington, a 13,000-square-foot home on a three-acre estate.[12]

When Ludwig announced that Amy Friend was joining his firm, he boasted about the fact that Friend had played a key role in shaping the Dodd-Frank bill and that at Promontory she would help clients with "the regulatory implementation of the Dodd-Frank Wall Street Reform and Consumer Protection Act of 2010, which, at 2,300 pages, is one of the most complex and wide-ranging overhauls of the financial regulatory framework in decades."[13]

But Friend was just one of many who crafted the convoluted bill, left government, and now command large fees from firms trying to make sense of it. Daniel Meade was the chief counsel on the Financial Services Committee under Chairman Barney Frank (the Frank of Dodd-Frank). Meade left Capitol Hill for Hogan Lovells, a well-established lobbying firm. When Meade arrived, the firm Hogan Lovells announced that Meade was "a principal draftsperson of substantial portions of the Dodd-Frank Wall Street Reform and Consumer Protection Act." The firm's publicity explained that Meade would be "representing financial services entities and other entities impacted by the regulation of those entities in connection with a broad range of regulatory and transactional matters, including issues related to the Dodd-Frank Act."[14] It makes all the sense in the world: if you can't understand a complex new legal regime, who better to help guide you than one of the people who drafted it? But think about it from the perspective of the congressional aide: your future wealth depends on crafting a complex bill.

Senator George LeMieux was surprised by the power that committee staff in particular wield on Capitol Hill. "I was stunned at how committee staff would address even senior senators." That power came from their grasp of the details, which was not only a source of power but a future source of riches as well.[15]

One of the most confusing sections of the Dodd-Frank Act concerns options and commodity trading. In the months after the law passed, at least nine employees of the Commodity Futures Trading Commission (CFTC) who helped write that section and establish its regulatory provisions left for lucrative jobs, helping large firms figure out how to comply. They went to positions at JP Morgan Chase, Deutsche Bank, Nomura Securities, PricewaterhouseCoopers, and the white-collar criminal defense law firm Covington & Burling. These firms either are subject to the confusing Dodd-Frank rules or advise other firms on how to comply with them.[16]

It's the perfect form of extortion: legal, obscure, lucrative, and impossible to avoid. Financial executives will pay just about anything to avoid legal vulnerability, especially when vulnerability can mean jail time. If they don't understand what the rules are, they will pay someone who does. Little surprise that Harvey Pitt, the former head of the Securities and Exchange Commission, calls Dodd-Frank "the Lawyers' and Lobbyists' Full Employment Act."[17]

Companies by and large want to comply with laws and regulations. Executives don't want to pay fines, or worse, go to jail. Cass Sunstein served in the Obama administration as the administrator of the White House Office of Information and Regulatory Affairs. "As OIRA administrator, I often heard the following plea from the private sector: 'Please, tell us what you want us to do!' On many occasions, companies said that they were prepared to comply with the rules, and to do so in good faith, but they needed to know what, specifically, compliance entailed." Sunstein is no free market libertarian. He is generally liberal, and as a colleague of the president back when Obama was a law professor at the University of Chicago, Sunstein was a known quantity to his boss. Yet even the liberal professor admits that "regulation is often confusing, inconsistent, redundant, and excessive."[18] On top of that, the vagueness of these laws provides opportunities for the government to investigate someone under a wide variety of statutes, even if it isn't clear that the party committed a crime. Robert H. Jackson, Franklin Delano Roosevelt's attorney general, warned his prosecutors that federal law books were "filled with a great assortment of crimes" and that a prosecutor "stands a fair chance of finding at least a technical violation of some act on the part of almost anyone." And that was back when the number of laws and regulations on the books was a fraction of its current number. It's always a temptation for a prosecutor to be "picking the man and then searching the law books, or putting investigators to work, to pin some offense on him."[19]

John Allison recalls instances when his bank hired firms "filled with ex-regulators" to deal with complex regulations. The bank was especially interested in those who had "just left the government. We felt we had to hire certain consultants who had the contacts and relationships."[20]

But of course there is no money for the Permanent Political Class in providing companies with simple rules to comply with the law. As Professor Joel Mintz, an authority on regulatory law at Nova Southeastern University, puts it, "Regulatory compliance is quite a different matter than compliance with traffic law."[21] Professor Anthony Heyes of the University of Ottawa's Department of Economics agrees. "Many firms are unaware of which regulations apply to them, how and when to comply, of when waivers and deferrals might be available, of how to keep and disclose appropriate records in the manner, and of the plethora of unwritten rules and conventions governing the way the regulator likes to do business."[22]

John Hofmeister, the former president of Shell Oil, saw how the process worked. "They deliberately write ambiguity into the law. It's part of a career-building process. If you are a congressional staffer, you spend your career crafting complex legislative language. This equips you to leverage your postgovernment competence." And complexity begets complexity. "The whole system builds on itself."[23]

Corporations and even investors themselves often hire consultants who wrote the law or rule in question. Those with detailed knowledge of what the Dodd-Frank law actually means can command salaries as high as $1 million from hedge funds. "Lawyers with Dodd-Frank Act and regulatory expertise are being wooed by private equity firms and hedge funds in need of an in-house compliance team," reported the *New York Law Journal* in 2012.[24]

For congressional staffers used to making 10 percent of that, it's a huge payday. Senator Ron Johnson was first elected to the U.S. Senate in 2010 from the state of Wisconsin. A businessman and entrepreneur, he has hired plenty of people over the years. When it came to hiring congressional staffers for his new job, he was struck by a phrase that some applicants used during the interview process: "cashing in." As in, "I want to work in public service for a while, before cashing in." "I had never heard that term before when hiring someone in the private sector," Johnson says. Time spent working at a lobbying firm or at a consultancy is "cashing in." Some people work on Wall Street until they have enough money to "cash out." In Washington, they set themselves up for those jobs in order to cash in.[25]

It's not just Dodd-Frank. Laws and regulations have become far more complex in every area. Why not? They're moneymakers for those who write them. Often, those rules and regulations are not written by elected officials and their staffs but by bureaucrats in government agencies. "Often the details of a regulation are too complex to sensibly be enriched in law, so Congress delegates rule-writing authority," explains Professor John Cochrane of the University of Chicago.[26] The Occupational Safety and Health Act (OSHA), for example, though passed by Congress, provided little about the rules and standards governing specific workplace settings. Instead, the law empowered OSHA bureaucrats to write safety laws based on their interpretation of the law and their own expertise. Other government agencies, like the Department of Housing and Urban Development, the Fish and Wildlife Service, and the Department of Agriculture, have similar opportunities. They also have judicial officers who essentially function as administrative judges.

In 2011 American businesses were required to comply with no fewer than 165,000 pages of federal regulations.[27]

High-powered and expensive consulting firms in Washington are littered with former regulators who are eager, for a nice fee, to clarify the confusing rules they once wrote. A former SEC senior associate director now at the power firm Murphy & McGonigle offers a "financial services advisory" practice. His bio notes that he "was responsible for the development and administration of Regulation M, Regulation SHO, and the SEC's interpretive guidance on Section 28(e) of the Securities Exchange Act of 1934."[28] In a press release the firm issued in 2011, it highlighted his "extraordinary breadth and depth of experience" and noted that he "will significantly enhance our ability to serve our financial services clients ... particularly during this period of rapid regulatory change."[29]

Another senior SEC official, who served as deputy director of trading and markets, went to work for the high-octane New York law firm Davis Polk to advise "on regulatory and compliance matters."[30] At the SEC, he "helped lead the development and implementation of investor protection policies, rules, and interpretations governing broker-dealers, securities markets, clearance and settlement systems, and transfer agents." At Davis Polk he would now be advising "on regulatory and compliance matters involving securities and derivatives for financial institutions."[31]

One SEC commissioner resigned his post in 2007 and joined Cooley Godward Kronish LLP, where he worked in the business litigation practice. His expertise? The opaque and convoluted Sarbanes-Oxley Act, which made executives potentially criminally liable for their actions. This ex-commissioner could help clear away the confusion (for a hefty fee) because he was "one of the key policy makers and architects of the SEC rules implementing SOX [Sarbanes-Oxley]. During his two terms, he helped lead the SEC in the study and crafting of the Commission's regulations implementing SOX."[32]

The D.C. power firm Skadden, Arps, Slate, Meagher & Flom LLP hired a deputy director of the SEC to help firms navigate through complex rules, boasting that he "assisted the commission with its consideration of significant rule amendments in a number of areas" and "advised the SEC's office of legislative affairs on a number of regulatory reform matters that were adopted in the Dodd-Frank Act."[33]

These are just a few of the dozens of executives who have made the same transition — and not just in the realm of financial regulation. This sort of legal extortion occurs in every aspect of economic life.

Health care regulations — which affect doctors, hospitals, drug companies, device makers, and insurance companies — provide another lucrative area for extraction. Part of the problem is that there are so many laws and regulations that doctors don't even know about, some of which could put them in jail. "The list of physicians subject to all-too-easy indictment for violations of federal laws is long because the governing statutes and regulations are deceptively easy to violate," says criminal defense attorney Harvey Silverglate. "These laws are not readily understood by medical practitioners operating in good faith because they are vague, complex, and often self-contradictory. If one adds up the number of physicians who are threatened by this state of affairs, it constitutes nearly every physician practicing medicine today."[34]

In 2004 the Department of Health and Human Services (HHS) was setting up rules for a massive expansion of the Medicare and Medicaid programs. At the center of that effort was Thomas Scully. A former Senate aide, White House official, and onetime head of the Federation of American Hospitals, he had been appointed by

President George W. Bush in 2001 to head the Centers for Medicare and Medicaid Services. Never heard of this government body? You should know it: CMS is a government agency that oversees more than $600 billion in annual spending of taxpayer money on health care. In 2003 Congress passed, and President Bush signed, a prescription drug benefit plan for seniors. It was the largest change in government health care policy involving seniors in a generation. Given the rules and parameters of the program written by HHS officials, it was also incredibly confusing and difficult to digest. Health care companies, insurance companies, pharmaceutical firms, and medical device manufacturers had a difficult time understanding it. Which is probably just how it was designed to be. Shortly after the law passed and the regulations were written, Scully quit his job and inked a deal with Alston & Bird, a powerful Washington, D.C., lobbying and consulting firm. He also signed on with Welsh, Carson, Anderson & Stone, a New York–based investment firm. His fees were reportedly $1,000 an hour.[35] His job? Advising "clients on how to navigate the complexities of the new Medicare law."[36]

The Affordable Health Care Act (aka "Obamacare") is a massive bill of more than two thousand pages. There are also thousands of pages of additional "rules." For example, HHS recently published just one 189-page rule setting out the regulations for doctors to form so-called accountable care organizations. Doctors complain that the requirements are "too complex and convoluted for them to understand."[37]

One of the key architects of the law was Elizabeth Fowler, who served as the chief health policy counsel to Senator Max Baucus, chairman of the Senate Finance Committee. It was Baucus's committee that took the lead in drafting the bill. As *Politico* put it at the time, "If you drew an organizational chart of major players in the Senate health care negotiations, Fowler would be the chief operating officer." After Obamacare became law, Fowler went to the

Obama White House to oversee implementation of the law. She served as a special assistant to the president for health care and economic policy at the National Economic Council. After she oversaw much of the infrastructure developed for the law's implementation, however, she cashed in, moving to the health care giant Johnson & Johnson, where she would lead "global health policy."[38]

The Affordable Health Care Act was passed in 2009. Another of its key draftsmen was Tom Daschle, the former senator from South Dakota who served as congressional point man on the bill for the Obama administration.[39] After Obamacare passed, he cashed in, working full-time at a lobbying and consulting firm, representing a new batch of health-related companies eager to know exactly what the law would mean for them. Daschle says that he is not a lobbyist but rather provides "strategic advice on public policy matters" — to a law firm that is one of the most powerful lobbying operations in Washington.[40]

Senator Arlen Specter's health care policy specialist, John Myers, left public service after the bill passed to work for the Glover Park Group, a consultancy and lobbying firm. He now represents health insurance and pharmaceutical companies.[41] Liz Engel, who was the health policy director at the Senate Democratic Policy Committee, joined him there.[42] Other congressional staffers, from Nancy Pelosi's top health care aide to staffers at the Senate Health Committee, House Democratic Policy Committee, and the powerful House Ways and Means Committee, also joined the consulting and lobbying business.[43] It's good and profitable work for those who crafted a bill that people still don't fully understand.[44]

Every aspect of regulatory life is now involved in the extortion racket. There is an "explosive growth of consultancy firms offering specialist advice on energy saving/compliance."[45] The Environmental Protection Agency (EPA) has passed a series of "self-audit" regulations that require businesses to monitor their own activities to ensure that they are in compliance with complex regulations. That, of course, requires regulatory expertise — jobs for ex-regulators.[46] One government official explained in 2009, "The best opportunities should be in consulting services ... in response to a growing demand for professionals to prepare environmental impact statements."[47] Many regulators suggest that businesses hire a consultant given the fact that they must deal with "complex environmental regulations."[48] There are even instances where a government agency like OSHA forced companies to hire "OSHA-approved safety directors" to comply with 'voluntary' guidelines.[49] Talk about a jobs bill! How about a closed-shop jobs bill for the ultimate insiders union?

When some banks were recently charged with foreclosure abuse, government regulators threatened to throw the book at them. To clean the mess up, they forced the large banks to hire expensive consultants — usually from firms that included their former colleagues. "The government insisted that the banks hire expensive consultants to do a review of every foreclosure that took place in 2009 and 2010," writes Joe Nocera in the *New York Times*.[50] The firm that Amy Friend joined, Promontory, made huge sums of money off the deal. "Promontory was a big winner, one of a couple of firms that earned more than $1 billion in fees."[51] A nice payday for those who are supposed to be helping victims. In the total settlement over foreclosures, only $3.3 billion actually went to people who were apparent victims, and most of them received an average of $868 per foreclosed home.[52]

Some regulators have been caught running dubious "side businesses," acting as regulators but also providing "advisory services" to corporations to help them get their environmental permits approved. In Utah, for example, a top regulator was sued by a company that claimed he was "extorting" money from it.[53]

Complex regulations create opportunities for bureaucrats and politicians in certain industries, who put ex-regulators on their boards of directors as a form of protection. Researchers have found, for instance, that when the natural gas industry was heavily deregulated, the number of new board members with a political background decreased by 35 to 58 percent.[54]

Paying an ex-regulator or bureaucrat is important not only for compliance efforts but also for the process of obtaining the exemptions, waivers, and loopholes that are now routinely included in some regulations. Often these exemptions are granted at the discretion of government officials. Hire a former colleague or boss and your chances of getting an exemption go up dramatically. Regulations are often ambiguous and confusing, and regulators have an immense amount of discretion in deciding how and whether certain regulations will be enforced, according to a study by Michael J. Licari, a professor at the University of Northern Iowa.[55]

Complex and obscure regulations are enormously profitable for the Permanent Political Class. But they are enormously damaging to the rest of us — like any extortion scheme. Alan Siegel has spent decades pushing for greater simplicity in communications and has consulted with major corporations on simplicity in branding. Dubbed "Mr. Plain English" by *People* magazine, Siegel says, "Complexity robs us of time, patience, understanding, money and optimism." He goes on: "The United States was founded and governed for over two centuries on the basis of a document that is six pages long. That is 0.1 percent of the length of the current income tax code, which currently runs a whopping fourteen thousand pages." (Even IRS commissioner Douglas Shulman admitted on C-SPAN that he can't do his own personal tax return anymore because "it's just too complicated.")[56] Law professor Michael Waggoner at the University of Colorado argues that "laws must be specific enough to solve a problem . . . suspicion is likely to grow among citizens that long and nearly unreadable laws are hiding things, a suspicion that may often be valid."[57] According to Waggoner, the trouble is that complicated laws enrich those who make the laws while making the rest of society poorer.[58]

Surveys consistently show that firms and individuals want to know what rules they need to comply with. In early 2009, Siegel conducted a survey and discovered that 79 percent of Americans wanted the president to "mandate that clarity, transparency, and plain-English be a requirement for every new law, regulation, and policy."[59] Another survey conducted in 2012 reveals that 85 percent of the people favor simplifying government rules and regulations, and 81 percent think that making regulations "simpler and less complex" would help create more jobs.[60] Jobs outside of Washington, for a change.

Simplicity is important, says Siegel, because simplicity in government will shorten the distance between government and citizens. And that, of course, is why the Permanent Political Class hates the idea: there is a huge amount of money to be made as the middleman. Ex-bureaucrats and politicians can interpret and navigate through the thicket of rules and laws. It is a lucrative service to offer.

For bureaucrats and other members of the Permanent Political Class, there are profits to be made in the notion that "why use one simple form when four difficult ones will do." Professor Anthony Heyes believes that "people working in regulatory agencies have too little incentive to make or keep procedures and practices simple, transparent or user-friendly." He argues that one-third of the costs of regulations are "transaction costs" — that is, "paying someone to help you jump through the 'hoops and hurdles' of the regulatory process."[61] The next time Congress debates a complex bill, ask yourself: who benefits?

8

PROTECTION FOR A PRICE

What About a Washington Corrupt Practices Act?

A little violence never hurt anyone.

— "LEFTY TWO GUNS" RUGGIERO

THE MAFIA DOESN'T JUST OPERATE on the street level. Mobsters hire lawyers who help them extend their system of extortion and intimidation through legal means. The role of the "mob lawyer" is to use the *legal system* to advance the interests of an organization that is constantly breaking the law.

Martin Light was once such a "mob lawyer." In 1986 he told the President's Commission on Organized Crime how he performed his job. Using legal tactics, intimidation, and bribery, his primary job was to "protect the family." Even when defending an individual mobster facing legal charges, his primary commitment was to the organization, not his client. Trust and loyalty were the key, he said. If you were loyal, it was profitable to be a mob lawyer. He claimed that at the time there were twenty to thirty lawyers in New York who were used by the Mafia. The list was carefully vetted. Legitimate lawyers could never expect to get in on the lucrative business, he said. "Who would trust *them?*"[1]

The Permanent Political Class does not operate outside of the law. They are not actively breaking laws, and they do not fear jail time. Instead, they use extralegal means to extort their money. It is what makes them so successful, and their "family" so profitable. Their extralegal options even extend to our legal system, which we expect and hope will be impartial and fair.

In theory, the American federal judicial system interprets rules and laws consistently for all citizens. It has been subverted by racial bias and economic leverage, but in theory, and in our collective great hopes, everyone is equal before the law. Yet in recent years it has been increasingly bent for the benefit of the Permanent Political Class. Who gets prosecuted, how aggressively they are prosecuted, and who avoids facing charges can and often does depend on the ability to pay protection money to the Permanent Political Class.

If you are going to extort people — whether using illegal or extralegal methods — it is best to target those who have lots of money and who really fear what you could do to them. You also need a weapon that can be wielded easily. In the case of American justice, nothing beats a vaguely written, broadly interpreted law that can send a powerful and wealthy person to jail.

There are now more than 4,450 criminal laws on the books. As Harvard's Alan Dershowitz warns, that creates opportunities for mischief. It creates a situation in which "citizens who believe they are law abiding may, in the eyes of federal officials, be committing three felonies each day."[2] But some laws are a lot worse than others, especially when they can be interpreted so broadly that they depend chiefly on the whims of prosecutors.

We would all like to think that presidential appointees at the Department of Justice or the Securities and Exchange Commission will administer justice without self-interest or political calculations in mind. Back in 1940, FDR's attorney general, Robert H. Jackson, assembled federal prosecutors in Washington to warn them about the ease with which DOJ power could be abused. Jackson expressed his concerns that a government official would "pick people that he thinks he should get, rather than pick cases that need to be prosecuted." Doing so would be quite simple, warned Jackson. The federal law books were "filled with a great assortment of crimes" and a federal investigator stood "a fair chance of finding at least a technical violation of some act on the part of almost anyone." The reality was that it would be rather easy to start by "picking the man and then searching the law books, or putting investigators to work, to pin some offense on him."[3]

The government has a great deal of discretion in how it pursues financial crimes. The Securities and Exchange Commission and the Department of Justice often work together investigating and prosecuting them. The SEC metes out only civil and administrative penalties. The DOJ handles both civil and criminal cases. But what sort of crimes do these agencies choose to focus on? Which companies do they choose to go after? How can companies and executives stay out of deep trouble? All of these questions are decided by senior government officials at these agencies and others who are appointed by the president and have their budgets set by Congress. And as we saw earlier, in recent years our top law enforcement officials were campaign fund-raisers.

There is an alarming amount of evidence that "protection money" determines how these cases are handled. One study by two business professors looked at 463 executives from 200 firms that had been in the crosshairs of the SEC. They found that those who paid their tithes to the Permanent Political Class in the form of campaign contributions got off far easier than those who didn't. Among their findings: "Accused executives at firms who make political contributions, either via a political action committee or via the CEO, are banned for three fewer years, serve probation five fewer years, prison for six fewer years, and are 46% less likely to receive both prison time and an officer ban" than those whose firms did not do so. Donations made by the executives themselves had a similarly dramatic effect. And the amounts mattered. Giving more money "significantly reduces the monetary penalty" that firms and individuals are forced to pay.[4]

They conclude that protection money makes a huge difference: "There is sufficient motive for executives [to] make political contributions in the hopes that regulatory authorities will be less inclined to bring charges, or at the very least, that penalties will be lessened."[5]

Another study found the same disturbing reality. Looking at a different set of data, the author of this study found that fund-raising and contributions are "effective at reducing the probability of enforcement and penalties." She also found evidence of "firms strategically using political expenditures to avoid prosecution by the SEC." They "target their political contributions to politicians serving on Committees with a strong relationship to the SEC."[6]

A third study found that hiring members of the Permanent Political Class (specifically, Washington-based lobbyists) is another effective form of paying protection money. The authors of this study looked at SEC and DOJ investigations of a number of firms and discovered that companies with lobbyists on the payroll were 38 percent less likely to have any fraud detected compared to those not involved in lobbying. Furthermore, if any fraud is detected at a company that employs lobbyists, that investigation takes an average of 117 days more work by the regulatory authorities in question.[7]

The reality is that the SEC chairman and his or her commissioners, as well as the U.S. attorneys — not to mention the top leadership at the Department of Justice — are directly selected and appointed by the president of the United States. And the budgets of both the SEC and the DOJ are determined by Congress. They are political appointees. As Jackson warned a long time ago, our government gives them enormous discretion, and they apparently use that discretion to bring fewer charges against firms that pay protection money.

There is also evidence that these government officials can and frequently do factor politics into their prosecutorial decisions, just as Jackson feared. The DOJ pursues cases against political opponents with greater vigor than it brings to cases against its political allies. It happens under both political parties. A study by Professor Sanford Gordon at New York University found that under Presidents George W. Bush and Bill Clinton, prosecutions tended to reveal a "partisan bias." Each administration was more aggressive in prosecuting suspects aligned with the other political party than those aligned with their own.[8] This is not exactly news. It has been a longtime criticism of the Department of Justice. Modern American history offers examples of widespread abuse under Presidents Lyndon Johnson and Richard Nixon when it came to using the Justice Department to punish or threaten their opponents.

Even the Internal Revenue Service (IRS) can function as a tool of protection in the hands of an administration. Richard Nixon had his famous enemies list — which led to tax audits for the unlucky members. But in a broader sense, there is evidence that the IRS serves to protect those who matter to a president. A more recent study of who gets audited by the agency found that "the fraction of individual income tax returns audited is significantly lower in districts that are important to a president electorally." The scholars conclude: "These findings suggest that the IRS is not a rogue government agency, but rather is an effective bureaucratic agent of its political sponsors."[9] More recently, the IRS has been engulfed in controversy concerning the targeting of conservative groups for additional IRS scrutiny and allegations of increased audits of opponents of the Obama administration.[10]

The Department of Justice has far more latitude and discretion than the IRS, which has only the tax code to use as a weapon. The DOJ has the entire criminal code. What is surprising is how it selects from among the many thousands of weapons hidden in our laws. Take, for example, the collapse of MF Global. The chairman of the financial firm was former New Jersey senator and governor Jon Corzine, an Obama fund-raiser who bundled over $500,000 for the president's campaign.[11] Corzine is the consummate insider. During the 2008 campaign, he was dubbed Obama's "financial guru."[12] And members of his now-defunct firm served on Obama administration advisory boards.

Then news struck that Corzine's firm vaporized $1.6 billion in client funds. Bankruptcy trustee reports on MF Global alleged that funds had been taken from customer accounts. Furthermore, the reports alleged that MF Global lacked adequate controls to prevent it from knowing it was using customer-segregated funds to meet liquidity needs. As James B. Stewart of the *New York Times* concluded, "It seems clear that serious violations of the law were committed."[13] The pattern of conduct demonstrated not only that serious violations had occurred but that senior executives, including Corzine, knew about them or were involved in their execution.

University of Washington securities law professor Anita Krug also believes that MF Global executives apparently filed a "false report."[14] As *Bloomberg* pointed out in April 2013, prosecutors could charge Corzine under the Sarbanes-Oxley Act, which allows for a CEO or executive who signs off on false financial reports to be sentenced to ten years in prison and ordered to pay a $1 million fine.[15] Samuel Tenenbaum, associate professor of law at Northwestern and director of the Investor Protection Center, concurs that "clearly the law was broken" in the MF Global case.[16] Louis Freeh, former FBI director, who served as a trustee in the MF Global bankruptcy case, called Corzine's conduct "grossly negligent" and a clear "breach of fiduciary duty."[17]

During the critical week before MF Global declared bankruptcy, and as funds were being shifted around, Commodity Futures Trading Commission chairman Gary Gensler was in regular contact with MF Global executives through a personal and private email account. The CFTC inspector general later would report that this was "troubling."[18] Clearly, this was not the sort of cozy arrangement other financial entities could expect to receive.

When MF Global filed for bankruptcy on October 31, 2011, over 99 percent of its customer accounts were commodity accounts. But federal regulators decided that the Securities Investor Protection Corporation (SIPC) would take over the liquidation. The CFTC should have been in charge, but Gary Gensler deferred to the SEC. This allowed MF Global Holdings to file a chapter 11 bankruptcy, enabling the firm to continue to transfer assets in and out of accounts. Had it been designated by regulators as a commodities firm (which it was), those accounts would have been frozen to protect customers.[19]

The CME Group is a diverse derivatives marketplace comprising five designated contract markets (CME, CBOT, NYMEX, COMEX, and KCBT). The CME Group was the "primary regulator" of MF Global. CME Group chairman Terry Duffy told a congressional committee that Corzine and MF Global executives knew they were raiding customer accounts to cover trading shortfalls. But then something interesting happened: the "primary regulator" was instructed by government officials to end its MF Global investigation. The CME Group had been focusing its regulatory investigation on the illegal raiding of customer accounts. As journalist and futures expert Mark Melin puts it:

> As documented on page 139 of the Trustees' report, on October 28, Mr. Corzine was faced with a decision. He was required to cover an internal margin call of $175 million in London with his only source of funding which was customer assets. It is at this moment, a willful decision to transfer customer funds to cover business expenses took place, which violated the law. This was said to be one of the clear focuses of a CME Group Investigation.[20]

So, despite Corzine having bundled at least $500,000 for the Obama campaign, the president's DOJ still charged him, right? Wrong. Industry observers were stunned when newspaper accounts quoted government regulators and law enforcement officials on background as saying that the "case was cold," even before MF Global executives had been questioned by authorities.[21] By August 2012, the *New York Times* was reporting that the criminal investigation was winding down, with no charges expected.[22] Legal observers were stunned that Edith O'Brien, the MF Global executive who was responsible for executing so many of the questionable trades, was neither charged nor granted immunity.

One might think that commodities traders would circle the wagons and defend the actions of Corzine and MF Global. After all, wouldn't that be to their own benefit? But that has hardly been the case. As futures trader Stanley Haar puts it, "If the crimes committed in this case are allowed to go unpunished . . . this will only serve to reinforce the widespread perception of pervasive cronyism and corruption in Washington, D.C."[23]

Lisa Timmerman, a seventeen-year employee of MF Global who

was the firm's assistant comptroller for five years, is more blunt: "Corzine is a major Obama fundraiser [which] is keeping prosecutors from bringing criminal charges against him."[24]

On June 27, 2013, the CFTC filed a civil complaint against Corzine that, among other things, he unlawfully used customer funds.[25] However, neither Jon Corzine nor any other MF Global employee has been criminally charged. What's more, neither Corzine nor any of the senior executives have been barred from trading in the futures markets. In fact, the New York Post reported that the criminal probe into Jon Corzine is now being dropped, according to a person knowledgeable of the probe.[26]

In recent years, the law of choice for legal extortion and intimidation has been the Foreign Corrupt Practices Act (FCPA). It was originally passed in 1977 in the shadow of Watergate, following investigations that revealed that U.S. corporations had been bribing foreign government officials in exchange for government contracts. In 1976, for example, Japanese prime minister Tanaka Kakuei was indicted after it was revealed that he received $2 million in cash from Lockheed Martin in exchange for arranging a large government contract.[27]

The FCPA is narrowly focused, or at least it appears to be. The law includes a bribery provision that requires a showing that the payment was "knowingly" made.[28] But a second provision of the law, the so-called record-keeping provision, holds that if you make "false or misleading statements on a company's books for any purpose whatsoever" involving money paid overseas, you could face a fine or even imprisonment. Furthermore, if you make legitimate "facilitating payments" but fail to account for them, you could face jail time — even if there is no evidence that bribery ever took place.[29] Into such ambiguous cracks, extortion can fall. The penalties in the law are steep: not only could a company and its executives pay steep fines, but executives, officers, directors, shareholders, and employees could face jail time. In some cases, a jail term could be as long as twenty years.[30]

Professor Mike Koehler, the most widely published legal scholar on FCPA, notes that Congress "specifically intended for its anti-bribery provisions to be narrow in scope."[31] At first, after the law was enacted in 1977, "enforcement was largely non-existent for most of its history."[32] On average, only two to three cases a year were pursued during the law's first thirty years. Then suddenly, within the past decade, enforcement of the law exploded. The results: it is one of the most profitable and aggressive forms of legal extortion in American history.

Shortly after Barack Obama was elected president in 2008, he appointed a team of experienced white-collar criminal defense attorneys to head up the Department of Justice. Eric Holder, the co-chair of his campaign, got the top job of attorney general. Holder had been head of the Washington office of Covington & Burling, a powerful D.C. white-shoe law firm. Joining him from Covington was Lanny Breuer, who became head of the Criminal Division. Steven Fagell, also of Covington, came over to serve as the deputy chief of staff and counselor to Breuer. Jim Garland moved over to serve as counselor and deputy chief of staff to Holder.

In early 2009, the United States was grappling with the financial crisis and the mortgage-backed securities implosion. While many people argued about real criminal conduct on the part of some investment bankers, mortgage companies, and others in the financial sector, Breuer's interest seemed to be elsewhere. When he took over as head of the DOJ's 900-lawyer Criminal Division, "the substantive law most of interest" to him proved to be . . . the FCPA.[33] Early on, he expressed his view that FCPA was one of his "top priorities."[34]

Breuer's and Holder's interest in the anticorruption law is curious because of Covington's role in actually drafting the bill. (The firm

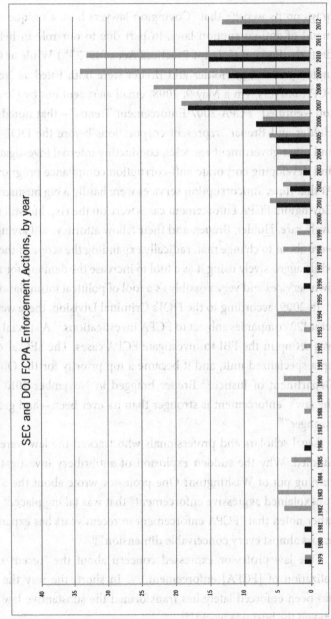

USING THE LEGAL SYSTEM TO EXTORT[35]

SEC and DOJ FCPA Enforcement Actions, by year

- Number of SEC FCPA Enforcement Actions
- Number of DOJ FCPA Actions

Number of Enforcement Actions

1979 1980 1981 1982 1983 1984 1985 1986 1987 1988 1989 1990 1991 1992 1993 1994 1995 1996 1997 1998 1999 2000 2001 2002 2003 2004 2005 2006 2007 2008 2009 2010 2011 2012

brags on its website that "Covington lawyers have a unique command of anti-corruption laws, in part due to our role in helping draft the Foreign Corrupt Practices Act of 1977."[36]) While at Covington & Burling, Holder and Breuer were both listed as "senior FCPA lawyers" (in a May 9, 2008, email alert sent out by Covington — entitled "FCPA-2007 Enforcement Trends" — that noted that Holder and Breuer "represent corporations before the DOJ, SEC and other government agencies, conducting internal investigations and developing corporate anti-corruption compliance programs"). At that time, anticorruption services were hardly a big business for Covington. FCPA enforcement cases were on the rise, but still relatively rare. Holder, Breuer, and their fellow attorneys at Covington were about to change that, radically expanding the scope of the law while aggressively using it as a tool to increase the demand for their own services and very possibly as a tool of political intimidation.

In 2009, according to the DOJ's Criminal Division, there were at least 120 companies subject to FCPA investigations.[37] A special unit was set up in the FBI to investigate FCPA cases. The SEC also set up a specialized unit, and it became a top priority for the Obama Department of Justice.[38] Breuer bragged in November 2010 that the law's "enforcement is stronger than it's ever been — and getting stronger."[39]

Legal scholars and professionals who tracked the law were befuddled. Why the sudden explosion of antibribery investigations coming out of Washington? One professor wrote about the SEC's "unexplained aggressive enforcement" that was taking place.[40] Another noted that "FCPA enforcement in recent years has expanded across almost every conceivable dimension."[41]

One law professor expressed concern about the "recent radicalization of [FCPA] enforcement.... In short, the way the Act has been enforced lately has transformed the substantive law and shaken the business world."[42]

The sort of cases that were being pursued and prosecuted bore little relationship to the bribery of foreign government officials to procure government contracts. Holder and Breuer were now charging companies and individuals "not alleged to have engaged in or even known about the wrongdoing."[43]

The Justice Department cast a remarkably wide net that included expansive definitions of what a "government official" was and what constituted a "bribe." How wide? Lanny Breuer admitted that essentially no company was immune from charges of misconduct, given the new standard. "There will always be rogue employees who decide to take matters into their own hands," he said. "They are a fact of life."[44] Ignorance of what a midlevel employee or overseas consultant might be doing was no defense. Large corporations were charged because they "directly or indirectly" gave gifts to overseas individuals. These gifts didn't need to be cash bribes. Offering "sightseeing trips" could get you into legal trouble.[45] A large pharmaceutical company made a contribution to a legitimate charity in Poland, but was charged with wrongdoing because it had not accurately reflected the contribution in its financial statements.[46] Royal Dutch Shell was charged with conspiracy to violate the antibribery law based "solely on the allegations that [its] express door-to-door courier service" offering expedited delivery into Nigeria paid money to Nigerian customs officials so equipment could be delivered quickly. Yet even if the company didn't know about the payments, it was deemed to have received an "improper advantage" in the African country.[47]

These were not exactly traditional examples of bribery. There were no large cash payments to government ministers or luxury sports cars purchased for a midlevel bureaucrat. Now firms were facing possible criminal charges for giving such gifts to overseas individuals as "bottles of wine, watches, cameras, kitchen appliances, business suits, television sets, laptops, tea sets, and office furniture."

Pharmaceutical companies that offered even very small gifts to a physician, nurse, or midwife might now face criminal prosecution under the Justice Department theory that these health care workers are "government officials."[48]

A former assistant chief of the DOJ Fraud Section noted that "some of the government's cases appear to blur the lines or muddy the waters when it comes to the limits of the statute."[49] That was putting it mildly.

Corporations and executives, of course, were eager to know how they could comply. A large corporation with thousands of employees around the world needed to have an effective compliance program. But Breuer explained that setting up a compliance system was not a defense. "We can't engage in some sort of formalistic solution from a script that says if you check the following six boxes you're guaranteed this outcome," he said.[50] So how *could* companies comply with the law and avoid the possibility of jail? As Professor Amy Westbrook noted, they had no guidance from the government.[51]

"The FCPA is enforced like no other law," wrote another legal scholar. "The FCPA simply means what the DOJ and SEC says it means and 'FCPA law' largely develops through privately-negotiated agreements, subject to little or no judicial scrutiny."[52] One partner at the power law firm Gibson, Dunn & Crutcher summarized the uncertainty: "In this environment, you need to anticipate that the [government] is going to pursue any legal theory that it feels is remotely supportable. To some extent, you have to expect the unexpected."[53]

The Holder regime didn't just target firms, it named names. As Lanny Breuer put it, "One cornerstone of our FCPA enforcement policy: the aggressive prosecution of individuals."[54] The prosecution of specific executives went up dramatically, putting directors, officers, and even shareholders at risk "even if they did not have actual knowledge of the corrupt nature of the payments."[55] Little surprise that "executives reportedly spend sleepless nights wondering if their company will be the next target of an FCPA enforcement action."[56]

Even more troubling is how the Justice Department selectively enforced the law, evidence that Jackson's warnings in 1940 were prophetic. Enforcement and penalties have been random. The Justice Department approach "penalizes similar bad actors with mismatched severity," said one legal expert.[57]

When asked by a congressional committee to explain how they chose which companies to go after, Assistant Attorney General Ronald Welch wouldn't provide a direct answer, but rather, referred to general principles of prosecution.[58] The DOJ admitted in an FCPA guideline that it had "declined to prosecute both individuals and corporate entities" in several dozen instances without explaining exactly why.[59]

One lawyer, writing in the *Northwestern Journal of International Law and Business,* put it bluntly: FCPA enforcement, he asserted, "has been largely inconsistent with traditional 'rule of law' values that emphasize the need to clearly define prohibited behavior, treat similar cases similarly, and apply a separation of powers structure."[60]

What with the Justice Department's aggressive and selective investigations and prosecutions, ambiguities in the law itself, and criminal investigations for small gifts of wine or cameras, the law has created real fear in the executive suite, which is what any extortion scheme is supposed to do: "throw fear." Even the *suspicion* that you have violated the law can be expensive. It can drive down a company's stock price, and class-action attorneys can file additional civil suits alleging executive "misconduct" whether the underlying charge is proven or not.

The question is: why? We have already seen why the Obama enforcers might not have prosecuted many bankers, and criminal prosecutors have laid off bundler Jon Corzine. They needed their campaign cash. But why, instead, prosecute so many transnational firms in such arbitrary ways?

The answer may not be hard to find. Panicked corporations and executives lawyered up — precisely what the extortionist had hoped for. Many corporations and executives turned to Holder's and Breuer's old law firm, Covington & Burling. The firm expanded its practice accordingly. Steven Fagell, who had migrated to the Justice Department from Covington to serve as counselor to Breuer, returned in 2010 to Covington, where he became the "co-chair of the global anti-corruption practice group."[61] Jim Garland, who had made a similar migration to serve as Holder's counselor, also returned to Covington to work on anticorruption and white-collar criminal defense issues. As Holder and Breuer pursue their aggressive and widespread strategy of investigation and possible prosecution, Covington is doing a roaring business representing the very firms in the Justice Department's crosshairs. The firm openly brags on its website that in 2010 it "successfully obtained two FCPA Opinion Releases from the U.S. Department of Justice" for its corporate clients, giving them guidance on particular issues. The firm also notes that it has performed "anti-corruption risk assessments for more than 30 global enterprises" and also represented an executive for KBR (Halliburton's subsidiary), which was under investigation into alleged bribery. Covington also has an enormous practice helping corporations doing business in China avoid bribery charges.[62]

Other government lawyers who had helped ramp up enforcement of FCPA have left public service to join other firms. Mark Mendelsohn left the Justice Department and headed to a New York law firm to defend corporations from FCPA charges. On its website the firm brags that Mendelsohn "was responsible for overseeing all investigations and prosecutions under the FCPA" and that his "background and experience will be an enormous asset to our clients, which are facing increased scrutiny." Mendelsohn is believed to be making $2.5 million a year in his new job.[63]

And the money to be made isn't just in defending corporations under investigation. Many large companies, concerned about the law, voluntarily approach the Justice Department when they uncover possible violations, to ask for guidance. This is a business opportunity for well-connected law firms.

The Department of Justice requires many companies to hire a "monitor" to make sure they are complying with the ambiguous FCPA law. Usually the choice is someone who — yes, you guessed it — previously worked at either the Justice Department or the SEC. The fees for this kind of work can be enormous — up to $10 million a year or more. When the chemical firm Innospec pled guilty in March 2010 to technical violations of the law, Judge Ellen Segal Huvelle was furious at the high "monitoring fees" the firm was forced to pay. "It's an outrage that people get $50 million to be a monitor," she said in her Washington, D.C., courtroom. "It's a boondoggle."[64]

Attorney General Jackson had warned that prosecutors could pick the man and then find a technical violation to selectively target him. That appears to be precisely what the Justice Department and the SEC have been doing with the antibribery law. As two lawyers put it in the *Securities Regulation Law Journal,* the DOJ creates a circumstance where "vague standards and policies hinder compliance and make enforcement inconsistent." This creates conditions for abuse.[65] The department doesn't choose to enforce the law broadly. Instead, it focuses on certain "targeted industries," to whom it sends "sweep letters," asking firms to come clean. The government makes it clear that investigators will go easier on these targeted firms if they turn in competitors. Hank Walther, the former assistant chief of the Foreign Corrupt Practices Act Unit at Justice, left in January 2012 (in order to work for the power firm Jones Day on antibribery compliance). He explained in an interview: "One of the purposes of DOJ's use of industry-wide investigations is to encourage each company to be the first one in the door to admit its own wrongdoing, then to tell DOJ everything it knows about its competitors who are also engaged in similar forms of wrongdoing. . . . Companies that are in the government's crosshairs are expected to disclose their own wrongdoing, then cooperate and provide information about their competitors."[66] As one legal scholar notes, however, these industrywide investigations can turn into "boundless enforcement agency fishing expeditions, the cost of which [is] borne by the companies subject to the sweeps."[67]

How are the industries targeted? Justice Department and SEC officials won't say. But it is interesting to note that the Holder regime's first "sweep" letter went to the oil and gas industry just days after the midterm elections in November 2010.[68] (In the elections held just days earlier, the oil and gas sector had given almost four times more money to the opposition party than it had given to the president's party.[69] Was that a factor?)

Hedge funds were also targeted after the 2010 elections. According to the *Wall Street Journal*, the SEC was launching a "sweep" of the hedge fund industry for possible FCPA violations. Federal investigators were apparently interested in whether hedge funds in the United States had provided "excessive entertainment or travel expenses" for employees of foreign government pension funds or government investment funds.[70] Curiously, the hedge fund industry during the 2010 election had begun a dramatic about-face.[71] In 2008 the industry had given over $13.2 million to Democrats and less than $6.6 million to the GOP. But in 2010, an off-year election, hedge fund firms donated $6 million to Republicans and $5.6 million to Democrats. Hedge fund managers continued their race to the right in 2012, giving $11.8 million to Republicans and only $3.8 million to Democrats.[72] Were these two events related? Possibly.

In October 2010, President Obama had told an audience bluntly, "We are going to punish our enemies and we're gonna reward our friends who stand with us on issues that are important to us."[73]

Other targeted industries included pharmaceuticals, tobacco, and arms manufacturers. (Each of these industries tended to favor Republicans over Democrats in 2010.) Why were these sectors selected? Politics? Legal strategy? A little of both?

I am not necessarily arguing that partisanship is paramount. Money may matter even more. Compare the FCPA cases with the Justice Department's treatment of Wall Street firms — which may be populated by Republican voters but have produced (as we have seen) plenty of donations for the Obama campaigns. Remember that prosecutors looked into the affairs of MF Global, which lost $1.6 billion of its investors' money and improperly mingled client funds with the company's own capital, yet in the end brought no criminal charges. Moreover, after executive Jon Corzine testified before Congress that the mingling was unintended by him, the government indicated that criminal charges could not be brought absent any intent to commit fraud. But this standard should be held for foreign corruption as well: if an executive has no knowledge of or intention to bribe, the government should not pursue that individual. Yet for the Obama Justice Department, foreign corrupt practices apparently require neither intent nor knowledge.

A troubling pattern emerged in 2012 during the heated presidential election. The Justice Department chose to pursue investigations and possible criminal indictments against a group of individuals who were heavily involved in supporting Mitt Romney in the general election. These antibribery charges focused on the records portion of the law, whether it was faulty record-keeping about donations to charities or actions by companies affiliated with the target firm, whose executives clearly did not have knowledge of wrongdoing. It should raise serious questions about Robert Jackson's warnings about identifying the person first and then looking for a technical violation of the law. Consider the targets:

- *Koch Industries:* The privately held company owned by Charles and David Koch came under investigation for potential FCPA violations after the company fired several employees from a European subsidiary who were involved in alleged payments to officials in Africa, India, and the Middle East.[74] The Koch brothers were among the largest contributors to the effort to defeat President Obama in November 2012.

- *Las Vegas Sands, Inc.:* This business is owned by Sheldon Adelson, and it suddenly found itself facing three FCPA investigations concerning its casinos in Macau, China. Adelson was a large and generous campaign contributor to Mitt Romney and to super PACs looking to defeat Obama (after having spent large sums on Newt Gingrich during the primaries). Adelson's company would later disclose in SEC filings that "there were likely violations of the books and records and internal controls provisions" of the law, not the actual bribing of foreign officials.[75]

- *News Corporation:* The global information and news corporation, headed by Rupert Murdoch — who was critical of Obama and owns Fox News — was investigated by the DOJ relating to the phone-hacking scandal in the United Kingdom using the FCPA. The law was intended for when government officials are bribed in exchange for government contracts. That of course didn't apply in this case.

- *Walmart:* Walmart had apparently hired agents in Mexico to help it expand its business, and those agents had given gifts — bribes — to spur movement on regulatory issues. But now the entire company, including executives and members of the board of directors who had no direct knowledge, was subject to possible legal sanction. Jim and Alice Walton, children of the founder of Walmart, were two of the largest contributors to efforts to unseat President Obama. Each contributed $200,000 to Restore Our Future, the super PAC supporting Mitt Romney.[76] Jim Walton sits on the Walmart board.[77] Again, it appears that bribery may have occurred. It is not at all clear that Walmart knew about it. According to the FCPA under Eric Holder, that apparently doesn't matter.

- *Hewlett-Packard:* The firm came under investigation for alleged bribes made by now former employees to help a subsidiary break into the Russia market.[78] CEO Meg Whitman and her husband had given a total of $200,000 to a pro-Romney super PAC.[79]

What motivated the Justice Department to pursue these particular investigations? We can't ultimately know. But given the history of the Justice Department and the SEC doing a president's bidding, using criminal investigations as a tool of leverage and intimidation cannot be dismissed. As Professor Sara Sun Beale of Duke University Law School puts it, the very structure of the DOJ makes this sort of concern real. "It will not be possible to preclude entirely the possibility that political considerations might improperly influence decisions in individual prosecutions." She goes on: "The nature of contemporary federal criminal law magnifies the potential for mischief, because the definitions of the relevant offenses are both broad and vague, giving the prosecutors extraordinarily wide discretion on which there are few checks." Beale adds, "In comparison to other agencies the Department [of Justice] has a disproportionate number of presidential appointees."[80] (And recall in the Obama Administration at least half a dozen bundlers as well.) Noted defense attorney

Harvey Silverglate is more blunt: "We must foster the realization that the Justice Department's tactics too often are not employed to protect, but to attack law-abiding society."[81]

Let me be clear: I am not trying to absolve any of these firms of all wrongdoing. Exactly how they are pursued, under exactly what statute, is an important question. But my real question is this: if the Justice Department has pursued these firms, why hasn't it gone after the Wall Street firms or MF Global? There was clear wrongdoing there too. Why does the government require intent by one set of executives (like Corzine), but not by another? Could it be that the key difference is that the Wall Street firms contributed heavily to the Obama campaign?

After the 2012 election, Lanny Breuer resigned as the head of the Department of Justice Criminal Division. He returned to Covington & Burling to become vice chair of the firm. The key author of the Justice Department's antibribery policy and its expansive, aggressive, opaque enforcement was now expected to earn "about $4 million" a year.[82] His job? To offer advice to clients on how to avoid prosecution from his former colleagues. At Covington, according to the firm, Breuer now "specializes in helping clients navigate anticorruption matters [among other things]." His biography on the law firm's website notes that while at DOJ he "oversaw numerous prosecutions that set new benchmarks across a host of enforcement areas, including anti-corruption."[83] He certainly did.

Dennis Kelleher, a former partner at another D.C. power firm, Skadden Arps, called the move a "blatant cashing-in."[84] And indeed, Breuer created a new demand for legal and accounting services that he and his colleagues leaving Justice and returning to Covington were now uniquely positioned to supply. Ethics laws require a one-year cooling-off period for Justice Department officials before they can represent defendants before their old department, "but these rules serve only to prevent the most egregious conflict of interest scenarios."[85] Breuer can still provide strategic advice and guidance behind the scenes. And his former Covington partner, Attorney General Eric Holder, is still calling the shots.

Covington, for its part, made clear that "we are one of the few firms in the world with lawyers who recently held senior positions" at the Department of Justice, "which enables us to offer highly sophisticated advice regarding U.S. enforcement environments."[86]

Breuer is not alone. Other Justice Department officials who had lit the fuse on the antibribery bomb had also departed and could now charge big fees to defuse it. Nathaniel Edmonds left DOJ and headed to the power firm Paul Hastings, which boasts, "Mr. Edmonds was responsible for directly supervising up to half of the DOJ's investigations into transnational bribery. . . . He also drafted portions of the FCPA Resource Guide published in November 2012, which details the contours of the FCPA legal regime."[87] Edmonds told the *Legal Times* after he left DOJ that with the expansion of FCPA investigations and prosecutions, "the practice would likely continue to be robust for attorneys."[88] The traditional mafiosi would have used more colorful language. Today's revolving-door lawyers are essentially earning a form of "vig" — the money the bookies and mobsters used to skim off of betting operations.

Many corporate executives are perplexed by the aggressive enforcement of this antibribery law, not because they defend bribery, but because the regime is *encouraging* it. As John Hofmeister, the former president of Shell Oil, told me, "The Foreign Corrupt Practices Act basically says you can't give gifts to foreign government officials — which includes campaign contributions and donations to certain charities. Of course, that's what we get asked to do all the time from Washington. Why doesn't the FCPA cover Washington? Why not have a Washington Corrupt Practices Act?"

Hofmeister, of course, is not holding his breath.

9

IT'S A FAMILY AFFAIR

> Do you spend time with your family? Good. Because a man that doesn't
> spend time with his family can never be a real man.
>
> – DON CORLEONE, *THE GODFATHER*

HOURS AFTER SENATOR HARRY REID was sworn in for his fourth term on January 4, 2005, a collection of high-powered lobbyists gathered with him at an expensive steak house near Capitol Hill. Reid had just been selected the new leader of the Senate Democrats. The previous leader, Senator Tom Daschle of South Dakota, had lost his reelection bid that past November. Reid was seated in the quiet backroom of the restaurant. The lobbyists, who represented the largest and most powerful corporations in the world, took turns saying hello to the new leader. "It was like a scene out of *The Godfather*," one lobbyist told *Roll Call*. "He was in the back room and people were lined up to greet him and pay homage."[1]

Senator Harry Reid rose to power in the Senate not because of natural charisma, good looks, or a gift for giving fine speeches. Instead, he has built a formidable political machine in Washington and in Nevada, a machine known for its toughness and ruthlessness. Susan McCue, then his chief of staff, said in 2005 that his methods were straightforward: Reid looks at a person's vulnerabilities to "disarm, to endear, to threaten, but most of all to instill fear."[2]

The Reid machine is largely a family-run enterprise. If Harry Reid is the don, his three sons and a son-in-law are the street captains. The machine has accumulated significant power. With that power has come an opportunity to extract money and make the family wealthy.

Halfway across the continental United States, Senator Roy Blunt of Missouri and his family have built an equally powerful and intimidating machine with many of the same characteristics as the Reid machine. Families engage in self-enrichment via extraction and piggybacking on power. The rise of these two families demonstrates how legal extortion has come to dominate the American political system.

Harry Reid may be one of the most powerful men in Washington, but he grew up in tiny Searchlight, Nevada, a small mining town south of Las Vegas. In his youth, the town hosted rough bars and whorehouses. The community pool, where young Harry could swim once a week, had actually been built by a bordello owner for his prostitutes, and his sense of civic duty led him to allow town kids to swim there every Sunday. Searchlight was a tough small town, and Harry's mom took in wash for money while his father mined in the hardscrabble hills. When Harry Reid entered high school, he would catch a ride to class in nearby Henderson, Nevada. It was there that he found his first mentor, a high school government teacher and boxing coach named Mike O'Callaghan. A Korean War vet who had lost his leg, O'Callaghan taught Reid how to box, or more accurately, how to fight. In 1970 O'Callaghan ran for governor and won. Reid ran as lieutenant governor.

In 1977 O'Callaghan made Reid chairman of the powerful Nevada Gaming Commission. Much of the job involved dealing with the mob. Reid knew how the game was played. He had represented an ex-con named Tony Domino, who had become a friend. "He had a big heart, and even though I suspected he had mob ties, there was nothing violent about him," said Reid later. Organized crime had always been involved in the Vegas gambling industry. But high profits were pushing the Chicago Outfit and others to drive harder to corner the casino business. They used various techniques to move assets around. They often brought in front men who acted as the face of the casino and served as "hidden associates" who collected the extortion money. It wasn't always clear who was who. One of Reid's first acts as chairman of the gaming commission was controversial precisely for that reason. He personally approved the sale of the Hacienda Hotel Casino to a group of investors, even though it was opposed by the state Gaming Control Board, which believed that hidden associate mob figures were deeply involved in the purchase.[3]

During his tenure, Reid did battle with mobsters, confronting wiseguys like Tony "The Ant" Spilotro, a figure in the Chicago mob, whom he barred from all casinos. That sort of behavior brought Reid death threats. In one particular case, police found a car bomb planted on the family station wagon. In July 1978, Reid was approached by a man named Jack Gordon, who offered him twelve grand to approve a new gaming machine for the casinos. Reid reported the incident to the FBI and wore a wire the next time he met with Gordon. The man was arrested and went to jail. (He later went on to marry LaToya Jackson.)[4] Later, when it became clear that Gordon might be trying to kill him, a close friend visited Reid and offered to kill Gordon. Reid politely declined. "No, Gary, thanks, but forget about it." Reid wrote later, "Wow, I thought, this is loyalty."[5]

By Reid's accounting, he fought the mob and helped to drive them largely out of the casino industry. But other accounts paint a more complicated picture. Reid's nickname as chairman of the commission was "Mr. Cleanface." Ironically, the moniker came from Tony Agosto, a Kansas City mobster involved in the Chicago Outfit's operations in Vegas. Agosto, who was the entertainment director of the Tropicana Hotel and Casino, had been monitored by the FBI and had once, in a visit with the Kansas City mob boss Nick Civella, bragged that "Mr. Cleanface" was on the mob payroll.[6] Agosto's testimony led to the conviction of several mob bosses from the Midwest. And the FBI believed that Mr. Cleanface was Reid. Agosto claimed that he channeled $10,000 a week to Reid through attorney Jay Brown, "an old and dear friend," as Reid described him.[7] But a five-month investigation of Reid by the Department of Justice revealed no evidence of criminal wrongdoing.

Reid did go after mobsters. But he also became longtime friends and business partners with individuals like Jay Brown, whose name has appeared several times in federal investigations involving organized crime. Reid recommended Brown to be Governor O'Callaghan's finance chairman for his 1974 reelection campaign. "The Browns and the Reids did spend a lot of time together, and we still do," Reid says. He did land deals with Brown and also counts him as a major donor.[8]

Of course, there is no need to use mob techniques for illegal ends when you can use them legally. That sense of using fear that Susan McCue talked about came not just out of the hardscrabble life of Searchlight but also from Reid's encounters with organized crime. Reid has a calm outward demeanor, but he is a fierce player who knows how to help his friends and destroy his enemies. "I believe in vengeance," he once told a reporter.[9] Former Nevada senator Richard Bryan, a fellow Democrat, says that the man from Searchlight "has a memory like a political elephant. You cross him, he'll never forget that. There will be a price to pay. Certainly there are people who paid the price." When asked by a reporter for examples, however, Bryan said he would "rather not get into it."[10] Reid himself has accused other lawmakers of moblike behavior. "Our nation's capital has been overrun by organized crime — Tom DeLay style," he wrote in an op-ed in the *Houston Chronicle*. "The gangsters are the lobbyists, cronies and lawmakers who have banded together and abused their power to serve their own self-interest."[11]

Let's see if Senator Reid was speaking from experience.

Harry Reid's godfather-like persona in Washington is a testament to the powerful machine that the Reid family has built in Nevada and Washington. Getting something done in Nevada usually means giving the Reids a piece of the action. You want to buy a large piece of land and develop it? You will probably have to deal with the Reids. Almost 87 percent of the land in Nevada is federal land.[12] Before he became Senate majority leader, Reid sat on the powerful Appropriations Committee and the Environment and Public Works Committee.[13] Reid had leverage over developers, builders, and corporations that wanted land because the federal government has to approve land swaps and land reclassifications involving federal land.[14]

His sons Rory, Key, and Joshua and son-in-law Steve Barringer have all worked as lobbyists or in the government relations field greasing the wheels for these sorts of deals. All four have worked at one point or another for Lionel Sawyer & Collins, the most powerful law firm in Nevada. The firm makes its money by representing developers, mining companies, and casinos. Key Reid helped establish the firm's office in Washington back in 2002. All four have also assumed important positions of power locally. Rory served for a time as the commissioner and vice chairman of Clark County, the most populous county in the state, and as vice chairman of the Southern Nevada Water Authority, a powerful institution in the sun-soaked desert state. Joshua Reid was appointed by President Obama to the governing board of the Tahoe Regional Planning Agency, which oversees development in the Lake Tahoe Basin. Reid has not been shy about pushing legislation that benefits his sons' clients. As the *Los Angeles Times* reported back in 2003, Reid pushed the innocuous-sounding Clark County Conservation of Public Land and Natural Resources Act of 2002, which provided a "cavalcade of benefits to real estate developers, corporations and local institutions that were paying hundreds of thousands of dollars in lobbying fees to his son's and son-in-law's firms, federal lobbyist reports show."[15]

Son-in-law Steve Barringer has earned millions representing large mining companies like Barrick Gold as a lobbyist.[16] According to one estimate based on lobbying records, he collected as much as $3.7 million between 1999 and 2009. During that decade, Senator Reid pushed to cut capital gains tax on collectible precious metals and pushed the U.S. Mint to produce more gold coins; both of these measures would increase demand and boost gold prices.[17] In return, Barrick Gold funneled money to the Reid family through a variety of fund-raising committees. Barrick Gold regularly pumps money into Reid's Senate campaign committee, joint fund-raising committees, and leadership PAC.[18]

Reid doesn't just pull the strings in Washington. When something is going on at the local level that he doesn't approve of, he will call and shut it down. When Bruce Woodbury, a Clark County commissioner, wanted to set up a land swap to prevent a new residential development from going up in Boulder City, Reid called Woodbury to say he didn't want the land swap to happen. "He was pretty blunt about it," Woodbury says. The call ended with Reid abruptly hanging up. The deal died.[19] When MGM was building a massive project called CityCenter, it ran into financial trouble. The project was under construction, but financing dried up. Harry Reid got on the phone and told banks to free up money so the project could be completed. They did.[20]

Nevada developer Chris Milam learned the perils of the Reid machine when he tried to develop an arena and bring an NBA team to Nevada. He hired Key Reid as a consultant in May 2011 and put him on a $5,000 retainer. But when it became clear that the Sacramento Kings of the NBA were not moving to Nevada, Milam tried to convert the project into a residential development. To make that happen he sued the City of Henderson, Nevada. The new city attorney was Harry Reid's son Josh. Josh Reid told Milam's legal team that "a longtime staffer of his father" was now in charge of the federal Bureau of Land Management, and even if they won the case in court, the feds would block him. Milam settled the case.[21]

How Josh Reid became the city attorney for Henderson was itself an expression of Reid family power in Nevada. After Josh Reid left law school, he became a shareholder and attorney in the powerful firm Brownstein Hyatt Farber Schreck in Las Vegas. With its large lobbying operation, the firm could boast of its connections and ability to help energy companies get government-backed loans and Department of Energy grants as part of the 2009 stimulus. The firm took out an ad in the *Wall Street Journal* that read, "Expertise in sustainable energy law is worth nothing without connections. Learn how we've helped clients obtain funding from the Department of Energy through the American Recovery and Reinvestment Act."[22] Josh Reid focused on environmental regulatory matters at the firm. His bio explains that he organized the sale and lease of significant wind and solar projects, advising clients "on federal and state renewable energy policy" and helping with "project development strategies" for clients that included large public utilities.[23]

When the opportunity to become city attorney of Henderson arose in 2011, Josh Reid was interested. The problem: the job called for ten years of experience. Josh had only eight. So the city council miraculously decided to change the rules and lower the requirement to eight years. Senator Harry Reid then called Henderson mayor Andy Hafen to discuss the merits of hiring his son.[24] Reid was soon on the payroll for the $199,000-a-year job.[25]

Even large corporations from halfway around the world have learned that all things must go through the Reids. The Chinese energy company ENN must have been reminded of its own country, where family payoffs and relationships are a regular part of doing business. ENN wanted to develop a $5 billion solar energy facility in Nevada when Harry Reid traveled to China in 2011 to meet with company executives. Shortly thereafter, executives at the company kicked in donations to two of Reid's separate fund-raising committees. Mu Meng, the vice president of ENN, contributed $10,000 on July 19, 2011, to Reid's Searchlight Tahoe Victory Fund. So, too, did the chief operating officer of the ENN Group, DeLing Zhou, who gave another $10,000 in two separate contributions on July 18 and July 20 of that year.[26] On August 10, 2011, Zhou also sent $5,000 to Reid's Searchlight Leadership Fund (his leadership PAC).[27]

ENN also hired Rory Reid's law firm to represent it. The firm helped to locate a 9,000-acre desert site for the project and managed to arrange for the Chinese firm to buy the Clark County land for well below its appraised value. (Rory Reid had been the former chairman of the Clark County Commission.) Meanwhile, in Washington, as *Reuters* put it, Harry Reid has been one of the project's "most prominent advocates."[28] Back in Nevada, the senator tried to "pressure Nevada's largest power company, NV Energy, to sign up as ENN's first customer," according to *Reuters*.[29]

Extracting money from wealthy interests and companies is a family affair. The growing number of Reid family finance committees and fund-raising operations led the Reids in 2003 to ask the Federal Election Commission to give son Rory flexible status when raising money. Reid was on the Clark County Commission at the time and had raised money for his father. But he also wanted to raise money for the Nevada state Democratic Party, which Harry Reid controlled as well. According to the family's filings with the FEC, they were asking for the government body to not consider Rory Reid "an agent of Senator Reid," even though he acted "and continues to act as the Senator's fundraising agent in certain circumstances." The distinction was important because there were different limits on how much money you could donate to a federal candidate or a state political party. The FEC declared that "Rory Reid's fundraising activities will only be attributed to a federal candidate or officeholder if he is acting on the authority of that candidate or officeholder." The beauty of this arrangement is that Nevada state law permitted the party to raise "unlimited amounts from individuals, corporations, and labor organizations." The FEC concluded, "So long as [Rory Reid's] fundraising for the state party is not done on the authority of the Senator, then it is permissible under federal law."[30]

Just as the Las Vegas mob was able to move funds through a combination of front men and silent partners, the Reids have been able to shift money through a network of fund-raising operations that go well beyond a simple campaign fund-raising committee.

Powerful companies or interests that have a stake in legislation in front of the Senate or that need help in Nevada can get tapped not only for a regular campaign donation but also by Reid's leadership PAC, a joint fund-raising committee, and even a Nevada state party committee. And like the manager of any good operation, Senator Reid is able to move the funds around. His campaign committee Friends for Harry Reid has received cash infusions from the Reid Majority Fund, the Reid Nevada Fund, and the Reid Victory Fund.[31] The Reid Majority Fund is a joint fund-raising operation that allows him to take in large donations. During the 2012 election cycle, for example, the largest contribution was $30,400 from a lobbyist at Elmendorf Strategies.[32] Another entity, the Reid Victory Fund, is also a joint fund-raising committee, which enables the senator to receive large contributions from lobbyists or hedge fund managers like Roger Altman, who kicked in $10,000 in June of 2010.[33] Many of the same corporate and labor PACs who give to Reid's Leadership Fund also send money to his Victory Fund.[34]

Harry Reid's Searchlight Leadership Fund is almost completely funded by corporate and labor PACs and lobbyists. During the two-year election cycle from 2011 to 2012, the fund collected donations from more than 250 PACs, from the American Dental Association to the National Association of Home Builders, to the United Auto Workers. Reid was not up for reelection — he had just been reelected in 2010 — but the fund took in $1.6 million in PAC contributions and another $817,000 in individual contributions. The majority of the individual donations were from executives at companies that had given PAC donations or were lobbyists.[35]

Like the lobbyists who gathered at that D.C. steak house after the 2004 election to pay tribute to Reid, these lobbyists and corporations gave to Reid because they had to. Failure to do so would mean possibly getting screwed when an important bill came up for a vote.

When Rory Reid decided to run for governor of Nevada in 2010, it quickly became clear that the apple had not fallen far from the tree. Rory's campaign set up an elaborate network of no less than *ninety-one* separate political action committees that could serve as conduits for money to his campaign. These were shell PACs formed in the fall of 2010 and then dissolved on December 31, 2010.[36] Veteran Nevada reporter Jon Ralston of the *Las Vegas Sun* broke the story. Ralston also discovered that all the PACs had the same Las Vegas residential address, which happened to be the home of Joanna Paul, a member of the Reid campaign's finance staff. (Ironically, she was in charge of compliance.)[37] Harry Reid solicited high-dollar donors for the Economic Leadership PAC, which subsequently brought in more than $800,000 over a five-month period. A PAC can give only a maximum of $10,000 to a candidate, but with the ninety-one PACs set up, the donations were disbursed in $10,000 increments to these other PACs, which then in turn quickly funneled the money to Rory Reid's campaign account. This arrangement allowed people like California film producer Steve Bing to funnel $200,000 to Reid's campaign.[38]

In April 2013, Harry Reid set up two new fund-raising organizations which he could use to extract donations and move money around.[39] The Reid Searchlight Fund was organized on April 5, 2013, according to FEC records.[40] Five days later, Senator Reid set up the Searchlight Lake Tahoe Victory Fund.[41] Both list Chris Anderson, the finance chair of his campaign committee, as the treasurer.[42] Apparently, one can never have too many fundraising committees.

While "Mr. Cleanface" runs the Democratic Party's toughest family extortion syndicate, on the other side of the aisle few Republican families can compete with the Blunts.

Roy Blunt grew up and spent much of his young adult life in southwestern Missouri, a decidedly less exciting place than Las Vegas. There's no evidence that he had to fight battles with the mob. His father sold milking equipment to dairy farmers, work that perhaps was prophetically symbolic. Like the Reid family in Nevada, the Blunts set up a "milking" operation in Missouri that would produce a strong brew of government power and profit-making potential.[43]

Roy Blunt was a schoolteacher who ran for county clerk as a young man. When he decided to run for Congress in 1996, he made a pilgrimage to Washington, where he met and consulted with a brash and powerful congressman named Tom DeLay. The Texas Republican was a fund-raising machine, which meant he was rising rapidly in the GOP ranks. Blunt took notice, and when he won his House seat race, he became an instant protégé to DeLay. Blunt and DeLay were equally impressed with each other. After only one term in Congress, Blunt was selected by DeLay to be chief deputy whip, the highest appointed position for House Republicans. His job was to be the chief vote-counter. But he also became a liaison between House Republicans and lobbyists. He followed DeLay's lead in setting up numerous political action committees, which allowed him to extract donations and establish a power base in Congress.[44]

As the *Washington Post* put it, Blunt came to "build a political machine of his own that extends from Missouri deep into Washington's K Street lobbying community."[45] The operation became known as "Blunt, Inc." As George W. Bush's White House political director Ken Mehlman put it, "There's nothing that happens in Congress that Roy Blunt isn't a major architect of."[46] And this architect didn't come cheap.

Blunt took responsibility for day-to-day meetings with lobbyists and formed an informal leadership team of twenty-five specific lobbyists to set the agenda. DeLay was constructing a political machine that included his congressional office and lobbyists who funneled money through a network of PACs and political committees run by his current and former staffers. At the center of the nexus was the Alexander Strategy Group, a lobbying firm founded by DeLay's former chief of staff. DeLay's wife, Christine, was on the payroll. Blunt made a similar arrangement in July 1999 with the Rely On Your Beliefs (RoyB) leadership PAC. Like DeLay's operation, RoyB was run by the Alexander Strategy Group. Blunt was able to transfer those funds to Missouri Republican organizations, which in turn could transfer the funds to help his son, Matt, who was running for secretary of state.[47]

Missouri Republicans nicknamed Matt Blunt "Baby Blunt" because he was young, just twenty-eight, when he announced his bid to become Missouri's secretary of state. Younger brother Andrew served as his campaign manager.[48]

Roy Blunt leveraged his position to steer money to the race. How could a D.C.-based lobbyist or corporation be motivated to send checks to a candidate for an office in Missouri with no real powers? Simple: by extraction. Roy was on the powerful Commerce Committee and was assigned to finance, telecommunications, and trade subcommittees. So checks arrived for the Missouri secretary of state race from Freddie Mac executives and railway transportation companies, as well as from Washington lobbyists. (Even famed motion picture industry lobbyist Jack Valenti sent a donation.) Never mind that as secretary of state, Baby Blunt would have no power to affect any of them. What mattered was that Roy Blunt had made it clear that he wanted the money to flow to his son. And with important legislation before his committees, they were eager to comply.[49]

Altria (parent company of Philip Morris) sent $100,000 to the Seventh District Congressional Republican Committee. (Roy Blunt represented Missouri's Seventh District.) The committee in turn donated $24,200 to Matt Blunt's campaign — the maximum amount permitted.[50] On March 16, 2000, Friends of Roy gave $50,000 to the same party organization. Eight days later, that committee transferred $40,000 to Missourians for Matt Blunt.[51] Later, an attorney for Roy Blunt would make a $3,000 payment to the Missouri Ethics Commission and admit that RoyB had violated campaign rules.[52]

Matt Blunt was elected secretary of state on November 7, 2000, in a tight race. He was the youngest person ever to win statewide office in Missouri. Days after he was sworn into office, his younger brother and campaign manager, Andy Blunt, registered as a lobbyist. By age twenty-six, Andy Blunt would boast an impressive list of clients that included Philip Morris, Miller Brewing Company, Southwestern Bell, UPS, and railroad companies Burlington Northern and Santa Fe.[53]

Blunt saw that government power gave you leverage over wealthy industries and companies that could be translated into money. He moved to solidify his relationship with the lobbying community. In 2003 his longtime chief of staff, Gregg Hartley, left to become vice chairman of the massive lobbying firm Cassidy & Associates. It didn't constitute a break with Blunt so much as simply a job change. "Blunt and I both conclude that I could still be a valuable part of his team," Hartley told *Washington Post* writer Robert Kaiser in an interview for Kaiser's book *So Damn Much Money*.[54] Indeed, Cassidy & Associates would become a key component in the Blunts' power structure. Andy Blunt would soon sign on as a consultant for Cassidy & Associates. "Mr. Blunt is available, on assignment, to augment Cassidy and Associates legislative and executive branch advocacy campaigns, at the state and federal level," said the lobbying outfit. The Cassidy website points out that Andy's clients include "Fortune 500 and 100 companies, state government vendors, and state trade associations."[55] Older brother Matt would also join Cassidy in 2009.[56]

Roy Blunt's climb to the top continued when he was elected majority whip in 2003. At the time nobody knew that the married Blunt was dating a lobbyist for Altria named Abigail Perlman on the side.[57] Surely not coincidentally, Blunt quietly tried to insert a provision in a Homeland Security bill that would prevent the Internet sale of tobacco products. It would have been a big win for Altria, which was the new name for Philip Morris, but the gambit was discovered by his Republican colleagues, who promptly killed it. Not only was Ms. Perlman a lobbyist for Altria, but so was Blunt's son Andy in Missouri. Later, Roy Blunt would divorce his wife and marry Abigail, who remains a high-profile lobbyist to this day. For their wedding, Blunt made sure to obtain a waiver from the House Ethics Committee from "all financial reporting requirements regarding all wedding gifts."[58]

Blunt became adept at using his powerful position in the House to do favors for his family members' lobbying clients. For example, his son Andy represented UPS. Roy Blunt inserted a provision into the Iraq War Emergency Appropriations Bill that would have required the U.S. military to move cargo only by majority-owned U.S. firms. It was a bid to block foreign competitors from getting any shot at winning some of the lucrative postal business shuttling supplies and packages between the United States and Iraq.[59]

In 2003 the family's climb to power took another turn when the young Missouri secretary of state Matt Blunt announced his plans to run for governor. There were two "first-class gubernatorial" candidates who were also looking at the race: the State Senate president, Peter Kinder, and Congressman Kenny Hulshof. But they both knew how it worked: you didn't run against the Blunts.[60] They both demurred, so the office was young Matt's for the taking. Andy, still a lobbyist, came over to run the campaign. They were joined by sister Amy Blunt, who served as a strategic adviser. Matt Blunt was only thirty-three, yet he won the election. Amy registered as a lobbyist for the firm Blackwell Sanders Peper Martin. The Blunts quickly announced that neither Amy nor Andy would lobby their brother. "My brother never lobbied the Secretary of State's office and my brother has been very clear that he's not going to lobby the executive branch of state government," said the governor-elect.[61]

Technically this was true. But there were easy ways around it. On December 9, 2004, Andy Blunt's firm hired a new associate named Jay Reichard, who was registered to lobby all branches of government. Reichard and Andy soon shared seventeen clients, thirteen of which were new clients signed after Matt had been elected governor. "Jay Reichard is not related to the governor," Andy Blunt said, "and is free to lobby anybody he wants."[62] True. And it was also true that Andy Blunt was right down the hall.

Soon it became clear that if you wanted something done, you had to hire a Blunt to help you.

In 2004 SBC Communications supported a Missouri state bill that would redefine competition between landline telephone companies and their wireless competitors. The bill would have given companies like SBC the opportunity to adjust their rates more quickly. But the bill died. In 2005 SBC hired Andy Blunt to "work behind the scenes" on the bill. Reintroduced as Senate Bill 237, it passed and was signed by his brother, the governor.[63]

It was part of a broader pattern of family profiteering — or attempted profiteering. Sometimes, when the family business became too public, their deals fell apart.

In 2005 Governor Blunt had to decide whether to sign a bill that would prohibit real estate brokers from offering homeowners barebones services in exchange for a low fee (H.B. 174). It was clearly an anticompetitive bill, and both the Justice Department and the Federal Trade Commission denounced it. But of course Realtors wanted it to pass, so they would be prohibited from undercutting one another's rates. The National Association of Realtors hired Gregg Hartley of Cassidy & Associates, under a one-month lobbying contract. They paid him $50,000 "to assist in pursuing its government affairs objectives. The nature of these objectives shall be working to ensure the enactment of HB 174 [the bill in question]." Sam Licklider, the chief lobbyist for Realtors in Missouri, said he believed Blunt would veto the bill. So they hired his father's old chief of staff to lobby him. The governor signed it.[64] There was no major public flap about conflict of interest, and the family business prospered. Whenever you hear Republicans proclaiming themselves to be in favor of free markets, you had better make sure they have no family members who are paid to squash that freedom.

On January 12, 2006, during his State of the State Address, Governor Matt Blunt pushed for a $25 million Healthcare Technology Fund. It was for the purpose of converting medical records into electronic records. Cerner Corporation, based in North Kansas City, was hoping to win a contract to help with the conversion. On November 12, 2005, Jeanne Patterson, wife of Cerner CEO Neal Patterson, had given $20,000 to the Republican Sixth Congressional District Committee, a party organization. Just four days earlier, the Sixth District Committee had transferred $10,000 to Blunt's campaign. Sixteen days after the Patterson contribution arrived, the Sixth District Committee gave $10,000 to yet another party committee, the Thirty-Second Republican Legislative District Committee, which naturally gave $10,000 to Blunt's campaign.[65] Cerner's lobbyist was a gentleman named Jewell Patek, a former state representative.[66] His lobbying firm had listed Andy Blunt as "of counsel" on several lobbying bids.

Also in 2006 Governor Blunt signed legislation requiring that gasoline sold in Missouri contain 10 percent ethanol. He also wanted full funding for an ethanol incentives fund, which would include a tax credit from the Missouri Agricultural and Small Business Development Authority. Andy Blunt was a founding member of a company called Central Missouri Biofuels, which was hoping to build a large ethanol plant that would produce 50 million gallons of ethanol per year. Partners in the project included the wife of Missouri congressman Sam Graves and a state representative and his wife. It fell to Sarah Steelman, the state treasurer and a fellow Republican, to kill the deal out of concerns relating to conflicts of interest. Andy Blunt was meanwhile also representing AGP, an Omaha, Nebraska, firm that was opening another ethanol production plant in Missouri.[67]

In another instance, Governor Matt Blunt proposed a dramatic increase in the cost of accessing driver's license records by the Department of Revenue to pay for a new computer contract. The State Department of Revenue, on May 1, 2007, announced that it was raising the fee to $7 per record.[68] In October, the Revenue Department signed a contract worth up to $50 million with BearingPoint, Inc., to refurbish the state's computer system for driver's license records.[69] BearingPoint's lobbyist in Missouri was Jay Reichard.[70] After the connection became public and questions were raised about the fee, the State Legislature balked and canceled the plan.

Among Andy Blunt's clients was Maximus, Inc., a Virginia-based firm that provides services to governments in the administration of health care. It ran the Missouri Medicaid payment system. Andy Blunt also represented a medical services contractor named ACS Heritage, which billed 10 million Medicaid prescriptions to the state Medicaid program every year.[71] When Governor Blunt set up a program for people to compare the prices of various prescriptions, the state chose ACS for the job.[72]

When Governor Matt Blunt announced in January 2008 that he would not seek reelection, Missourians were stunned. He explained that he had accomplished all that he set out to do, but many assumed that, with low poll numbers, he didn't want to fight what might prove to be a losing battle. (Among those disappointed were not only his family members but also a libertarian, pot-smoking gubernatorial candidate from Salem, Missouri, who had changed his name to Chief Wana Dubie and had hoped to produce bumper stickers that read: Dubie versus Blunt.)[73]

Back in Washington, Roy Blunt suffered from his close association with lobbyist Jack Abramoff. Abramoff had been sentenced to prison for bribing government officials and politicians with expensive meals, vacations, and cash. He had signed letters for some of the lobbyist's clients and had received campaign contributions. He was also on the FOO (Friends Of Owner) comp list at the lobbyist's restaurant, Signatures. Blunt could eat there for free, dining on $74 steaks and a $140 tasting menu, although his spokesperson said he never did.[74]

When the Abramoff scandal erupted, it took down Tom DeLay but actually helped Blunt, at least at first. Roy Blunt took DeLay's place as majority leader, serving in an interim capacity from September 2005 to February 2006. His son was still governor of Missouri, and two of his children and his wife were all lobbyists. Blunt seemed to be the natural permanent successor to DeLay. *The Hill* newspaper ran a poll that reportedly showed Blunt beating his nearest competitor, Congressman John Boehner, by a two-to-one margin.[75] Blunt ran a hard-nosed campaign, described by one veteran observer as "an old-style machine campaign based on subtle and not-so-subtle signals to other members that they dare not cross him."[76] But reformers in the House were worried about his connections to Abramoff, and Blunt lost in an upset to Boehner. "In the end," said Congressman Jeff Flake of Arizona, "we needed a course correction."[77]

But Blunt was far from defeated in his quest for yet more power and influence. In 2009 he announced his plans to run for the U.S. Senate. Like Harry Reid, Blunt knew the value of setting up an elaborate system of fund-raising entities that allows a politician to extract donations from the same contributor several times. For his 2010 Senate run, in addition to his campaign committee and his leadership PAC, he also created the Blunt Victory Committee, which transferred money both to his campaign and to the National Republican Senatorial Committee, which in turn also helped his campaign. He created yet another committee called the Road to Senate Victory Fund, which collected more than $1 million from donors and then transferred a chunk of it to Blunt and a handful of others.[78]

Blunt put his son Andy, a senior adviser to Thompson Communications, on the payroll as campaign manager.[79] But Blunt's campaign committee also paid almost $7 million to Thompson Communications for the race. It was by far his biggest expense, more than ten times the amount he paid to the next vendor. How much of this money ended up in Andy's pocket is impossible to say.[80]

Roy Blunt won his Senate race and returned to Washington, where he joined the powerful Senate Appropriations Committee and the Senate Commerce, Science, and Transportation Committee. His son Andy continues to work as a lobbyist; his clients include American Airlines, railroad companies, and many other major corporations.[81] In February 2011, former governor Matt Blunt took a job in Washington as head of the American Automotive Policy Council, an association created by the "Big Three" automakers to lobby for them (convenient, since his father had just joined the Transportation Committee in the Senate).[82] Daughter Amy Blunt has worked in recent years for Lathrop & Gage, a large Kansas City law firm with a Washington, D.C., lobbying and government affairs practice.[83] And the senator's wife continues to work as a lobbyist, now for Kraft Foods.[84]

For Roy Blunt, family enrichment is just part of the way the game is played. When Congressman Tom DeLay was criticized for putting his daughter and wife on the payroll and for his brother's lobbying work, Blunt defended him: "The things that Tom has been criticized about in one way or another every member of Congress could be criticized about." Indeed. DeLay's student has greatly surpassed his teacher.[85]

The Reids and the Blunts are particularly powerful and successful political families. In *The Godfather*, the New York–area Mafia was divided into five families. In Washington today, there are many more—but some are more powerful than others.

10

CONCLUSION

Protection for the Rest of Us

D ISGRACED GOVERNOR ROD BLAGOJEVICH, who tried to sell Barack Obama's U.S. Senate seat in Illinois to the highest bidder, is the modern symbol of corrupt politics. He seems perfectly suited to the role: the extortionist with his cartoonish hair, foul mouth, and equally foul-mouthed wife, sentenced to fourteen years in the state pen.

But what is the difference between his attempted extortion and the legal forms we have examined in this book? Perhaps Blago's real crime was simply a blunder: he lacked the soft touch and deftness that other politicians have mastered. Knowing he was the target of a federal investigation, he told a colleague (while the FBI was listening), "Assume everybody's listening; the whole world is listening." But he blathered on anyway. The Senate seat, Blago said, was a "f—— valuable thing, you just don't give it away for nothing."[1] He told an aide, "We were approached, 'pay to play,' you know, he'd raise me 500 grand, an emissary came, then the other guy would raise a million if I made him a senator."[2] He thought he could make "a play here" for his wife: get her a lucrative job in Washington or get her placed on some corporate boards.[3]

Extorting campaign donations and favors from powerful people. Getting a job for a family member. Sound familiar? Blago was certainly less sophisticated about it than most players in Washington. This is a guy who, on the day his wife was going to testify at his trial, told the media her new haircut was "beautiful," adding, "I say that to her every day — and I'm not just saying that because she's testifying."[4] And when he was caught renovating his house with non-union labor (a problem for a pro-union Democrat), he told the media that he had indeed used a "politically correct" list of contractors "and the landscaper was a lesbian."[5]

Blago — must it be said? — lacks the soft touch. Intelligence and gaffes aside, Blago also became too greedy. The key to maximizing the returns of extortion is to restrain "piggish propensities below their full porcine potential."[6]

Blago's ultimate mistake was not that he extorted — *but that he extorted in broad daylight.* What he did — trading government action for money or favors — happens all the time in Washington. He was often referred to as a classic "Chicago pol," suggesting that corrupt machine rule is a local affair. Yet most people forget that Blago served three terms in Congress. As Thomas G. Donlan of *Barron's* posits, "Since Blagojevich is apparently not smart enough to think up these ploys by himself, it's unpleasant but fair to believe that he learned them from experience in Washington while he was a congressman."[7] Chicago is a one-party town; Washington is not. But corruption can work perfectly well in either context.

What happened to Blago seems to personify the solution to political corruption: get rid of the "bad people" in government and replace them with "good people." Certainly individuals are responsible for their misdeeds and ought to be held to account. But there shouldn't be style points when it comes to corruption. If others are doing what Blago did, but doing it in a more subtle and sophisticated manner, that is a problem. Indeed, it might be a more severe problem because it is so hard to detect.

FBI investigations alone will never take corruption out of politics. They take too much effort, and they attack the problem serially, one target at a time. Instead, we need to start with a simple proposition: bureaucrats and politicians are just like other people. That may sound obvious, yet it is a real departure from the traditional way we think about government. We like to think our leaders are pursuing the common good. Yet if politicians and bureaucrats are ordinary people, they are going to make most of their decisions based on what benefits them personally.

This is not to say that there are no good, honest, and decent people in politics and government. But by and large people are people: politicians and bureaucrats are as self-seeking as members of other professions, such as bankers on Wall Street or film producers in Hollywood.

We also need to recognize that in Washington today corruption is driven more by extortion than by bribery. The power equation in Washington has shifted from the buyers to the sellers of influence. We all denounce "special interests," that is, lobbying by firms and industries. We should turn our attention to their counterparts. Our reform efforts have been almost exclusively devoted to restricting the activities of these special interests — in other words, ourselves — as opposed to the activities of the Permanent Political Class. This is unusual because when it comes to most industries in America — insurance, finance, and so on — most regulatory requirements fall on sellers, not buyers. Perhaps that doesn't happen in this case because it's the sellers who get to make the rules.

Reforms designed to protect the Permanent Political Class from outside special interests usually backfire and end up being a tool for further extortion. Let me give you a small example of how this fake is played in Washington. In 2006, in the wake of the Jack Abramoff scandal, Congress introduced a series of ethics reforms that were supposed to dramatically limit lobbyists' influence on Congress by restricting their ability to buy expensive meals or offer other favors to congressional staff.[8] Sounds like a good idea, doesn't it? But here's what happened: with lobbyists buying meals for staffers now out of the question, politicians started organizing fund-raisers where lobbyists paid to meet with the staffers! Lobbyist Stewart Van Scoyoc noted: "Particularly with the ethics package, it'll put more pressure on fundraising because it will limit the interaction between lobbyists and staff and push more of it into the fundraising context." As another lobbyist put it, "Members tap us all year, so why not the staff?"[9]

While some have proposed public financing of presidential campaigns as a possible solution, this proposal has huge problems. It is more likely to aid incumbents than challengers, since incumbents have many built-in advantages. If a challenger cannot raise money to take on an incumbent and cannot outspend that person, the incumbent will win almost every time. And the courts have repeatedly found that "checkbook activism is no less protected by the First Amendment than grassroots organizing." Donating money is a form of freedom of speech, in the eyes of our courts.[10] The famous Supreme Court case on campaign finance limits, *Buckley v. Valeo*, noted that "virtually every means of communicating ideas in today's mass society requires the expenditure of money" and that the ability to donate money for the causes you believe in is a constitutional right.[11] Many people have bitterly denounced this decision, but I do not believe any court will ever stop wealthy individuals from spending large sums to express their political views. We could tinker with various rules about what candidates may or may not do to coordinate with those individuals, but we cannot stop the "buyers" — ourselves — from entering the fray.

If spending money is a First Amendment right, the restrictions should not be placed on the spenders so much as on the candidates soliciting their help. Limiting the political extortion racket means regulating politicians and bureaucrats, not the American public.

Here are some necessary reforms:

1. Ban the solicitation or receipt of campaign contributions while Congress is in session in Washington. Extortion works best when the threat is imminent. The Mafia street thug who has a bat with him is more likely to get protection money than the distant extortionist making a phone call. The same holds true when it comes to the Permanent Political Class. Important bills that can make or ruin a company or an industry create the perfect baseball bat to use. Holding a fund-raiser in the shadow of the U.S. Capitol, where important legislation might be on the docket, is an extortionist's dream. Twenty-seven states already have similar laws or rules in place for their state legislatures. In *Buckley v. Valeo*, the Supreme Court ruled that "the appearance of corruption may persist whenever a favorable legislative outcome follows closely on the heels of a financial contribution."[12] Timing and location (proximity) are important. We need to divorce fund-raising from lawmaking as much as we can — as in Florida House rule 15.3(b):

> A House member may neither solicit nor accept any campaign contribution during the 60-day regular legislative session or any extended or special session on the member's own behalf, on behalf of a political party, on behalf of any organization with respect to which the member's solicitation is regulated under s. 106.0701, Florida Statutes, or on behalf of a candidate for the House of Representatives; however, a member may contribute to the member's own campaign.[13]

The Florida Senate has a similar restriction.

Extortion can occur at any time. But there is no question that there is no more advantageous time to bring leverage on and extort money than when Congress is about to vote.

Some might object that such a rule would put incumbents at a severe disadvantage. After all, Congress can be in session for months, and challengers would be free to raise money throughout that time. But if anything this restriction would force members of Congress to make efficient use of their time. So much of what happens in Washington is related to fund-raising: milker bills, congressional hearings designed to extract, and so on. Eliminating politicians' ability to raise money while in session would force them to devote their time exclusively to their job: lawmaking.

In 2007, Speaker of the House Nancy Pelosi announced that Congress would be moving to a five-day workweek rather than the traditional three-day week. It sounded like a good idea, but what did members do with the extra time? They held more fund-raisers! "Honestly we've already begun to schedule them," said Monica Notzon, a political fund-raiser. "I think we're going to see events every day of the week."[14] A lobbyist for the National Federal of Independent Business, Dan Danner, said, "If they're here more that's what they'll do. There'll be more fundraisers."[15]

Imposing this ban would not completely purify all fund-raising, of course. But it would help nudge fund-raising events in the direction of genuine support rather than extraction. As one scholar puts it, "There is little reason to believe that the genuine supporter of a candidate" would not give when Congress is out of session and when supporters are allowed to give.[16]

2. *Place an outright ban on contributions and solicitations involving lobbyists or government contractors.* Many states already have these sorts of restrictions in place.[17] For example, Connecticut General Statutes §9-704 (c) provides in part that:

contributions from (1) communicator lobbyist; (2) members of the immediate family of a communicator lobbyist; or (3) principals of a state contractor or prospective state contractors shall not be deemed to be qualifying contributions and shall be returned by the campaign treasurer of the candidate committee to the contributor or transmitted to the State Elections Enforcement Commission for deposit in the Citizens' Election Fund.

3. Restrict the ability of the Permanent Political Class to convert campaign money into a lifestyle subsidy. If you want to loan money to your campaign, that's fine. But you shouldn't collect interest in doing so. You have a First Amendment right to spend money on your campaign and loan money to your campaign, but you have no constitutional right to make a profitable investment out of it.

4. Ban leadership PACs. Leadership PACs have essentially become money-laundering operations. As Congressman Joe Hefley of Colorado put it, "My impression is that a lot of people use leadership PACs as a slush fund."[18] Even former FEC chairman Bradley Smith, who generally opposes restrictions on campaign financing on free speech grounds, believes that leadership PACs have to go because of how they are abused. Sometimes they are used to enhance a politician's lifestyle, sometimes to bribe colleagues for votes. As one member of Congress put it, "Having a leadership PAC helps me tremendously with my colleagues, whether it's getting legislation through [or] getting their support for it."[19] Members of Congress horse-trade all the time. They call it log-rolling: if you support building a bridge in my district, I will support beach restoration in yours. We cannot stop such trades. But leadership PACs are not about benefits for districts: they are about benefits for members of Congress.

Right now, politicians enjoy a nice loophole. They are provided an exemption from the provision in the *Ethics Manual* that prohibits soliciting or receiving contributions in congressional office buildings from fellow members. We need to extend the solicitation ban to members of Congress: selling your vote is selling your vote, whether it's to a special interest or a colleague.

5. *Restrict the ability of the Permanent Political Class to extort money for their families through political power.* We need to ban immediate family members (spouses and children) from registering as lobbyists. Period. We also need to prevent members of Congress from putting family members on the payroll. Campaigns and public service should not be about self-enrichment. Putting your kids on the campaign payroll can often be a simple way of moving campaign dollars into the family bank account.

But beyond restricting the extortionist avenues for the Permanent Political Class, we must also have transparency in the legislative process so that the practice can be exposed. If the military-industrial complex has been cause for worry, today there exists a legislative-lobbyist complex as well. Laws are so complicated that bills are not even read by members of Congress. Extortive practices are easy to carry out in a cloud of legal words.

All sorts of stuff is packed into bills. In an article for the *Washington Post* entitled "We Need to Read the Bills," Congressman Brian Baird wrote about a particularly embarrassing episode in which someone inserted a provision into a spending bill that would have allowed House and Senate Appropriations Committee chairmen and their staffs to examine any individual American's income tax returns.[20]

We can fix this problem by doing a couple of things. First, we should adopt a single-subject rule for all bills. Article III of the Florida Constitution "requires that every law shall embrace but one subject and matter properly connected therewith." In other words, each bill needs to be focused on one specific subject. You shouldn't be able to slip something in on an unrelated subject.

Second, we need to require members of Congress to actually read the bills they are going to vote on. This sounds like common sense to most people outside of Washington. But politicians, of course, think it's ridiculous that lawmakers should actually read the laws they are making! Several bills that have already been introduced would try to accomplish this in some way. Some would require a seven-day waiting period between the time when a bill is ready to be voted on and when the final vote actually takes place. During this period, members of Congress would be required to read the bill. Others suggest that all bills scheduled for a full vote on the floor be read out loud — even the two-thousand-page monsters. Back in 2009, thanks to a legislative maneuver, it appeared that a monster bill with four hundred amendments might need to be read aloud on the House floor. Congressional leaders actually hired a speed-reader to comply, even though no one would have been able to understand what he was reading. "Judging by the size of the amendments, I can read a page about every 34 seconds," said the speed-reader. Based on that estimate, it would have taken him nine hours to read the bill.[21] If we can pass a law to make reading aloud a permanent requirement, it will need to guard against such shenanigans. (Imagine all-night readings to empty chambers.) How about simply requiring members to read the bills before a vote and to sign a legal affidavit attesting to that fact?

Such laws have to have teeth. Current Senate rules require that any bill that will be voted on be posted online beforehand, so that the general public can read it.[22] But that rule is regularly suspended or ignored, without any penalty. So those who ignore the requirement to read a bill should face some sort of real sanction. After all, they are paid to be lawmakers. That is their job. How can they make laws if they don't even read them?

Government is getting bigger — and it is getting meaner. One key reason: it is profitable for the Permanent Political Class. We need to change this reality. Dante, in *The Inferno*, placed corrupt politicians in the eighth circle of hell, the penultimate in eternal damnation. Yet as Lord Acton famously said, power corrupts. We must assume that the temptation to corruption is universal in Washington, and we must create earthly punishments to deter it.

APPENDIX 1

REPUBLICAN PARTY DUES LISTS, 2013[1]

First Name	Last Name	2012 Cycle Outstanding	2013 March Dinner Outstanding Overage	2013 Dues Assessment	2013 Dues Pledged	2013 Dues Paid	Percentage of March Dinner Paid
John	Boehner		$0	$200,000	$418,347	$418,347	100%
Eric	Cantor		$0	$200,000	$200,000	$200,000	100%
Kevin	McCarthy		$0	$200,000	$200,000	$200,000	100%
Greg	Walden		$0	$165,000	$165,000	$165,000	100%
Cathy	McMorris Rodgers		$0	$165,000	$39,600	$39,600	100%
Lynn	Westmoreland		$0	$125,000	$125,000	$125,000	100%
Dave	Camp		$0	$165,000	$15,400	$15,400	100%
Jeb	Hensarling		$0	$165,000	$237,200	$89,600	100%
Harold	Rogers		$0	$165,000	$8,250	$8,250	100%
Peter	Roskam		$0	$165,000	$3,555	$3,555	100%
Pete	Sessions		$0	$165,000	$165,000	$148,700	100%
Fred	Upton		$0	$165,000	$138,500	$98,150	100%
Virginia	Foxx		$0	$125,000	$43,150	$25,000	100%
Doc	Hastings		$0	$125,000	—	—	100%
Darrell	Issa		$0	$125,000	$32,800	$32,800	100%
Lynn	Jenkins		$0	$125,000	$53,510	—	100%
John	Kline		$0	$125,000	$47,550	$40,050	100%

REPUBLICAN PARTY DUES LISTS, 2013

First Name	Last Name	2012 Cycle Outstanding	2013 March Dinner Outstanding Overage	2013 Dues Assessment	2013 Dues Pledged	2013 Dues Paid	Percentage of March Dinner Paid
James	Lankford		$0	$125,000	$500	$500	100%
Paul	Ryan		$0	$125,000	$125,000	—	100%
Bill	Shuster		$0	$125,000	$60,600	$46,000	100%
Kevin	Brady		$0	$85,000	$42,600	$42,600	100%
John	Campbell		$0	$85,000	$175,500	$175,500	100%
John	Carter		$0	$85,000	—	—	100%
Scott	Garrett		$0	$85,000	$9,700	—	100%
Sam	Johnson		$0	$85,000	$30,800	$30,800	100%
Timothy	Murphy		$0	$85,000	$7,000	$1,000	100%
Randy	Neugebauer		$0	$85,000	$47,800	$29,800	100%
Joseph	Pitts		$0	$85,000	$10,000	$10,000	100%
Patrick	Tiberi		$0	$85,000	$550	$550	100%
Ed	Whitfield		$0	$85,000	$44,750	$44,750	100%
Diane	Black		$0	$67,500	$248,650	$170,150	100%
Mike	Burgess		$0	$67,500	$0	$0	100%
Ken	Calvert		$0	$67,500	$97,566	$76,366	100%

REPUBLICAN PARTY DUES LISTS, 2013

First Name	Last Name	2012 Cycle Outstanding	2013 March Dinner Outstanding Overage	2013 Dues Assessment	2013 Dues Pledged	2013 Dues Paid	Percentage of March Dinner Paid
Tom	Cole		$0	$67,500	$140,250	$43,550	100%
Tom	Cotton		$0	$67,500	$54,533	$54,533	100%
Mario	Diaz-Balart		$0	$67,500	$77,500	$77,500	100%
Stephen	Fincher		$0	$67,500	$67,500	—	100%
Chuck	Fleischmann		$0	$67,500	$4,900	$4,900	100%
Cory	Gardner		$0	$67,500	$5,000	$5,000	100%
Sam	Graves		$0	$67,500	$8,500	$8,500	100%
Brett	Guthrie		$0	$67,500	$12,500	$2,500	100%
Ralph	Hall		$0	$67,500	$52,500	$52,500	100%
Gregg	Harper		$0	$67,500	$3,700	$3,700	100%
Andy	Harris		$0	$67,500	$7,500	$6,500	100%
Jaime	Herrera Beutler		$0	$67,500	$6,800	$6,800	100%
Mike	Kelly		$0	$67,500	$27,900	$27,900	100%
Leonard	Lance		$0	$67,500	$15,600	$15,600	100%
Billy	Long		$0	$67,500	$500	$500	100%
David	McKinley		$0	$67,500	Unclear	Unclear	100%
Jeff	Miller		$0	$67,500	$56,500	$56,500	100%

REPUBLICAN PARTY DUES LISTS, 2013

First Name	Last Name	2012 Cycle Outstanding	2013 March Dinner Outstanding Overage	2013 Dues Assessment	2013 Dues Pledged	2013 Dues Paid	Percentage of March Dinner Paid
Mick	Mulvaney		$0	$67,500	$23,350	$23,350	100%
Alan	Nunnelee		$0	$67,500	$2,421	$2,421	100%
Erik	Paulsen		$0	$67,500	$18,900	$8,900	100%
Tom	Price		$0	$67,500	$31,600	$28,100	100%
Tom	Rooney		$0	$67,500	$13,000	$13,000	100%
Steve	Scalise		$0	$67,500	$2,500	$2,500	100%
Adrian	Smith		$0	$67,500	$27,250	$16,500	100%
Lamar	Smith		$0	$67,500	$53,400	$6,000	100%
Steve	Stivers		$0	$67,500	$68,900	$68,900	100%
Ann	Wagner		$0	$67,500	$138,400	$112,600	100%
Steve	Womack		$0	$67,500	$73,100	$73,100	100%
Kevin	Yoder		$0	$67,500	$6,700	$6,700	100%
Vern	Buchanan		$0	$67,500	$69,425	—	100%
Spencer	Bachus		$0	$67,500	—	—	100%
Jason	Chaffetz		$0	$50,000	$11,000	$11,000	100%
Mike	Conaway		$0	$50,000	$5,000	$5,000	100%
Jeff	Denham		$0	$50,000	$10,466	$666	100%

REPUBLICAN PARTY DUES LISTS, 2013

First Name	Last Name	2012 Cycle Outstanding	2013 March Dinner Outstanding Overage	2013 Dues Assessment	2013 Dues Pledged	2013 Dues Paid	Percentage of March Dinner Paid
John	Fleming		$0	$50,000	$26,900	$26,900	100%
Randy	Forbes	($177,000)	$0	$50,000	—	—	100%
Joe	Heck		$0	$50,000	$37,300	$37,300	100%
Duncan	Hunter		$0	$50,000	$14,200	$14,200	100%
Jim	Jordan		$0	$50,000	$5,000	$5,000	100%
Frank	LoBiondo		$0	$50,000	$15,200	$15,200	100%
Tom	McClintock		$0	$50,000	—	—	100%
Kristi	Noem		$0	$50,000	$6,800	$4,300	100%
Thomas	Petri		$0	$50,000	$22,225	$17,225	100%
Ted	Poe		$0	$50,000	$3,400	$3,400	100%
Phil	Roe		$0	$50,000	$5,900	$5,900	100%
Todd	Rokita		$0	$50,000	$7,400	$2,400	100%
David	Schweikert		$0	$50,000	$14,500	—	100%
Steve	Southerland		$0	$50,000	$1,000	$1,000	100%
Glenn	Thompson		$0	$50,000	$9,400	$7,400	100%
Mac	Thornberry		$0	$50,000	$5,000	$5,000	100%

REPUBLICAN PARTY DUES LISTS, 2013

First Name	Last Name	2012 Cycle Outstanding	2013 March Dinner Outstanding Overage	2013 Dues Assessment	2013 Dues Pledged	2013 Dues Paid	Percentage of March Dinner Paid
Michael	Turner		$0	$50,000	$23,500	$23,500	100%
Ileana	Ros-Lehtinen		$0	$50,000	—	—	100%
Susan	Brooks		$0	$32,500	$1,000	$1,000	100%
Chris	Collins		$0	$32,500	$43,400	$23,400	100%
Doug	Collins		$0	$32,500	$0	$0	100%
Paul	Cook		$0	$32,500	$20,266	$20,266	100%
Kevin	Cramer		$0	$32,500	$26,900	$26,900	100%
Steve	Daines		$0	$32,500	$50,800	$25,000	100%
Rodney	Davis		$0	$32,500	$3,000	$3,000	100%
George	Holding		$0	$32,500	$17,500	$17,500	100%
Richard	Hudson		$0	$32,500	$34,700	$34,700	100%
Mark	Meadows		$0	$32,500	$23,900	$23,900	100%
Scott	Perry		$0	$32,500	$5,900	$5,900	100%
Tom	Rice		$0	$32,500	$3,500	$3,500	100%
Keith	Rothfus		$0	$32,500	$54,000	$53,000	100%
Roger	Williams		$0	$32,500	$377,800	$151,100	100%
Tim	Griffin		($3,500)	$67,500	—	—	95%

REPUBLICAN PARTY DUES LISTS, 2013

First Name	Last Name	2012 Cycle Outstanding	2013 March Dinner Outstanding Overage	2013 Dues Assessment	2013 Dues Pledged	2013 Dues Paid	Percentage of March Dinner Paid
Robert	Pittenger		($4,150)	$67,500	—	—	94%
Marsha	Blackburn		($5,350)	$67,500	—	—	92%
Gus	Bilirakis		($5,600)	$67,500	—	—	92%
Blake	Farenthold	($119,800)	($7,700)	$50,000	—	—	85%
David	Reichert		($10,600)	$85,000	—	—	84%
Stevan	Pearce		($11,500)	$67,500	—	—	83%
Dennis	Ross		($11,500)	$67,500	—	—	83%
Andy	Barr		($12,500)	$67,500	—	—	81%
Jim	Gerlach		($15,000)	$67,500	—	—	78%
Mo	Brooks		($7,500)	$32,500	—	—	77%
Reid	Ribble		($12,925)	$50,000	—	—	74%
Buck	McKeon		($35,400)	$125,000	—	—	72%
Rob	Woodall	($230,000)	($19,500)	$67,500	—	—	71%
Luke	Messer		($9,500)	$32,500	—	—	71%
Patrick	McHenry		($25,400)	$85,000	$36,200	—	70%
Tom	Reed		($20,500)	$67,500	—	—	70%
Kerry	Bentivolio		($10,000)	$32,500	—	—	69%

REPUBLICAN PARTY DUES LISTS, 2013

First Name	Last Name	2012 Cycle Outstanding	2013 March Dinner Outstanding Overage	2013 Dues Assessment	2013 Dues Pledged	2013 Dues Paid	Percentage of March Dinner Paid
John	Mica		($15,500)	$50,000	—	—	69%
Bill	Flores		($17,000)	$50,000	$88,200	—	66%
Lou	Barletta		($18,500)	$50,000	—	—	63%
Ron	DeSantis		($12,500)	$32,500	$2,500	—	62%
Jackie	Walorski		($12,500)	$32,500	$18,300	—	62%
Dan	Benishek		($20,000)	$50,000	—	—	60%
Pete	Olson		($27,300)	$67,500	—	—	60%
Vicky	Hartzler		($20,500)	$50,000	—	—	59%
Morgan	Griffith		($28,000)	$67,500	$3,000	—	59%
Rodney	Frelinghuysen		($35,500)	$85,000	—	—	58%
Jon	Runyan		($21,900)	$50,000	$2,500	$2,500	56%
Ted	Yoho		($15,000)	$32,500	—	—	54%
Mike	Coffman		($24,500)	$50,000	$0	—	52%
Bob	Gibbs		($25,000)	$50,000	—	—	50%
Scott	Rigell		($25,000)	$50,000	—	—	50%
Kenny	Marchant		($34,100)	$67,500	—	—	49%
Chris	Stewart		($16,500)	$32,500	—	—	49%
Randy	Hultgren		($25,500)	$50,000	—	—	49%

REPUBLICAN PARTY DUES LISTS, 2013

First Name	Last Name	2012 Cycle Outstanding	2013 March Dinner Outstanding Overage	2013 Dues Assessment	2013 Dues Pledged	2013 Dues Paid	Percentage of March Dinner Paid
Tom	Latham		($44,000)	$85,000	—	—	48%
Mike	Rogers (AL)		($26,500)	$50,000	—	—	47%
Joe	Barton	($220,646)	($35,900)	$67,500	—	—	47%
Jo	Bonner		($36,300)	$67,500	—	—	46%
Paul	Gosar		($26,900)	$50,000	—	—	46%
Brad	Wenstrup		($17,500)	$32,500	—	—	46%
Cynthia	Lummis		($27,000)	$50,000	—	—	46%
Daniel	Webster		($37,000)	$67,500	—	—	45%
Michelle	Bachmann		($37,500)	$67,500	—	—	44%
Doug	Lamborn		($28,500)	$50,000	—	—	43%
Aaron	Schock		($39,000)	$67,500	—	—	42%
Kay	Granger		($50,000)	$85,000	—	—	42%
Larry	Bucshon		($30,000)	$50,000	—	—	40%
John	Duncan		($30,000)	$50,000	—	—	40%
Bill	Johnson		($40,500)	$67,500	—	—	40%
Pat	Meehan		($30,000)	$50,000	—	—	40%

REPUBLICAN PARTY DUES LISTS, 2013

First Name	Last Name	2012 Cycle Outstanding	2013 March Dinner Outstanding Overage	2013 Dues Assessment	2013 Dues Pledged	2013 Dues Paid	Percentage of March Dinner Paid
Scott	Tipton		($30,000)	$50,000	—	—	40%
Rick	Crawford		($31,500)	$50,000	—	—	37%
Doug	LaMalfa		($20,500)	$32,500	—	—	37%
Bob	Goodlatte		($79,000)	$125,000	—	—	37%
Matt	Salmon		($20,900)	$32,500	—	—	36%
Jeff	Duncan		($32,500)	$50,000	—	—	35%
Bill	Posey		($44,500)	$67,500	—	—	34%
Thomas	Massie		($21,500)	$32,500	—	—	34%
Jack	Kingston		($56,300)	$85,000	—	—	34%
David	Valadao		($45,000)	$67,500	—	—	33%
Randy	Weber		($22,100)	$32,500	—	—	32%
Mike	Rogers (MI)		($46,500)	$67,500	—	—	32%
Candice	Miller		($46,500)	$67,500	—	—	31%
Chris	Gibson		($34,500)	$50,000	—	—	31%
Tim	Walberg		($34,500)	$50,000	—	—	31%
Rob	Wittman		($34,500)	$50,000	—	—	31%
Mike	Fitzpatrick		($47,000)	$67,500	—	—	30%
Michael	Grimm	($206,578)	($47,000)	$67,500	—	—	30%

REPUBLICAN PARTY DUES LISTS, 2013

First Name	Last Name	2012 Cycle Outstanding	2013 March Dinner Outstanding Overage	2013 Dues Assessment	2013 Dues Pledged	2013 Dues Paid	Percentage of March Dinner Paid
Mark	Amodei		($35,000)	$50,000	—	—	30%
Steve	Chabot		($35,000)	$50,000	—	—	30%
Louie	Gohmert		($35,000)	$50,000	—	—	30%
Steve	King		($35,000)	$50,000	—	—	30%
Tom	Marino		($35,000)	$50,000	—	—	30%
Austin	Scott		($35,000)	$50,000	—	—	30%
Lee	Terry		($59,500)	$85,000	—	—	30%
Robert	Hurt		($47,500)	$67,500	—	—	30%
Jim	Renacci		($47,500)	$67,500	—	—	30%
John	Culberson		($60,500)	$85,000	—	—	29%
Rob	Bishop		($49,000)	$67,500	—	—	27%
Richard	Hanna	($86,928)	($36,500)	$50,000	—	—	27%
Renee	Ellmers		($49,475)	$67,500	—	—	27%
Bill	Cassidy		($50,000)	$67,500	—	—	26%
Sean	Duffy		($50,000)	$67,500	—	—	26%
Todd	Young		($50,000)	$67,500	$14,900	—	26%

REPUBLICAN PARTY DUES LISTS, 2013

First Name	Last Name	2012 Cycle Outstanding	2013 March Dinner Outstanding Overage	2013 Dues Assessment	2013 Dues Pledged	2013 Dues Paid	Percentage of March Dinner Paid
Blaine	Luetkemeyer		($51,000)	$67,500	—	—	24%
Devin	Nunes		($64,500)	$85,000	—	—	24%
Charles	Dent		($51,500)	$67,500	—	—	24%
Frank	Wolf		($65,000)	$85,000	—	—	24%
Markwayne	Mullin		($25,000)	$32,500	$3,500	$3,500	23%
David	Joyce		($52,000)	$67,500	—	—	23%
Richard	Nugent		($52,000)	$67,500	—	—	23%
Peter	King		($52,500)	$67,500	—	—	22%
Adam	Kinzinger		($52,500)	$67,000	$45,000	$45,000	22%
Bob	Latta		($52,500)	$67,500	—	—	22%
John	Shimkus		($66,500)	$85,000	—	—	22%
Michael	McCaul		($98,000)	$125,000	—	—	22%
Bill	Huizenga		($53,000)	$67,500	—	—	21%
Michael	Pompeo		($53,000)	$67,500	—	—	21%
Ed	Royce		($100,100)	$125,000	—	—	20%
Robert	Aderholt		($69,000)	$85,000	—	—	19%
Michael	Simpson		($69,000)	$85,000	—	—	19%

REPUBLICAN PARTY DUES LISTS, 2013

First Name	Last Name	2012 Cycle Outstanding	2013 March Dinner Outstanding Overage	2013 Dues Assessment	2013 Dues Pledged	2013 Dues Paid	Percentage of March Dinner Paid
Ander	Crenshaw		($69,500)	$85,000	—	—	18%
Bill	Young	($329,500)	($69,500)	$85,000	—	—	18%
Charles	Boustany	($434,984)	($70,000)	$85,000	—	—	18%
Gary	Miller	($359,299)	($56,000)	$67,500	—	—	17%
Trent	Franks	($227,600)	($41,900)	$50,000	—	—	16%
Christopher	Smith		($41,900)	$50,000	—	—	16%
Trey	Radel		($27,500)	$32,500	—	—	15%
Joe	Wilson		($42,500)	$50,000	—	—	15%
Phil	Gingrey		($57,500)	$67,500	—	—	15%
Trey	Gowdy		($44,000)	$50,000	—	—	12%
Scott	Deslarlais		($44,600)	$50,000	—	—	11%
Frank	Lucas		($111,975)	$125,000	—	—	10%
Howard	Coble	($230,000)	($45,000)	$50,000	—	—	10%
Martha	Roby		($45,000)	$50,000	—	—	10%

DEMOCRATIC CONGRESSIONAL CAMPAIGN COMMITTEE

Dues Lists[2]

DCCC 2013 – 2014 Member Dues

Member Category	Dues Goal	Raised Goal
Leadership		
o Nancy Pelosi	$800,000	$25,000,000
o Steny Hoyer	$800,000	$2,500,000
o Jim Clyburn	$600,000	$1,500,000
o Xavier Becerra	$450,000	$1,000,000
o Joe Crowley	$450,000	$3,000,000
o Steve Israel	$450,000	$10,000,000
o Rob Andrews	$450,000	$500,000
o Rosa DeLauro	$450,000	$500,000
DCCC Advisory Chairs		
o John Larson	$300,000	$500,000
o Chris Van Hollen	$300,000	$500,000
DCCC Vice Chairs		
o Jared Polis	$300,000	$500,000
o Allyson Schwartz	$300,000	$3,000,000
DCCC Council Chairs	$300,000	$500,000
Chief Deputy Whips	$300,000	$500,000
Exclusive Committee Ranking Members	$500,000	$1,000,000
Ranking Members	$250,000	$250,000
Exclusive Subcommittee Ranking Members	$250,000	$250,000
Exclusive Committee Members	$200,000	$250,000
Non-Exclusive Subcommittee Ranking Members	$150,000	$100,000
Members	$125,000	$75,000

DEMOCRATIC CONGRESSIONAL CAMPAIGN COMMITTEE

Dues Lists[2]

DEMOCRATIC CONGRESSION			
2013 - 2014 ELECTION CYCLE DUE$			
MEMBER	**COH 12/31/12**	**Dues Goal**	**Dues Received**
LEADERSHIP			
Pelosi, Nancy	$449,327.33	$800,000.00	$250,000.0(
Hoyer, Steny	$777,032.09	$800,000.00	$280,000.0(
Clyburn, Jim	$1,233,310.01	$600,000.00	$200,000.0(
Becerra, Xavier	$901,779.45	$450,000.00	$400,000.0(
Crowley, Joe	$788,652.14	$450,000.00	$115,000.0(
Israel, Steve	$336,023.60	$450,000.00	$450,000.0(
Andrews, Robert	$491,519.32	$450,000.00	$100,000.0(
DeLauro, Rosa	$10,971.26	$450,000.00	$90,000.0(
DCCC NATIONAL CHAIRS			
Himes, Jim	$762,091.15	$300,000.00	$48,000.0(
Polis, Jared	$25,376.55	$300,000.00	$100,900.0(
CHIEF DEPUTY WHIPS			
Butterfield, GK	$238,368.30	$300,000.00	$0.0(
Degette, Diana	$62,321.36	$300,000.00	$0.0(
Ellison, Keith	$56,569.76	$300,000.00	$7,000.0(
Lewis, John	$206,616.12	$300,000.00	$0.0(
Lujan, Ben Ray	$314,480.27	$300,000.00	$32,500.0(
Matheson, Jim	$16,841.59	$300,000.00	$0.0(
Schakowsky, Jan	$273,011.52	$300,000.00	$40,800.0(
Sewell, Terri	$377,613.87	$300,000.00	$45,000.0(
Wasserman Schultz, Debbie	$530,196.58	$300,000.00	$30,000.0(
Welch, Peter	$1,239,101.19	$300,000.00	$100,000.0(
EXCLUSIVE COMMITTEE RANKING MEMBERS			
Levin, Sander	$238,137.97	$500,000.00	$115,000.0(
Lowey, Nita	$417,573.87	$500,000.00	$300,000.0(
Slaughter, Louise	$24,826.60	$500,000.00	$0.0(
Waters, Maxine	$46,683.21	$500,000.00	$0.0(
Waxman, Henry	$220,611.74	$500,000.00	$0.0(
RANKING MEMBERS			
Brady, Robert	$578,057.76	$250,000.00	$0.0(
Conyers, John	$63,322.67	$250,000.00	$15,000.0(
Cummings, Elijah	$780,052.38	$250,000.00	$55,000.0(
Engel, Eliot	$51,286.29	$250,000.00	$10,000.0(
Johnson, Eddie Bernice	$67,820.46	$250,000.00	$5,000.0(

DEMOCRATIC CONGRESSIONAL CAMPAIGN COMMITTEE
2011 - 2012 ELECTION CYCLE DUES & MONEY RAISED (November 5, 2012)

MEMBER	Cash on Hand 9/30/12	2011-2012 Dues Goal	2011-2012 Dues Received	2011-2012 Raised for DCCC Goal	2011-2012 Raised for DCCC	2011-2012 Frontline and Red to Blue Contributions/Raised	2011-2012 Member Points
LEADERSHIP							
Pelosi, Nancy	$423,418	$800,000	$1,000,000	$25,000,000	$52,962,359	5,197,792	632
Hoyer, Steny	$1,503,478	$800,000	$1,100,000	$2,500,000	$4,983,604	3,861,700	583
Clyburn, Jim	$1,612,178	$600,000	$1,000,000	$1,500,000	$5,324,161	1,949,700	472
Larson, John	$389,754	$450,000	$510,000	$1,000,000	$734,277	263,000	133
Becerra, Xavier	$987,803	$450,000	$500,000	$800,000	$1,078,600	387,000	30
Israel, Steve	$931,087	$450,000	$475,000	$10,000,000	$20,136,170	2,161,700	341
DeLauro, Rosa	$106,364	$450,000	$450,000	$500,000	$611,200	151,000	34
Miller, George	$265,478	$450,000	$450,000	$500,000	$1,077,843	471,000	83
DCCC VICE CHAIRS							
Crowley, Joe	$1,067,858	$300,000	$320,000	$6,000,000	$8,452,552	1,379,500	143
Ellison, Keith	$175,199	$300,000	$200,000	$500,000	$513,913	48,910	73
Pierluisi, Pedro	$360,977	$300,000	$300,000	$500,000	$516,684	7,500	15
Schwartz, Allyson	$3,092,911	$300,000	$345,000	$500,000	$1,780,845	1,257,400	74
CHIEF DEPUTY WHIPS							
Butterfield, GK	$314,521	$300,000	$175,000	$500,000	$40,000	107,845	17
Degette, Diana	$121,442	$300,000	$300,000	$500,000	$430,840	7,000	10
Lewis, John	$225,574	$300,000	$300,000	$500,000	$82,956	20,000	4
Matheson, Jim	$306,662	$300,000	$30,000	$500,000	$73,750	37,500	5
Pastor, Ed	$1,344,934	$300,000	$300,000	$500,000	$133,482	237,000	96
Schakowsky, Jan	$380,853	$300,000	$300,000	$500,000	$635,827	11,000	
Waters, Maxine	$213,656	$300,000	$265,000	$500,000	$50,000	132,000	53
Welch, Peter	$1,335,964	$300,000	$200,000	$500,000	$20,000		
EXCLUSIVE COMMITTEE RANKING MEMBERS							
Dicks, Norm	$254,635	$500,000	$305,000	$1,000,000	$499,700	18,000	13
Frank, Barney	$31,696	$500,000	$275,000	$1,000,000	$1,096,634	68,700	38
Levin, Sander	$399,183	$500,000	$525,000	$1,000,000	$571,000	503,000	30
Slaughter, Louise	$410,709	$500,000	$60,000	$1,000,000	$20,000	3,000	1
Waxman, Henry	$1,144,281	$500,000	$300,000	$1,000,000	$122,000	58,000	3
RANKING MEMBERS							
Berman, Howard	$393,998	$250,000	-	$250,000	$110,350	1,000	2

MEMBER	Cash on Hand 9/30/12	2011-2012 Dues Goal	2011-2012 Dues Received	2011-2012 Raised for DCCC Goal	2011-2012 Raised for DCCC	2011-2012 Frontline and Red to Blue Contributions/Raised	2011-2012 Member Points
Brady, Robert	$504,299	$ 250,000	$ 250,000	$	$ -	$ 1,000	11
Conyers, John	$113,972	$ 250,000	$ 50,000	$ 250,000	$ 25,000		
Cummings, Elijah	$800,057	$ 250,000	$ 250,300	$ 250,000	$ 76,000	$ 21,500	
Filner, Bob	$0	$ 250,000	$ -	$ 250,000	$ -	-	
Johnson, Eddie Bernice	$134,406	$ 250,000	$ 35,000	$ 250,000	$ 271,271		2
Markey, Ed	$3,213,927	$ 250,000	$ 350,000	$ 250,000	$ 1,026,800	$ 46,500	45
Peterson, Collin	$657,400	$ 250,000	$ 150,000	$ 250,000	$ 55,000		1
Rahall, Nick	$160,388	$ 250,000	$ 100,000	$ 250,000	$ 203,336	$ 59,700	5
Ruppersberger, Dutch	$954,735	$ 250,000	$ 270,000	$ 250,000	$ 261,000	$ 22,000	2
Sanchez, Linda	$261,458	$ 300,000	$ 50,000	$ 500,000	$ 109,000	$ 51,000	37
Smith, Adam	$272,230	$ 250,000	$ 250,000	$ 250,000	$ 276,900	$ 141,000	45
Thompson, Bennie	$1,376,987	$ 250,000	$ 250,000	$ 250,000	$ 101,500	$ 5,000	13
Van Hollen, Chris	$2,283,819	$ 300,000	$ 400,000	$ 500,000	$ 493,043	$ 197,000	27
Velazquez, Nydia	$243,125	$ 250,000	$ 250,000	$ 250,000	$ 27,100	$ 7,750	3
EXCLUSIVE SUBCOMMITTEE RANKING MEMBERS							
Bishop, Sanford	$378,127	$ 250,000	$ 30,000	$ 250,000	$ 22,500		
Capuano, Mike	$499,351	$ 250,000	$ 100,000	$ 250,000	$ 15,000	$ 42,000	1
Clay, Lacy	$65,685	$ 250,000	$ -	$ 250,000	$ 15,000		
Doggett, Lloyd	$2,592,707	$ 250,000	$ 250,000	$ 250,000	$ 32,000	$ 22,500	12
Eshoo, Anna	$545,304	$ 250,000	$ 305,000	$ 250,000	$ 508,159	$ 207,000	3
Farr, Sam	$89,464	$ 250,000	$ 45,500	$ 250,000	$ 11,000	$ 34,000	2
Fattah, Chaka	$49,434	$ 250,000	$ 150,000	$ 250,000	$ 184,925	$ 7,000	2
Green, Gene	$854,995	$ 250,000	$ 250,000	$ 250,000	$ 108,300	$ 34,000	2
Gutierrez, Luis	$371,657	$ 250,000	$ -	$ 250,000	$ -	$ 1,000	
Honda, Mike	$275,493	$ 250,000	$ 251,000	$ 250,000	$ 37,500	$ 99,500	65
Lowey, Nita	$1,048,364	$ 250,000	$ 249,994	$ 250,000	$ 333,500	$ 307,000	18
Maloney, Carolyn	$648,760	$ 250,000	$ 250,000	$ 250,000	$ 300,892	$ 229,000	72
McCarthy, Carolyn	$941,560	$ 250,000	$ 60,000	$ 250,000	$ 60,000	$ 3,000	17
McDermott, Jim	$60,806	$ 250,000	$ 70,000	$ 250,000	$ -	$ 15,000	13
Moran, James	$339,912	$ 250,000	$ 250,000	$ 250,000	$ 408,100	$ 26,500	10
Neal, Richard	$1,990,888	$ 300,000	$ 300,000	$ 500,000	$ 350,900	$ 86,000	13
Olver, John	$2,563	$ 250,000	$ 170,000	$ 250,000		$ 40,000	11
Pallone, Frank	$3,463,830	$ 250,000	$ 250,000	$ 250,000	$ 530,500	$ 70,500	9
Price, David	$147,017	$ 250,000	$ 50,000	$ 250,000	$ 87,500	$ 3,000	
Rush, Bobby	$42,639	$ 250,000		$ 250,000	$ 20,000	$ 25,000	
Serrano, Jose	$44,837	$ 250,000	$ 92,500	$ 250,000	$ 5,000	$ 1,000	2
Stark, Pete	$537,749	$ 250,000	$ -	$ 250,000	$ 378,500	$ 75,000	8

MEMBER	Cash on Hand 9/30/12	2011-2012 Dues Goal	2011-2012 Dues Received	2011-2012 Raised for DCCC Goal	2011-2012 Raised for DCCC	2011-2012 Frontline and Red to Blue Contributions/Raised	2011-2012 Member Points
Visclosky, Pete	$297,910	$ 250,000	$ 250,000	$ 250,000	$ 61,000	$ 33,500	17
WAYS & MEANS							
Berkley, Shelley	$924,918	$ 200,000	$ -	$ 250,000	$ 10,000	3,000	
Blumenauer, Earl	$604,531	$ 200,000	$ 225,000	$ 250,000	$ 130,300	302,100	18
Kind, Ron	$737,725	$ 200,000	$ 30,000	$ 250,000	$ 563,900	694,500	2
Pascrell, Bill	$434,279	$ 200,000	$ -	$ 250,000	$ 15,000	1,000	
Rangel, Charles	$26,600	$ 200,000	$ 60,000	$ 250,000	$ 6,000		5
Thompson, Mike	$1,402,213	$ 200,000	$ 255,000	$ 250,000	$ 211,500	251,500	86
APPROPRIATIONS							
Hinchey, Maurice	$23,893	$ 200,000	$ -	$ 250,000	$ 15,000	2,500	10
Jackson Jr., Jesse	$113,056	$ 200,000	$ -	$ 250,000	$ 5,000		
Kaptur, Marcy	$245,270	$ 200,000	$ 200,000	$ 250,000	$ 20,000	353,200	41
Lee, Barbara	$76,547	$ 200,000	$ 175,000	$ 250,000	$ 282,100	61,500	18
McCollum, Betty	$180,300	$ 200,000	$ 70,000	$ 250,000	$ 325,600	50,670	33
Rothman, Steven	$61,403	$ 200,000	$ 72,501	$ 250,000	$ 10,000	1,000	20
Roybal-Allard, Lucille	$129,665	$ 200,000	$ 75,000	$ 250,000	$ -	18,500	1
Schiff, Adam	$2,069,429	$ 300,000	$ 300,000	$ 500,000	$ 54,891	111,500	16
ENERGY & COMMERCE							
Baldwin, Tammy	$3,472,763	$ 200,000	57,142	$ 250,000	$ 110,100		
Barrow, John	$1,196,804	$ 200,000	$ -	$ 250,000	$ 93,500	48,000	1
Capps, Lois	$1,060,405	$ 200,000	$ -	$ 250,000	$ 21,000	40,000	2
Castor, Kathy	$785,721	$ 179,548	125,000	202,278	$ 23,500	10,000	1
Christian-Christensen, Donna	$34,900	$ 200,000	20,000	260,000	$ 59,760	9,000	10
Dingell, John	$485,254	$ 200,000	$ -	$ 250,000	$ 28,000		3
Doyle, Mike	$298,527	$ 200,000	100,000	$ 250,000	$ 37,760	56,500	10
Engel, Eliot	$134,192	$ 200,000	205,000	$ 250,000	$ 15,000	57,000	13
Gonzalez, Charles	$43,379	$ 200,000	55,000	$ 250,000	$ 196,450	1,000	
Matsui, Doris	$224,875	$ 200,000	201,020	$ 250,000	$ 442,151	87,500	23
Ross, Mike	$10,652	$ 200,000	$ -	$ 250,000	$ 20,000	21,000	1
Towns, Edolphus	$10,201	$ 200,000	$ -	$ 250,000	$ -	1,000	2
RULES							
Hastings, Alcee	$335,077	$ 200,000	40,000	$ 250,000	$ 20,000	6,500	1
McGovern, Jim	$337,548	$ 200,000	200,000	$ 250,000	$ 15,000	21,000	1
Polis, Jared	$309,108	$ 300,000	325,000	$ 500,000	$ 1,089,529	849,142	284

MEMBER	Cash on Hand 9/7/2012	2011-2012 Dues Goal	2011-2012 Dues Received	2011-2012 Raised for DCCC Goal	2011-2012 Raised for DCCC	2011-2012 Frontline and Red to Blue Contributions/Raised	2011-2012 Member Points
FINANCIAL SERVICES							
Ackerman, Gary	$221,814	$200,000	$40,083	$250,000	$-	$4,000	12
Baca, Joe	$283,366	$200,000	$-	$250,000	$30,800	$4,500	
Carney, John	$754,347	$300,000	$150,000	$500,000	$161,000	$30,000	20
Carson, Andre	$560,037	$200,000	$30,000	$250,000	$104,000	$7,000	5
Cleaver, Emanuel	$534,143	$200,000	$80,000	$266,000	$157,500	$2,000	6
Donnelly, Joe	$936,136	$200,000	$-	$250,000	$50,800		1
Green, Al	$148,042	$200,000	$25,000	$250,000	$-		1
Himes, Jim	$1,622,624	$300,000	$300,000	$500,000	$998,119	$1,049,500	33
Hinojosa, Ruben	$270,111	$200,000	$25,000	$250,000	$5,000	$17,000	
Lynch, Stephen	$683,160	$200,000	$-	$250,000	$12,500		1
Meeks, Gregory	$74,284	$200,000	$10,000	$250,000	$25,000	$7,000	4
Miller, Brad	$84,977	$200,000	$-	$250,000	$-	$1,000	
Moore, Gwen	$66,934	$200,000	$55,000	$250,000	$149,400	$43,325	52
Perlmutter, Ed	$229,910	$200,000	$30,000	$250,000	$137,000	$28,500	2
Peters, Gary	$460,099	$200,000	$25,000	$250,000	$25,000	$38,000	21
Scott, David	$225,606	$200,000	$20,500	$250,000	$22,500	$2,000	1
Sherman, Brad	$1,847,715	$200,000	$15,000	$250,000	$4,000	$76,000	93
Watt, Mel	$311,455	$200,000	$200,000	$250,000	$20,500		
NON-EXCLUSIVE SUBCOMMITTEE RANKING MEMBERS							
Altmire, Jason	$2,007	$150,000	$30,000	$100,000	$522,900	$705,000	
Andrews, Robert	$595,362	$150,000	$150,000	$100,000	$230,645	$3,000	17
Bishop, Tim	$909,003	$150,000	$30,800	$100,000	$-		
Bordallo, Madeleine	$185,657	$150,000	$5,000	$100,000	$-		
Boren, Dan	$683,498	$150,000	$-	$100,000	$163,200	$1,000	
Boswell, Leonard	$226,277	$150,000	$2,500	$100,000	$-		1
Braley, Bruce	$574,785	$150,000	$-	$100,000	$117,500	$2,000	1
Brown, Corrine	$24,020	$150,000	$-	$100,000	$102,350		
Carnahan, Russ	$2,318	$150,000	$-	$100,000	$32,500	$2,000	3
Chu, Judy	$1,199,054	$150,000	$174,999	$100,000	$23,611	$28,500	16
Clarke, Yvette	$45,288	$150,000	$15,000	$100,000	$9,750	$3,000	2
Cohen, Steve	$906,077	$150,000	$120,700	$100,000	$12,500	$24,500	1
Connolly, Gerry	$1,339,586	$150,000	$25,000	$100,000	$40,000	$21,000	2
Cooper, Jim	$834,589	$150,000	$-	$100,000	$-		
Costa, Jim	$566,090	$150,000	$-	$100,000	$11,500		
Costello, Jerry	$1,779,416	$150,000	$150,000	$100,000	$22,500	$61,000	11

199

MEMBER	Cash on Hand 9/30/12	2011-2012 Dues Goal	2011-2012 Dues Received	2011-2012 Raised for DCCC Goal	2011-2012 Raised for DCCC	2011-2012 Frontline and Red to Blue Contributions/Raised	2011-2012 Member Points
Critz, Mark	$364,298	$ 150,000	$ -	$ 100,000	$ 39,500	$	1
Cuellar, Henry	$1,015,621	$ 300,000	$ 300,000	$ 500,000	$ 384,904	$ 75,000	3
Davis, Danny	$224,874	$ 150,000	$ 125,000	$ 100,000	$ 500	$ 2,000	21
Davis, Susan	$291,423	$ 150,000	$ 150,000	$ 100,000	$ 17,000	$ 14,000	15
DeFazio, Peter	$622,277	$ 150,000	$ 5,000	$ 100,000	$ 56,300	$ 1,000	45
Edwards, Donna	$108,650	$ 300,000	$ 145,000	$ 500,000	$ 261,130	$ 210,285	
Faleomavaega, Eni	$52,117	$ 150,000	$	$ 100,000	$	$	1
Fudge, Marcia	$248,078	$ 150,000	$ 150,000	$ 100,000	$ 92,100	$ 25,000	
Grijalva, Raul	$89,386	$ 150,000	$ -	$ 100,000	$ 1,500	$	
Holden, Tim	$0	$ 150,000	$	$ 100,000	$	$	8
Holt, Rush	$1,036,658	$ 150,000	$ 175,004	$ 100,000	$ 170,586	$ 66,500	
Holmes Norton, Eleanor	$207,280	$ 150,000	$ 165,002	$ 100,000	-	$	10
Jackson Lee, Sheila	$118,793	$ 300,000	$ 153,179	$ 500,000	$ 127,900	$	2
Kildee, Dale	$14,126	$ 150,000	$ -	$ 100,000	$ 110,400	$ 2,500	15
Kucinich, Dennis	$42,067	$ 150,000	$	$ 100,000	-	$	
Langevin, Jim	$412,692	$ 150,000	$ 90,000	$ 100,000	$ 203,200	$ 20,000	
Larsen, Rick	$587,838	$ 150,000	$ 175,000	$ 100,000	$ 544,500	$ 655,500	3
Lipinski, Dan	$881,380	$ 150,000	$	$ 100,000	$ 20,500	$ 14,000	
Lofgren, Zoe	$590,077	$ 150,000	$ 170,000	$ 100,000	$ 172,436	$ 129,000	18
McIntyre, Mike	$593,171	$ 150,000	$	$ 100,000	$ 10,000	$	1
McNerney, Jerry	$1,037,825	$ 150,000	$ 60,000	$ 100,000	$ 500	$	3
Michaud, Mike	$620,873	$ 150,000	$	$ 100,000	$ 16,000	$ 13,500	6
Nadler, Jerry	$631,950	$ 150,000	$ 175,948	$ 100,000	$ 30,800	$ 73,000	44
Napolitano, Grace	$236,013	$ 150,000	$ 20,000	$ 100,000	$ 30,800	$ 1,000	2
Quigley, Mike	$511,789	$ 150,000	$ 150,000	$ 100,000	$ 20,500	$ 136,500	57
Reyes, Silvestre	$17,035	$ 150,000	$	$ 100,000	$ 30,500	$	10
Richardson, Laura	$68,498	$ 150,000	$ 70,000	$ 100,000	$ 75,000	$ 1,000	3
Richmond, Cedric	$258,848	$ 150,000	$ 1,500	$ 100,000	$ 26,000	$ 11,000	5
Sablan, Gregorio	$75,494	$ 150,000	$	$ 100,000	$	$	
Sanchez, Loretta	$1,134,386	$ 150,000	-	$ 100,000	$ 26,000	$ 48,000	1
Scott, Bobby	$101,984	$ 150,000	$ 94,000	$ 100,000	$ 20,000	$ 1,000	15
Tierney, John	$424,517	$ 150,000	$	$ 100,000	$ 32,500	-	1
Woolsey, Lynn	$13,881	$ 150,000	$ 1,000	$ 100,000	$	$ 3,500	1
MEMBERS							
Barber, Ron	$550,279	$ 28,409	$ -	$ 17,045	$ -	$	
Bass, Karen	$126,735	$ 300,000	$ 220,640	$ 500,000	$ 487,592	$ 56,500	91
Bonamici, Suzanne**	$318,487	$ 51,136	$ 7,500	$ 30,682	$ 221,300	$	5

MEMBER	Cash on Hand 9/30/12	2011-2012 Dues Goal	2011-2012 Dues Received	2011-2012 Raised for DCCC Goal	2011-2012 Raised for DCCC	2011-2012 Frontline and Red to Blue Contributions/Raised	2011-2012 Frontline Member Points
Chandler, Ben	$833,100	$125,000	$ -	$75,000	$2,500		1
Cicilline, David	$240,963	$125,000	$5,000	$75,000	$147,125		10
Clarke, Hansen	$5,575	$125,000	$5,000	$75,000			1
Courtney, Joe	$605,018	$125,000	$125,000	$75,000	$34,000	26,000	1
Deutch, Ted	$558,992	$300,000	$166,724	$500,000	$406,816	35,000	11
Garamendi, John	$162,452	$125,000	$10,000	$75,000	$200		1
Hahn, Janice**	$131,727	$90,909		$54,545			
Hanabusa, Colleen	$397,674	$125,000	$10,000	$75,000	$1,500		1
Heinrich, Martin	$1,010,688	$125,000	$ -	$75,000	$30,400		1
Higgins, Brian	$617,919	$125,000	$125,000	$75,000	$21,000	251,550	35
Hirono, Mazie	$688,826	$125,000		$75,000	$ -		
*Hochul, Kathy** *	$924,542	$96,591	$3,500	$57,955	$ -	1,000	16
Johnson, Hank	$47,574	$125,000	$31,000	$75,000	$ -		1
Keating, William	$418,917	$125,000		$75,000	$53,000		1
Kissell, Larry	$560,986	$125,000	$ -	$75,000	$ -		1
Loebsack, Dave	$668,125	$125,000	$ -	$75,000	$15,000		10
Lujan, Ben Ray	$473,369	$125,000	$140,000	$75,000	$377,200	66,750	51
Murphy, Chris	$512	$125,000		$75,000	$ -		1
Owens, Bill	$770,032	$125,000	$4,000	$75,000	$69,100	5,000	31
Pingree, Chellie	$205,123	$125,000	$125,000	$75,000	$187,700	35,250	5
Ryan, Tim	$252,523	$125,000	$115,000	$75,000	$6,500	31,000	11
Sarbanes, John	$822,908	$125,000	$125,000	$75,000	$21,500	73,000	
Schrader, Kurt	$1,026,454	$125,000	$130,000	$75,000	$42,500	36,000	2
Sewell, Terri	$464,166	$125,000	$125,000	$75,000	$50,835	25,750	13
Shuler, Heath	$110,501	$125,000		$75,000	$ -		3
Sires, Albio	$106,076	$125,000	$ -	$75,000			
Speier, Jackie	$1,099,085	$300,000	$250,300	$500,000	$411,881	67,000	10
Sutton, Betty	$1,213,601	$300,000		$500,000	$190,800		2
Tonko, Paul	$517,289	$125,000	$136,000	$75,000	$5,000	163,000	86
Tsongas, Niki	$371,937	$125,000	$61,990	$75,000	$144,400		2
Wasserman Schultz, Debbie	$1,614,428	$300,000	$300,000	$4,000,000	$777,236	1,008,500	121
Walz, Tim	$789,381	$300,000	$2,500	$500,000	$260,300	4,000	4
Wilson, Frederica	$86,380	$125,000	$10,000	$75,000	$ -		1
Yarmuth, John	$559,780	$125,000	$125,000	$75,000	$ -	49,000	

*Frontline Members in italics

**Recalculated for partial term in 112th Congress

Dues subject to increase based on committee assignments

2011-2012 Raised for DCCC Goals are subject to change

LEADERSHIP PAC SPENDING ON OTHER CANDIDATES DURING THE 2012 ELECTION CYCLE[3]

PAC NAME	POLITICIAN	TOTAL AMOUNT SPENT	SPENT ON OTHER CANDIDATES	% SPENT ON OTHER CANDIDATES
America Forward PAC	John Conyers Jr. (D-MI)	$102,802	$1,430	1%
Leading Us in Success PAC	Luis Fortuno (R-PR)	$140,869	$4,500	3%
Reclaim America PAC	Marco Rubio (R-FL)	$1,699,784	$72,984	4%
Reinventing a New Direction	Rand Paul (R-KY)	$1,436,120	$150,000	10%
MICHELE PAC	Michele Bachmann (R-MN)	$1,372,174	$146,500	10%
Build America PAC	Gregory Meeks (D-NY)	$156,141	$20,000	12%
Tenn PAC	Lamar Alexander (R-TN)	$954,825	$155,500	16%
Dakota PAC	John Hoeven (R-ND)	$153,840	$26,000	16%
Vote to Elect Republicans Now PAC	Vernon Buchanan (R-FL)	$382,480	$65,250	17%
Texas Freedom Fund	Joe Barton (R-TX)	$141,683	$24,500	17%

Note: Listed are the leadership PACs of sitting members of Congress that spent more than $100,000 during the election cycle and gave the least to other candidates.

NOTES

1. INTRODUCTION: "THROW FEAR"

1. *Congressional Record*, vol. 145, pt. 19, October 26–November 3, 1999, p. 26957.
2. MapLight, "U.S. Congress—Find Contributions: Contributor, Apache Corporation; Election Cycle, 2002, 2004, 2006, 2008, 2010, 2012," http://maplight.org/us-congress/contributions (accessed April 12, 2013).
3. Ray Plank, interview with the author.
4. Robert H. Sitkoff, "Politics and the Business Corporation," *Regulation* (2003–2004): 1136.
5. HBR IdeaCast, "How Campaign Finance Reform Could Help Business," *Harvard Business Review* (September 6, 2012), http://blogs.hbr.org/ideacast/2012/09/how-campaign-finance-reform-co.html.
6. Robert Dreyfuss, "Reforming Reform," *The American Prospect* (December 18, 2000).
7. CREW (Citizens for Responsibility and Ethics in Washington), "Family Affair Report Details Nepotism in Congress," http://www.citizensforethics.org/pages/family-affair-report-reveals-nepotism-abuse-in-congress.
8. Sitkoff, "Politics and the Business Corporation," p. 1132.
9. Ibid., 1135.
10. "Cash from the Packers: Story of a Republican Demand While the Beef Inquiry Was On," *New York Times*, September 17, 1905.

11. Sitkoff, "Politics and the Business Corporation," p. 1135.

12. Ibid.

13. Fred Wertheimer, "Soft Money and Political Extortion," *Baltimore Sun*, June 5, 2000.

14. U.S. Senate, "Résumé of Congressional Activity," http://www.senate.gov/pagelayout/reference/two_column_table/Resumes.htm; Josh Tauberer, "Kill Bill: How many bills are there? How many are enacted?" Govtrack.com, August 4, 2011.

15. MapLight, "U.S. Congress — Find Contributions: Contributor, Apache Corporation; Election Cycle, 2002, 2004, 2006, 2008, 2010, 2012" (see ch. 1, n. 2; accessed April 15, 2013).

16. Ray Plank, interview with the author.

17. "Basically Taking Over," *Las Vegas Review-Journal*, June 11, 2008.

18. John Hofmeister, interview with the author.

19. Bob Herbold, interview with the author.

20. John Hofmeister, interview with the author.

21. Former FBI agent Bill Roemer, quoted in Kirsten Lindberg, Joseph Petrenko, Jerry Gladden, and Wayne A. Johnson, "Traditional Organized Crime in Chicago," *International Review of Law, Computers, and Technology* (March 1998): 47–73.

22. John Bresnahan, "Tim Bishop's Bar Mitzvah Episode Could Spell Trouble," *Politico*, August 15, 2012.

23. Brittany H. Bramlett, James G. Gimpel, and Frances E. Lee, "The Political Ecology of Opinion in Big-Donor Neighborhoods," *Political Behavior* 33 (2011): 565–600.

24. Gary J. Miller, "Confiscation, Credible Commitment, and Progressive Reform in the United States," *Journal of Institutional and Theoretical Economics* 145, no. 4 (December 1989): 686–92.

25. John Hofmeister, interview with the author.

26. "Shakedown on K Street," *BloombergBusinessweek*, February 19, 2006, http://www.businessweek.com/stories/2006-02-19/shakedown-on-k-street.

27. Ruth Marcus, "Intoxicated on Fundraising," *Washington Post*, June 2, 2010.

28. *New York Times*, June 19, 1974, p. 35; David Burnham, *New York Times*, February 26, 1975, p. 16.

29. Susan E. Dudley and Richard D. Otis Jr., "eRulemaking: A Case Example of eGov Transformation," Working Paper 57, Mercatus Center, George Mason University.

30. Harvey A. Silverglate, *Three Felonies a Day: How the Feds Target the Innocent* (New York: Encounter Books, 2011). See also the introduction by Alan Dershowitz.

31. William Blackstone, *Commentaries on the Laws of England, vol. IV, Of Public Wrongs* (1857), 1, p. 146.

32. *United States v. Barber*, 668 F.2d 778 (4th Cir., 1982) at 783.

33. Posner quoted in "Casenotes: Criminal Law," *University of Dayton Law Review* 19, 251, p. 272.

34. Fred S. McChesney, *Money for Nothing: Politicians, Rent Extraction, and Political Extortion* (Cambridge, MA: Harvard University Press, 1997), p. 45.

35. Frank Bovenkerk, "'Wanted: Mafia Boss'—Essay on the Personology of Organized Crime," *Crime, Law, and Social Change* 33 (2000): 237.

36. "Corruption Perception Index," http.//www.transparency.org/research/cpi/overview.

37. World Bank, "Worldwide Governance Indicators," http://info.worldbank.org/governance/wgi/sc_chart.asp.

38. Klaus Schwab, ed., *The Global Competitiveness Report, 2012–2013* (Geneva: World Economic Forum, 2013), pp. 390–92, http://www3.weforum.org/docs/WEF_GlobalCompetitivenessReport_2012-13.pdf.

39. A. Block, "Mafia," in *International Encyclopedia of the Social and Behavioral Sciences*, ed. Neil J. Smelser and Paul B. Bates (Oxford: Elsevier Science, 2001), p. 9125.

2. AMERICA'S MOST EXPENSIVE TOLLBOOTH

1. Robert Longley, "Salaries and Benefits of U.S. Congress Members," About.com, U.S. Government Info, http://usgovinfo.about.com/od/uscongress/a/congresspay.htm (accessed April 17, 2013).

2. "Federal Employees, 2011," Asbury Park Press, http://php.app.com/fed_employees11/search.php.

3. Library of Congress Thomas, "Bill Text Versions—112th Congress (2011–2012), H.R. 1002," http://thomas.loc.gov/cgi-bin/query/z?c112:H.R.1002: (accessed April 17, 2013).

4. Molly Zelvonberg, "Wireless Tax Fairness Act of 2011 Passed," *Examiner*, November 1, 2011, http://www.examiner.com/article/wireless-tax-fairness-act-of-2011-passed (accessed April 17, 2013).

5. Opensecrets.org, "Donor Lookup: AT&T," https://www.opensecrets.org/indivs/search.php?sort=D (accessed April 17, 2013).

6. Thomas Catan, "Washington Wire: Echoes of Nixon's Order on ITT Deal in Democrats' Letter to Obama on AT&T," *Wall Street Journal*, September 15, 2011, http://blogs.wsj.com/washwire/2011/09/15/echoes-of-nixons-order-on-itt-deal-in-democrats-letter-to-obama-on-att/ (accessed April 17, 2013).

7. Brendan Sasso, "House Republicans Put Pressure on Obama to Drop AT&T Lawsuit," *The Hill*, September 20, 2011.

8. MapLight, "U.S. Congress—Find Contributions: Legislator, John Boehner; Interest Group, Communications and Electronics Industry; Election Cycle, 2012" (see ch. 1, n. 2; accessed April 12, 2013).

9. MapLight, "U.S. Congress—Find Contributions: Interest Group, Communications and Electronics Industry; Election Cycle, 2012" (see ch. 1, n. 2; accessed April 12, 2013).

10. MapLight, "U.S. Congress — Find Contributions: Legislator, John Boehner, Interest Groups, Communications and Electronics Industry and Telephone Utilities; Election Cycle, 2012" (see ch. 1, n. 2; accessed April 12, 2013).

11. Illustration source: MapLight, "U.S. Congress — Find Contributions: Legislator, John Boehner; Election Cycles, 2006, 2008, 2010, 2012" (financial disclosure documents, 2005–2012), http://maplight.org/us-congress/contributions?s=1&p olitician=155&office_party=Senate%2CHouse%2CDemocrat%2CRepublican%2 CIndependent&election=2008%2C2010%2C2012&string=AT%26T&business_ sector=any&business_industry=any&source=All.

12. MapLight, "U.S. Congress — Find Contributions: Contributor, Verizon; Election Cycle, 2012" (see ch. 1, n. 2; accessed April 12, 2013).

13. Opensecrets.org, "Lobbying: Hastert, Joshua," http://www.opensecrets.org/ lobby/lobbyist.php?id=Y0000028642L (accessed April 17, 2013).

14. Lynn Sweet, "Against History," *Illinois Issues Online,* September 2002, http://illi-noisissues.uis.edu/features/2002sept/hastert.html (accessed April 17, 2013).

15. Opensecrets.org, "Lobbying: Clyburn, William Jr.," http://www.opensecrets.org/ lobby/lobbyist.php?id=Y0000019707L (accessed April 17, 2013).

16. Federal Communications Commission (FCC), "Acting Chairwoman Mignon Clyburn," http://www.fcc.gov/leadership/mignon-clyburn (accessed April 12, 2013).

17. Library of Congress Thomas, "Bill Text Versions — 112th Congress (2011–2012), H.R. 2940," http://thomas.loc.gov/cgi-bin/query/z?c112:H.R.2940: (accessed April 17, 2013).

18. Library of Congress Thomas, "Bill Text Versions — 112th Congress (2011–2012), H.R. 1070," http://thomas.loc.gov/cgi-bin/query/z?c112:H.R.1070: (accessed April 17, 2013).

19. Govtrack.us, "H.R. 1070 (112th): Small Company Capital Formation Act of 2011," March 14, 2011, http://www.govtrack.us/congress/bills/112/hr1070 (accessed April 12, 2013); and "H.R. 2940 (112th): Access to Capital for Job Creators Act," September 15, 2011, http://www.govtrack.us/congress/bills/112/hr2940 (accessed April 12, 2013).

20. MapLight, "U.S. Congress — Find Contributions: Legislator, John Boehner; Date, October 1–December 1, 2011" (see ch. 1, n. 2; accessed April 15, 2013).

21. Ibid.

22. Ibid.

23. Ibid.

24. Ibid.

25. Deirdre Shesgreen, "Speaker John Boehner Displays 'Deft Touch with Fundraising,'" *Cincinnati Enquirer,* January 9, 2012, http://westchesterbuzz.com/2012/01/10/ speaker-john-boehner-displays-deft-touch-with-fundraising (accessed April 17, 2013).

26. "DealBook: Boehner to Bankers: Stand Up to 'Punk' Staffers," *New York Times,*

March 18, 2013, http://dealbook.nytimes.com/2010/03/18/boehner-to-bankers-stand-up-to-punk-staffers (accessed April 17, 2013).

27. Steptoe & Johnson LLP, "Daily Tax Update—January 31, 2012: Tax Extenders Focus of Finance Tax Reform Hearing," http://www.steptoe.com/resources-detail-8002.html (accessed April 17, 2013).

28. Anna Palmer, "K Street Mounts Blitz for Tax Breaks," *Politico*, December 4, 2011.

29. Kent Hoover, "Five Tax Breaks That Business Groups Want Extended," *The Business Journals*, April 26, 2012.

30. Palmer, "K Street Mounts Blitz for Tax Breaks."

31. "Tax Support for Oil and Gas Debated," *Albuquerque Journal*, December 4, 2011.

32. MapLight, "U.S. Congress—Find Contributions: Legislator, Max Baucus; Date, January 1–December 31, 2011" (see ch. 1, n. 2; accessed April 16, 2013).

33. Ibid.

34. Opensecrets.org, "PACs: Contributors," https://www.opensecrets.org/pacs/pacgave2.php?cycle=2012 (accessed April 17, 2013).

35. Jay Costa, "What's the Cost of a Seat in Congress?" MapLight, March 10, 2013, http://maplight.org/content/73190.

36. Lee Drutman, "Ways and Means, Financial Services, and Energy and Commerce Are Top House Fundraising Committees," Sunlight Foundation, April 2, 2012, http://sunlightfoundation.com/blog/2012/04/02/housecommittees.

37. Elizabeth Williamson, "A Conversation with Rep. Dave Camp," *Wall Street Journal*, November 21, 2010.

38. MapLight, U.S. Congress—Find Contributions: Legislator, Dave Camp; Election Cycle, 2012 (see ch. 1, n. 2; accessed April 15, 2013).

39. Ernst & Young, "Tax Extenders Have Expired—Again," *Technical Line*, no. 2012-10 (February 9, 2012), http://www.ey.com/Publication/vwLUAssets/TechnicalLine_BB2279_TaxExtenders_9February2012/$FILE/TechnicalLine_BB2279_TaxExtenders_9February2012.pdf.

40. MapLight, "U.S. Congress—Find Contributions: Legislator, Dave Camp; Election Cycle, 2012" (see ch. 1, n. 2; accessed April 15, 2013).

41. Howard Gleckman, "Is House Review of Tax Breaks a Donation Shakedown, or Could We See Reform?" *Forbes*, April 26, 2012.

42. House Committee on Ways and Means, "Chairman Tiberi Announces Hearings on Certain Expiring Tax Provisions" (hearing advisory), April 26, 2012.

43. MapLight, "U.S. Congress—Find Contributions: Legislator, Dave Camp; Election Cycle, 2012" (see ch. 1, n. 2; accessed April 20, 2013).

44. MapLight, "U.S. Congress—Find Contributions: Legislator, Dave Camp; Date, March 1–April 26, 2012" (see ch. 1, n. 2; accessed April 17, 2013).

45. Maplight, "U.S. Congress—Find Contributions: Legislator, Patrick Tiberi; Date, March 1–April 26, 2012" (see ch. 1, n. 2; accessed April 17, 2013).

46. Tim Weiner, "Struggles in His Past, Burdens in His Present," *New York Times*, August 5, 1999.

47. "The New Team: Ray LaHood," *New York Times,* December 26, 2011.

48. U.S. House of Representatives, "Department of Defense Appropriations Bill, 2013," Report 112-, 112th Cong., 2nd sess., http://appropriations.house.gov/uploadedfiles/defense-fy13-fullcommitteereport.pdf.

49. U.S. House of Representatives, Committee on Appropriations, "Press Release: House Appropriations Committee Releases Fiscal Year 2013 Defense Appropriations Bill," May 7, 2012, http://appropriations.house.gov/news/documentsingle. aspx?DocumentID=294116 (accessed April 17, 2013).

50. "Operating Expenditures—Congressman Bill Young Campaign Committee (2012 Election Cycle)," available at: FEC.Gov, http://www.fec.gov/fecviewer/CandCmteTransaction.do.

51. MapLight, "U.S. Congress—Find Contributions: Legislator, C. Young; Date, March 15–31, 2012" (see ch. 1, n. 2; accessed April 17, 2013).

52. Ibid.

53. MapLight, "U.S. Congress—Find Contributions: Legislator, C. Young; Date, January 1–March 31, 2012" (see ch. 1, n. 2; accessed April 17, 2013).

54. MapLight, "U.S. Congress—Find Contributions: Legislator, C. Young; Date, April 1–December 31, 2012" (see ch. 1, n. 2; accessed April 17, 2013).

55. Van Scoyoc Associates, "Our People," http://www.vsadc.com/people (accessed April 17, 2013).

56. Van Scoyoc Associates, "Our Clients," http://www.vsadc.com/clients (accessed April 17, 2013).

57. David S. Fallis and Dan Keating, "In Congress, Relatives Lobby on Bills Before Family Members," *Washington Post,* December 29, 2012.

58. Bill Adair and Wess Allison, "Rep. Young's Earmarks Help His Children's Employers," *Tampa Bay Times,* April 8, 2008.

59. Ibid.

3. PROTECTION: FOR A PRICE

1. "Couple Plans 'Mafia-Free' Wedding," *BBC News,* April 1, 2009.

2. "A Bullet for a Businessman," *Bloomberg Businessweek,* November 3, 1991.

3. Alan Dershowitz, introduction to Silverglate, *Three Felonies a Day.*

4. Opensecrets.org, "Bundlers," http://www.opensecrets.org/pres08/bundlers. php?id=n00009638 (accessed May 3, 2013).

5. Chart sources: http://www.opensecrets.org/pres08/bundlers.php?id=N00009638 (2008 election); www.opensecrets.org/pres12/bundlers.php (2012 election).

6. "Obama Slams 'Fat Cat Bankers,'" CBS News, December 13, 2009, http://www. cbsnews.com/video/watch/?id=5975092n (accessed May 03, 2013).

7. Roger Parloff, "Why Wall Street Could Go to Jail," CNNMoney, http://money.cnn. com/galleries/2008/fortune/0812/gallery.parloff_quotes.fortune (last updated January 6, 2009; accessed May 3, 2013).

8. Tom Gardner, "Hundreds Should Go to Jail," The Motley Fool, January 29, 2009, http://www.fool.com/investing/general/2009/01/29/hundreds-should-go-to-jail. aspx (accessed May 3, 2013).

9. Lindsey Ellerson, "The Note: Obama to Bankers: I'm Standing 'Between You and the Pitchforks,'" ABC News, April 3, 2009, http://abcnews.go.com/blogs/politics/2009/04/obama-to-banker (accessed May 3, 2013).

10. Eamon Javers, "Inside Obama's Bank CEOs Meeting," Politico, April 3, 2009.

11. Lucy Madison, "Obama: 'Occupy Wall Street' Reflects 'Broad-Based Frustration,'" CBS News, October 9, 2011, http://www.cbsnews.com/8301-503544_162-20116707-503544/obama-occupy-wall-street-reflects-broad-based-frustration (accessed May 3, 2013).

12. Jessica Desvariex, "Pelosi Supports Occupy Wall Street Movement," ABC News, October 9, 2011, http://abcnews.go.com/Politics/pelosi-supports-occupy-wall-street-movement/story?id=14696893 (accessed May 3, 2013).

13. Joshua Altman, "DNC Chairwoman: Occupy Wall Street Embodies How 'Working People Feel,'" The Hill, October 11, 2011.

14. Robert Reich, "Only $4.2 Billion to Buy This Election?" October 27, 2010, http://robertreich.org/post/1419481402 (accessed May 3, 2013).

15. Peter H. Aranson, American Government: Strategy and Choice (Cambridge, Mass.: Winthrop Publishers, 1981), pp. 252–53.

16. "Links to Printed United States Senate Permanent Subcommittee on Investigations: Hearings and Reports 106th–112th Congresses," March 15, 2013, http://www.hsgac.senate.gov/download/report-and-exhibit-links-wall-street_the-financial-crisis (accessed May 3, 2013).

17. Halah Touryalai, "Goldman Sachs CEO Lawyers Up Amid DOJ Investigation," Forbes, August 22, 2011.

18. April 8, 2011 — One week before the report is released, Goldman managing director Bruce Heyman gives $30,800 to the Democratic National Committee and $5,000 to Barack Obama.

April 11, 2011 — Two days before the report is released, Goldman senior director John Farmer writes a $25,800 check to the Democratic National Committee.

June 7, 2011 — Susan Scher, a banker at Goldman in New York City, contributes $5,000 to Barack Obama and $5,000 to the Democratic National Committee.

June 19, 2011 — Goldman managing director Sanjeev Mehra gives $5,000 to the Obama campaign and $30,800 to the Democratic National Committee. His wife also makes a donation. Mehra had never given to Obama before.

June 21, 2011 — Jonathan Lopatin, a senior executive at Goldman, writes a $20,000 check to the Democratic National Committee and a $5,000 check to the Obama campaign. This is his first-ever contribution to Obama, and by far his largest contribution ever to an individual candidate (Opensecrets.org, "Donor Lookup," http://www.opensecrets.org/indivs/index.php; MapLight, "U.S. Congress — Find Contributions" http://maplight.org/us-congress/contributions).

19. Goldman Sachs reported in its Form 10-Q that the Justice Department announced on August 9, 2012, that it would not press criminal charges against the firm or its employees arising out of the issues raised by the staff report of the Senate Permanent Subcommittee on Investigations. See U.S. Securities and Exchange Commission, "The Goldman Sachs Group: Form 10-Q," September 30, 2012, http://www.sec.gov/Archives/edgar/data/886982/000119312512458820/d41105 3d10q.htm (accessed May 3, 2013).

20. Peter Wallsten, "Obama Plans to Turn Anti–Wall Street Anger on Mitt Romney, Republicans," *Washington Post,* October 14, 2011.

21. Josh Gerstein, "Carney Defends Obama Meeting Wall Street Donors at White House," *Politico,* June 14, 2011.

22. Heidi Przybyla, "Obama Seen as Anti-Business by 77% of U.S. Investors," *Bloomberg,* January 21, 2010.

23. Eamon Javers, "For Fundraising, Obama Relies Even More on Wall Street," CNBC, July 22, 2011, http://www.cnbc.com/id/43854224 (accessed May 03, 2013).

24. Anna Sale, "Graphic: Obama Campaign Sees Fundraiser Turnover," WNYC, February 17, 2012, http://www.wnyc.org/articles/its-free-country/2012/feb/17/ amongst-glitzy-galas-ny-finance-and-business-bundlers-still-raise-most-obama (accessed May 3, 2013).

25. Devin Banerjee, "Levy: Obama Needs McDonald's Fundraiser for Wall Street," *Bloomberg,* June 20, 2012.

26. Permanent Subcommittee on Investigations, "Opening Statement of Senator Carl Levin at Hearing on Tax Haven Banks and U.S. Tax Compliance: Obtaining the Names of U.S. Clients with Swiss Accounts," March 4, 2009, http://www.levin. senate.gov/newsroom/press/release/?id=1cc17ddd-d117-4dc1-83e3-7dc150a9e168 (accessed May 3, 2013).

27. "UBS in Settlement Talks with SEC over Mortgage Bond Deal—WSJ," *Reuters,* March 23, 2013; "SEC Charges UBS Global Asset Management for Pricing Violations in Mutual Fund Portfolios," January 17, 2012, www.sec.gov/News/PressRelease/1365171488750#.UgLEmbYnhFs.

28. Andrew Ramonas, "DOJ Drops UBS Tax Evasion Case," Main Justice: Politics, Policy, and the Law, October 22, 2010, http://www.mainjustice.com/2010/10/22/ doj-drops-ubs-tax-evasion-case (accessed May 3, 2013).

29. Opensecrets.org, "2012 Presidential: Barack Obama's Bundlers"; see, for example, U.S. Department of Justice, "Justice Department Reaches Settlement with Bank of America to Resolve Allegations of Discrimination Against Recipients of Disability Income," September 13, 2012, http://www.justice.gov/opa/pr/2012/ September/12-crt-1116.html; U.S. Department of Justice, "Federal Government and State Attorneys General Reach $25 Billion Agreement with Five Largest Mortgage Servicers to Address Mortgage Loan Servicing and Foreclosure Abuses," February 9, 2012, http://www.justice.gov/opa/pr/2012/February/12-ag-186.html; Phil Mattingly, "U.S. Won't Prosecute Goldman Sachs, Employ-

ees over CDO Deals," *Bloomberg Businessweek,* August 10, 2012, http://www
.businessweek.com/news/2012-08-09/justice-finds-no-viable-basis-for-charges
-against-goldman.

30. Opensecrets.org, "2012 Presidential: Barack Obama's Bundlers," March 25, 2013,
http://www.opensecrets.org/pres12/bundlers.php (accessed May 3, 2013).

31. Matthew Goldstein, "SEC Closes Fairfax Investigation on Hedge Funds—
Sources," *Reuters,* December 8, 2011.

32. Jen Sabella, "Obama New York Fundraiser with Rahm Emanuel Moved," *Huffington Post,* July 14, 2011.

33. Opensecrets.org, "Barack Obama's Bundlers."

34. Katie Thomas, "Pfizer Settles U.S. Charges of Bribing Doctors Abroad," *New York
Times,* August 8, 2012.

35. Sarah Fulmer and April Knill, "Political Contributions and the Severity of Government Enforcement," paper presented at the meeting of the American Finance
Association, San Diego, March 1, 2012, p. 16.

36. "Obama, Wall Street, and Lobbyists," *Christian Science Monitor,* April 22, 2010.

37. Mike Allen, "Obama Campaign Adds Senior Adviser," *Politico,* October 24, 2011.

38. Justin Elliott, "Top Obama Campaign Aide Lobbied for Bank Bailout," *Salon,* January 9, 2012.

39. Keach Hagey, "NPR Host's Husband Joins Obama Campaign," *Politico,* October
24, 2011.

40. Collins Johnson Group, "About Us," http://thecollinsjohnsongroup.com/about.
html (accessed May 5, 2013).

41. Nicholas D. Kristof, "Taxes and Billionaires," *New York Times,* July 7, 2011.

42. MapLight, "U.S. Congress —Find Contributions: Legislator, John Boehner; Interest Group, Finance/Insurance/Real Estate and Securities & Investment; Date,
June 8–9, 2011 (see ch. 1, n. 2; accessed May 5, 2013).

43. Ibid.

44. "Know Your Power Couples," *The Daily Beast,* http://www.thedailybeast.com/
newsweek/galleries/2008/12/24/photos-know-your-power-couples.html   (accessed May 5, 2013).

45. Timothy P. Carney, "K Street: More Shakedown Than Bribery?" *Washington Examiner,* February 14, 2012.

46. SKDKnickerbocker, "Anita Dunn," www.skdknick.com/about/anita-dun (accessed May 5, 2013).

47. Patrick Howley, "The Democrats' Hedge Fund Shakedown Comments," *Washington Free Beacon,* January 14, 2012.

48. "Bio: Hilary Rosen," *Huffington Post,* http://www.huffingtonpost.com/hilary-
rosen (accessed May 5, 2013).

49. Elizabeth Wasserman and Jonathan Allen, "Barack Obama, Trustbuster?" *Politico,* August 16, 2012; Eric Lichtblau and Eric Lipton, "Strategizing for the President, and Corporate Clients, Too," *New York Times,* October 19, 2012.

50. Thomas Catan, Jeffrey A. Trachtenberg, and Chad Bray, "U.S. Alleges E-Book Scheme," *Wall Street Journal,* April 11, 2012.

51. John Aloysius Farrell, "Obama Sues Publishers, Who Respond with a Fundraiser," *National Journal,* March 25, 2012, http://www.nationaljournal.com/blogs/decoded/2012/05/obama-sues-publishers-who-respond-with-a-fundraiser-25 (accessed May 5, 2013).

52. Library of Congress Thomas, "Bill Text Versions — 112th Congress (2011–2012), H.R. 3523," http://thomas.loc.gov/cgi-bin/query/z?c112:H.R.3523: (accessed May 5, 2013).

53. MapLight, "U.S. Congress — Find Contributions: Legislator, James Clyburn; Interest Group, Communications and Electronics Industry; Date, March 1–April 30, 2012 (see ch. 1, n. 2; accessed May 5, 2013).

54. Opensecrets.org, "Lobbyist Profile: Alexander, Stacey," http://www.opensecrets.org/lobby/lobbyist.php?id=Y0000039600L&year=2012; and "Lobbyist Profile: Mason, Marcus," http://www.opensecrets.org/lobby/lobbyist.php?id=Y000001141 11L (accessed May 5, 2013).

55. Govtrack.us, "House Vote #192 in 2012: H.R. 3523 (112th): Cyberspace Intelligence Sharing and Protection Act," April 26, 2012, http://www.govtrack.us/congress/votes/112-2012/h192.

56. Alicia Mundy, "U.S. Effort to Remove Drug CEO Jolts Firms," *Wall Street Journal,* April 26, 2011.

57. John Stanton, "Former Baucus Aide at Center of Flap over Insurer's Mailings on Health Reform," *Roll Call,* September 23, 2009.

4. THE UNDERGROUND WASHINGTON ECONOMY

1. Matthew Mosk, "Fundraisers Tap Those Who Can't Say No," *Washington Post,* August 7, 2009; and Clyde Wilcox, "Design Campaign Finance Disclosure in the States: Tracing the Tributaries of Campaign Finance," *Election Law Journal* (December 2005): 376.

2. Sunlight Foundation, Political Party Time, http://politicalpartytime.org/www/partytime_dump_all.csv.

3. George Mitchell quoted in Mark C. Alexander, "Let Them Do Their Jobs: The Compelling Government Interest in Protecting the Time of Candidates and Elected Officials," *Loyola University Chicago Law Journal* 37: 14–15.

4. Ryan J. Reilly and Melissa Jeltsen, "House Ethics: Timing on Fundraisers, Financial Reform Was a Coincidence," *TPMMuckraker,* January 27, 2011, http://tpmmuckraker.talkingpointsmemo.com/2011/01/house_ethics_timing_on_fundraisers_financial_reform_was_coincidence.php?p=0.

5. Ibid.

6. Ibid.

7. Stanley Brubaker, "The Limits of Campaign Spending Limits," *Public Interest* (Fall 1998): 40.

8. Benjamin S. Feuer, "Between Political Speech and Cold, Hard Cash: Evaluating the FEC's New Regulations for 527 Groups," *Northwestern University Law Review* 100, no. 2 (2006): 932.

9. Andrew B. Hall, "How Much of the Incumbency Advantage Is Financial?" January 10, 2013, p. 2, http://polmeth.wustl.edu/media/Paper/HallHowMuch.pdf.

10. Chris Murphy, "I Didn't Get Elected to Be a Fundraiser: How Trolling for Donations Detracts From Lawmakers' Mission," *Hartford Courant,* February 3, 2008.

11. Larry Makinson, "Speaking Freely: Washington Insiders Talk About Money in Politics," Center for Responsive Politics, 2003.

12. Stephen Ansolabehere, John M. de Figueiredo, and James M. Snyder Jr., "Why Is There So Little Money in U.S. Politics?" Working Paper 9409, National Bureau of Economic Research, December 2002, p. 15.

13. Douglas D. Roscoe and Shannon Jenkins, "A Meta-Analysis of Campaign Contributions' Impact on Roll Call Voting," *Social Science Quarterly* 86, no. 1 (2005): 52–68.

14. David Mills and Robert Weisberg, "Corrupting the Harm Requirement in White-Collar Crime," *Stanford Law Review* 60, no. 5 (March 2008): 1381.

15. Thomas Brunell, "The Relationship Between Political Parties and Interest Groups: Explaining Patterns of PAC Contributions for Congress," *Political Research Quarterly* 58 (2005): 682.

16. Amy J. Hillman, Gerald D. Keim, and Douglas Schuler, "Corporate Political Activity: A Review and Research Agenda," *Journal of Management* 30, no. 6 (2004): 848.

17. See Appendix 1.

18. U.S. Congressman Fred Upton, "Committee Assignments," http://upton.house.gov/biography/committees.htm; see Appendix 1. The dues listed are one-sixth of the total assessment for the cycle.

19. U.S. Congressman Dave Camp, "Biography," http://camp.house.gov/biography/; see Appendix 1. The dues listed are one-sixth of the total assessment for the cycle.

20. U.S. Congressman Lamar Smith, "Biography," http://lamarsmith.house.gov/biography/; see Appendix 1. The dues listed are one-sixth of the total assessment for the cycle.

21. U.S. House of Representatives, Democratic Caucus, "The Democratic Caucus," http://www.dems.gov/democratic-caucus.

22. National Republican Congressional Committee, "NRCC Patriot Program," http://electgoppatriots.com/; "U.S. Rep. Allyson Schwartz Reappointed to Powerful Ways and Means Committee in 113th Congress," *Times Herald* (Montgomery County, Penn.), December 12, 2012.

23. Stuart Rothenberg, "The Most Vulnerable House Incumbent(s) of 2013," Rothen-

berg Political Report, April 17, 2013, http://rothenbergpoliticalreport.com/news/article/the-most-vulnerable-house-incumbents-of-2014.

24. Mark Wegner, "Congress Daily: House Races, Hoyer Links Fundraising to Keeping Seats on Key Panels," *National Journal Daily*, February 2, 2011.

25. Congressman Jim Cooper, "Forum: Fixing Congress," *Boston Review*, May 2, 2011.

26. Molly K. Hooper, "House Republican Campaign Chief Furious After Leak on Party Dues," *The Hill, March 17, 2011.*

27. For this exemption, see *Committee on Standards of Official Conduct, House Ethics Manual*, 110th Cong., 2nd sess. (Washington, D.C.: U.S. Government Printing Office, 2008), p. 145, http://ethics.house.gov/sites/ethics.house.gov/files/documents/2008_House_Ethics_Manual.pdf.

28. See Cornell University Law School, Legal Information Institute, "2 USC § 439A — Use of Contributed Amounts for Certain Purposes," http://www.law.cornell.edu/uscode/text/2/439a.

29. William Bernhard and Tracy Sulkin, "Following the Party? Member-to-Member Campaign Contributions and Cue-Taking in the U.S. House," paper presented at the annual meeting of the American Political Science Association, Seattle, September 1–4, 2011, p. 10.

30. James Valvo and Carl Oberg, "Exposing the Special Interests Behind Waxman-Markey," Policy Paper 0909, *Americans for Prosperity*, September 2009, http://americansforprosperity.org/files/Policy_Paper_0909_0.pdf.

31. Govtrack.us, "House Vote #477 in 2009: H.R. 2454 (111th): American Clean Energy and Security Act of 2009," June 26, 2009, http://www.govtrack.us/congress/votes/111-2009/h477.

32. Keenan Steiner and Jake Harper, "In GOP Leadership Race, McMorris Rodgers Has the Dough Behind Her," Sunlight Foundation Reporting Group, November 14, 2012, http://reporting.sunlightfoundation.com/2012/gop-leadership-race-mc-morris-rodgers-has-dough-behind-her/.

33. Federal Election Commission (FEC), "Candidate and Committee Viewer: "PAC TO THE FUTURE," http://www.fec.gov/fecviewer/CandidateCommitteeDetail.do.

34. Jonathan Tamari, "Andrews Used Wife to Vet Use of Campaign Funds on Trip," *Philadelphia Inquirer*, September 12, 2012.

35. Robert Pear and Jennifer Steinhauer, "House Rebukes GOP Leaders over Spending," *New York Times*, September 21, 2011.

36. Ibid.

37. Major Garrett, "Beyond Mediation," *National Journal*, September 30, 2011.

38. Federal Election Commission (FEC), "Candidate and Committee Viewer: Freedom Project," http://www.fec.gov/fecviewer/CandidateCommitteeDetail.do.

39. Govtrack.us, "House Vote #72 in 2012: H.R. 3630 (112th): Middle-Class Tax Relief and Job Creation Act of 2012," February 17, 2012, http://www.govtrack.us/congress/votes/112-2012/h72.

40. "2012 House Races," *Politico*, http://www.politico.com/2012-election/map/#/House/2012/TN.

41. Jennifer Steinhauer and Robert Pear, "House Set to Vote Down Payroll Tax Cut Extension," *New York Times*, December 19, 2011.

42. Federal Election Commission (FEC), "Candidate and Committee Viewer: Majority Committee PAC," http://www.fec.gov/fecviewer/CandidateCommitteeDetail.do; "Election 2010," *New York Times*, http://elections.nytimes.com/2010/results/house.

43. Federal Election Commission (FEC), "Candidate and Committee Viewer: AmeriPAC: The Fund for a Greater America," http://www.fec.gov/fecviewer/CandidateCommitteeDetail.do.

44. Govtrack.us, "House Vote #477 in 2009: H.R. 2454 (111th): American Clean Energy and Security Act of 2009," June 26, 2009, http://www.govtrack.us/congress/votes/111-2009/h477.

45. Kristin Kanthak and George A. Krause, *The Diversity Paradox: Political Parties, Legislatures, and the Organizational Foundations of Representation in America* (New York: Oxford University Press, 2012), p. 79.

46. Kathryn Pearson, *Party Discipline in the Contemporary Congress: Rewarding Loyalty in Theory and Practice* (Berkeley: University of California Press, 2005), p. 11.

47. Ibid.

48. Suzanne Robbins, "Cash Flows: Leadership PACs in the U.S. Congress from 1992 to 2008," Proceedings of the Forty-Third Hawaii International Conference on Systems Science, IEEE Computer Society, Koloa Kauai, Hawaii, January 5–8, 2010, p. 2.

49. Quoted in Marian Currinder, *Money in the House: Campaign Funds and Congressional Party Politics* (Boulder, Colo.: Westview, 2009), p. 252 (ellipses in original).

50. Federal Election Commission (FEC), "Candidate and Committee Viewer: Mountaineer," http://www.fec.gov/fecviewer/CandidateCommitteeDetail.do.

51. Federal Election Commission (FEC), "Candidate and Committee Viewer: AmeriPAC: The Fund for a Greater America," http://www.fec.gov/fecviewer/CandidateCommitteeDetail.do.

52. Timothy J. Burger, "California's Napolitano Makes $220,000 from 1998 Campaign Loan," *Bloomberg*, February 13, 2009, http://www.bloomberg.com/apps/news?sid=aUZXCuqGb_Lw&pid=newsarchive.

53. Ibid.

54. See CREW (Citizens for Responsibility and Ethics in Washington), *Family Affair Report* (2012), p. 41, http://www.citizensforethics.org/page/-/PDFs/Reports/Family_Affair_House_2012_CREW.pdf?nocdn=1. The author has independently verified these numbers by examining FEC files.

55. Ibid.

56. Ibid.

57. "Rep. Rodney Alexander (R)," *National Journal*, http://www.nationaljournal.com/almanac/member/8.

58. Katherine Skiba, "Numerous Battles Haven't Slowed Rep. Bobby Rush," *Chicago Tribune*, September 19, 2011.

59. See Elliott Peterson's LinkedIn profile at: http://www.linkedin.com/pub/elliott-peterson/59/215/9a9; CQ MoneyLine, "Peterson, Collin C., 2009–2010 Election Cycle" (itemized disbursement data), http://www.politicalmoneyline.com/tr/tr_mg_cand.aspx?&sCandID=H2MN07014&sCycle=2010 (subscription required).

60. "Election Results [1992–2012]: District 4 in Texas," PoliGu.com, http://www.thepoliticalguide.com/Profiles/House/Texas/Ralph_Hall/ElectionResults.

61. "Election Results [1992–2012]: District 6 in Texas," PoliGu.com, http://www.thepoliticalguide.com/Profiles/House/Texas/Joe_Barton/ElectionResults.

62. "Election Results [1992–2010]: District 9 in North Carolina," PoliGu.com, http://www.thepoliticalguide.com/Profiles/House/North_Carolina/Sue_Myrick/ElectionResults.

63. Federal Election Commission (FEC), "Candidate and Committee Viewer: Randy Forbes," http://www.fec.gov/fecviewer/CandidateCommitteeDetail.do.

64. Federal Election Commission (FEC), "Candidate and Committee Viewer: Gary Miller," http://www.fec.gov/fecviewer/CandidateCommitteeDetail.do.

65. CREW, *Family Affair Report*, pp. 205–6.

5. THE DOUBLE-MILKER: *YOU MAY NOT BE INTERESTED IN WASHINGTON, BUT WASHINGTON IS INTERESTED IN YOU*

1. Bruce Bouton, "RMA Members Attend GRAMMYs on the Hill," *International Musician* 109, no. 6 (June 2011).

2. "Internet Piracy and How to Stop It: A Senate Bill Has Commendable Goals, but Needs Some Work Before It Can Be Law" (editorial), *New York Times*, June 9, 2011.

3. Business Software Alliance, "Shadow Market: 2011 BSA Global Software Piracy Study," 9th ed., May 2012, http://globalstudy.bsa.org/2011/downloads/study_pdf/2011_BSA_Piracy_Study-Standard.pdf.

4. Maria Pallante, John Clark, Michael O'Leary, Linda Kirkpatrick, Katherine Oyama, and Paul Almeida, testimony before House Judiciary Committee hearing on H.R. 3261 (Stop Online Piracy Act), 112th Cong., 1st sess., November 16, 2011.

5. Paul Harris, "Veep Vows War on Fakes," *Daily Variety*, December 16, 2009, p. 5.

6. Ted Johnson, "Veep on Piracy Pulpit," *Daily Variety*, April 13, 2011.

7. Matthew K. Dames, "Why the Frame of 'Piracy' Matters," *Information Daily* 26, no. 6 (June 2009): 22.

8. Johnson, "Veep on Piracy Pulpit."

9. Dave Boyer and Susan Crabtree, "Obama Presses China on Rights, Trade; Vice

President Xi Jinping Visits U.S.," *Washington Times,* February 15, 2012; Jonathan Weisman and Greg White, "Biden Decries Russian Corruption During Visit," *Wall Street Journal,* March 11, 2011.

10. Tom Barkley and Jarod Favole, "U.S. Sets Coordinated Response to Intellectual-Property Threats," *Wall Street Journal,* June 23, 2010.

11. Govtrack.us, "H.R. 3261 (112th): Stop Online Piracy Act," October 26, 2011, http://www.govtrack.us/congress/bills/112/hr3261 (accessed April 2, 2013); Govtrack.us, "S. 968 (112th): Preventing Real Online Threats to Economic Creativity and Theft of Intellectual Property Act of 2011," May 12, 2011, http://www.govtrack.us/congress/bills/112/s968 (accessed March 2, 2013).

12. Paul Sexton, "Business Diary: Glen Barros," *Financial Times,* February 14, 2011.

13. Cecilia Kang and Perry Bacon Jr., "Obama's Fundraising Faces Key Test in California," *Washington Post,* April 19, 2011.

14. Tina Daunt, "Disappointed Hollywood Giving Obama Cold Shoulder," *Hollywood Reporter,* September 15, 2011.

15. Nicholas Confessore, "Small Donors Are Slow to Return to the Obama Fold," *New York Times,* September 24, 2011.

16. Carla Marinucci, "Fans Resent Lack of Public Obama Events," *San Francisco Chronicle,* June 2, 2013.

17. Dave Rosenberg, "Sony Pictures CEO Hates the Internet," CNet News, May 16, 2009, http://news.cnet.com/8301-13846_3-10242526-62.html (accessed May 6, 2013).

18. Jamie Crawford, "Obama Makes Stop in Los Angeles, Wraps Up Campaign Swing," CNN, April 22, 2011.

19. Seema Mehta and Maeve Reston, "Obama Makes His Case in California," *Los Angeles Times,* April 21, 2012; Jackie Calmes and Brooks Barnes, "Obama Makes His Case in Mostly Friendly Territory," *New York Times,* April 21, 2012.

20. Calmes and Barnes, "Obama Makes His Case in Mostly Friendly Territory."

21. Michael O'Brien, "DNC Raises $12.4 Million in April," *The Hill,* May 20, 2011.

22. Govtrack.us, "S. 968 (112th): Preventing Real Online Threats to Economic Creativity and Theft of Intellectual Property Act of 2011," May 12, 2011, http://www.govtrack.us/congress/bills/112/s968 (accessed May 5, 2013).

23. Greg Sandoval, "Senate Panel OKs Controversial Antipiracy Bill," CNet News, May 26, 2011, http://news.cnet.com/8301-31001_3-20066456-261.html (accessed May 5, 2013).

24. Gautham Nagesh, "Google Chairman Says Online Piracy Bill Would 'Criminalize' the Internet," *The Hill,* December 12, 2011.

25. Richard Verrier and Jim Puzzanghera, "Piracy Legislation Pits Hollywood Against Silicon Valley," *Los Angeles Times,* December 5, 2011.

26. Declan McCullagh, "Senate Bill Amounts to Death Penalty for Web Sites," CNet News, May 12, 2011, http://news.cnet.com/8301-31921_3-20062398-281.html (accessed May 6, 2013).

27. John Carey, "Scott and Bill Went Up the Hill," *BusinessWeek,* March 5, 1998.

28. Timothy P. Carney, "How Hatch Forced Microsoft to Play K Street's Game," *Washington Examiner,* June 24, 2012.

29. Microsoft News Center, "Microsoft Brings Innovation and Excitement of Kinect for Xbox 360 to Policymakers and Families on Capitol Hill," June 24, 2011, http://www.microsoft.com/en-us/news/press/2011/jun11/06-24FamilyGameNightPR.aspx (accessed May 5, 2013).

30. "Party with a Purpose, Lobbying Lobby Squawks About Limits on Largesse," *St. Louis Post Dispatch,* April 16, 2012.

31. Ibid.

32. Carney, "How Hatch Forced Microsoft."

33. Janie Lorber, "Influence: GOP Woos High-Tech Industry," *Roll Call,* January 30, 2012.

34. Brent Lang, "MPAA Chief Chris Dodd Makes Top Level Appointments," The Wrap, September 15, 2011, http://www.thewrap.com/movies/column-post/mpaa-chief-chris-dodd-makes-top-level-appointments-31006?utm_source=feedburner&utm_medium=feed&utm_campaign=Feed%3A%20thewrap%2Flatest-news%20(The%20Wrap%20RSS) (accessed May 5, 2013).

35. "Executive Profile: Michael O'Leary," *Bloomberg Businessweek,* http://investing.businessweek.com/research/stocks/people/person.asp?personId=53569702.

36. Jonathan Allen and Jennifer Martinez, "Generation X Joining K Street," *Politico,* March 25, 2012.

37. Alex Ben Block, "Why Both Sides of the Piracy Issue Applaud SOPA Delay (Analysis)," *Hollywood Reporter,* December 16, 2011.

38. Jennifer Martinez, "Shootout at the Digital Corral," *Politico, November 16,* 2011; David Goldman, "SOPA and PIPA Attract Huge Lobbying on Both Sides," CNN Money, January 25, 2012.

39. Martinez, "Shootout at the Digital Corral."

40. Viveca Novak, "SOPA and PIPA Spur Lobbying Spike," Opensecrets.org, January 26, 2012, http://www.opensecrets.org/news/2012/01/sopa-and-pipa-create-lobbying-spike.html (accessed May 6, 2013).

41. Viveca Novak and Michael Beckel, "Lobbying Expenditures Slump in 2011," Opensecrets.org, January 26, 2012, http://www.opensecrets.org/news/2012/01/lobbying-expenditures-slump-in-2011.html (accessed May 6, 2013).

42. U.S. Senate Committee on Commerce, Science, and Transportation, "Majority Members," http://www.commerce.senate.gov/public/index.cfm?p=Committee Members.

43. Opensecrets.org, "Lugar Hellman Group," http://www.opensecrets.org/lobby/firm_reports.php?id=F27967&year=2011 (accessed May 6, 2013).

44. David Levinthal and Anna Palmer, "Huge Day on Campaign Finance Playing Field—Newt Shaking K Street Money Tree—House Administration Committee Gets Its Documents," *Politico,* December 1, 2011.

45. Opensecrets.org, "Lobbying Profile: Gephardt, Richard," http://www.opensecrets. org/lobby/lobbyist.php?id=Y0000033482L&year=2011 (accessed May 5, 2013); "Lobbying Profile: Molinari, Susan," http://www.opensecrets.org/lobby/lobbyist.php?id=Y0000040464L&year=2012 (accessed May 5, 2013); Cecilia Kang, "Google Names Former GOP House Member Susan Molinari to Head D.C. Office," *Washington Post*, February 24, 2012.

46. Abby Goodnough, "Susan Molinari, Out of Congress and on Camera," *New York Times*, September 14, 1997.

47. Kim Eisler, "People and Politics: Hired Guns: The City's 50 Top Lobbyists," *Washingtonian* (June 1, 2007).

48. Opensecrets.org, "Lobbyist Profile: Bill Paxon," http://www.opensecrets.org/lobby/lobbyist.php?id=Paxon%2C%20Bill&id=Y0000040464M&year=2012 (accessed May 6, 2013).

49. LD-2 lobbying disclosure forms for Gray Global Advisors' relationship with Comcast for 2011, quarters 1–4, http://www.opensecrets.org/lobby/client_reports. php?id=D000000461&year=2011.

50. LD-2 lobbying disclosure forms for Akin, Gump et al.'s relationship with AT&T for 2011, quarters 1–4, http://www.opensecrets.org/lobby/client_reports. php?id=D000000461&year=2011.

51. See the Madison Group website at: http://www.madisongr.com/; LD-2 lobbying disclosure forms for Madison Group's relationship with Google, Inc., for 2011, quarters 2–4, http://www.opensecrets.org/lobby/client_reports.php?id= D000022008&year=2011.

52. Lonnae O. Parker, "Ron Brown and Michael A. Brown: Amid a Father's Legacy, a Son's Own Path," *Washington Post*, March 30, 2011; Opensecrets.org, "Lobbyist Profile: Michael Arrington Brown," http://www.opensecrets.org/lobby/lobbyist. php?id=Brown%2C%20Michael%20Arrington&id=Y0000037265L&year=2012 (accessed May 6, 2013).

53. LD-2 lobbying disclosure forms for Dutko Graylings's relationship with Google, Inc., for 2011, quarters 1–4, http://www.opensecrets.org/lobby/client_reports. php?id=D0000022008&year=2011.

54. Grayling, "Our People," http://us.grayling.com/OurPeople (accessed March 20, 2013); Wayne Barrett, "New York's Bush Boys," *Village Voice*, January 23, 2001.

55. Google Finance, "Podesta Group, Inc." http://www.google.com/finance? cid=3338214 (accessed May 6, 2013).

56. The White House, "Visitor Access Records," http://www.whitehouse.gov/briefing-room/disclosures/visitor-records (accessed May 6, 2013).

57. Opensecrets.org, "Podesta Group," http://www.opensecrets.org/lobby/firmsum. php?id=D000022193 (accessed May 6, 2013).

58. Opensecrets.org, "FIRST Group," http://www.opensecrets.org/lobby/firmlbs. php?id=D000061270 (accessed May 6, 2013).

59. Anna Palmer, "GOP Aides Head to K St. for Tech War," *Politico*, December 8, 2011.

60. MapLight, "U.S. Congress—Find Contributions: Legislator, Debbie Wasserman Shultz; Date, April 27–May 2, 2011" (see ch. 1, n. 2; accessed May 6, 2013).

61. "Standing Committees of the House" (Washington, D.C.: U.S. Government Printing Office, 2011), p. 426, http://www.gpo.gov/fdsys/browse/collection.action?collectionCode=CDIR&browsePath=112%2F2011-12-01&isCollapsed=false&leafLevelBrowse=false&ycord=0; Govtrack.us, H.R. 3261—112th Congress: Stop Online Piracy Act (2011)," http://www.govtrack.us/congress/bills/112/hr3261 (accessed March 20, 2013); MapLight, "U.S. Congress—Find Contributions: Legislator, Lamar Smith; Date, June 1–December 31, 2011" (see ch. 1, n. 2; accessed April 21, 2013).

62. Gibson Group, "About Us," http://gibsongroupdc.com/about.shtml (accessed March 20, 2013); LD-2 lobbying disclosure form regarding Gibson Group's relationship with Clear Channel Communication Holdings for 2011, quarters 1–4, http://www.opensecrets.org/lobby/client_reports.php?id=D000059056&year=2011.

63. MapLight, "U.S. Congress—Find Contributions: Legislator, Lamar Smith; Contributor, Clear Channel; Date, March 25, 2011" (see ch. 1, n. 2; accessed May 6, 2013).

64. Martinez, "Shootout at the Digital Corral."

65. MapLight, "U.S. Congress—Find Contributions: Legislator, Lamar Smith; Interest Group, Communications and Electronics Industry; Date, 2010, 2012" (see ch. 1, n. 2; accessed May 6, 2013).

66. Federal Election Commission (FEC), "Candidate and Committee Viewer: Longhorn PAC," http://www.fec.gov/fecviewer/CandidateCommitteeDetail.do.

67. Zach Carter, "SOPA Vote Delayed, Allowing for More Corporate Fundraising from Censorship Bill," *Huffington Post*, December 16, 2011.

68. La Toya Gratten, "SOPA Fundraisers," Political Party Time, January 27, 2012, http://politicalpartytime.org/blog/2012/01/27/sopa-fundraisers; Govtrack.us, "S. 968—112th Congress: Preventing Real Online Threats to Economic Creativity and Theft of Intellectual Property Act of 2011," May 12, 2011, http://www.govtrack.us/congress/bills/112/s968 (accessed March 20, 2013); U.S. Government Printing Office, "Standing Committees of the Senate," p. 375, http://www.gpo.gov/fdsys/browse/collection.action?collectionCode=CDIR&browsePath=112%2F2011-12-01&isCollapsed=false&leafLevelBrowse=false&ycord=0.

69. Gratten, "SOPA Fundraisers."

70. Ibid.

71. Alex Ben Block, "Hollywood's Top Brass Lobby for Anti-Piracy Laws in Washington, D.C.," *Hollywood Reporter*, December 7, 2011.

72. Howard Berman, testimony before the House Judiciary Committee hearings on H.R. 3261, November 16, 2011, pp. 130–35.

73. Alex Ben Block, "Why Both Sides of the Piracy Issue Applaud SOPA Delay (Analysis)," *Hollywood Reporter,* December 16, 2011.

74. Nick Baumann and Siddhartha Mahanta, "SOPA Aftermath: Winners and Losers," *Mother Jones,* January 23, 2012.

75. Jon Swartz, "Obama Attends Private Fundraiser in Silicon Valley," *USA Today,* April 21, 2011.

76. Glenn Thrush, "At California Dinner, President Obama Woos Technology Leaders," *Politico,* February 17, 2011.

77. Carla Marinucci, "Obama Dines with Tech Stars of Silicon Valley," *San Francisco Chronicle,* February 18, 2011.

78. Adam Clark Etes, "Some Perspective on Obama's Bromance with Eric Schmidt," *The Atlantic Wire,* June 24, 2011, http://www.theatlanticwire.com/politics/2011/06/obamas-bromance-googles-eric-schmidt-out-hand/39225/.

79. Joshua Green, "The Amazing Money Machine," *The Atlantic,* June 1, 2008.

80. Michelle Quinn, "Obama Gets No Bounce from Silicon Valley Boom," *Politico,* August 19, 2011.

81. Thrush, "President Obama Woos Technology Leaders."

82. Josh Smith, "Presidential Candidates Gather Silicon Valley Contributions," *National Journal,* August 17, 2011.

83. Jim Brunner, "Obama Will Visit Area for Fundraisers," *Seattle Times,* September 22, 2011.

84. "Lady Gaga Joins Obama's Silicon Valley Fundraiser," *Silicon Valley Business Journal,* September 26, 2011, http://www.bizjournals.com/sanjose/news/2011/09/26/lady-gaga-joins-obama-valley-fundraiser.html (accessed May 6, 2013).

85. Devin Dwyer, "Obama Taps Veteran Hollywood Bundlers for Campaign Cash," ABC News, September 26, 2011.

86. Govtrack.us, "H.R. 3261 (112th): Stop Online Piracy Act," October 26, 2011, http://www.govtrack.us/congress/bills/112/hr3261 (accessed May 6, 2013).

87. House Judiciary Committee, hearing on H.R. 3261, the "Stop Online Piracy Act," November 16, 2011, http://judiciary.house.gov/hearings/hear_11162011.html (accessed May 6, 2013).

88. Block, "Why Both Sides of the Piracy Issue Applaud SOPA Delay."

89. Josh Richman, "Palo Alto Online: Tech Leaders Meet with Vice President Joe Biden," January 18, 2012, http://www.paloaltoonline.com/news/show_story.php?id=24016 (accessed May 6, 2013).

90. Micah L. Sifry, "After SOPA/PIPA Victory, Tech Is Thinking About Tackling Political Reform," *TechPresident,* January 24, 2012, http://techpresident.com/news/21674/after-sopapipa-victory-tech-thinking-about-tackling-political-reform (accessed May 6, 2013).

91. Lou Dobbs, comments on *Lou Dobbs Tonight,* Fox Business Network, January 19, 2012.

92. Richard Verrier, "Obama Administration Expresses Concern About Anti-Piracy Bills," *Los Angeles Times,* January 14, 2012.

93. "Lawmakers Withdraw Support of Anti-piracy Bills after Online Protest," CNN Wire, January 19, 2012, http://www.cnn.com/2012/01/19/tech/sopa-blackouts (accessed May 6, 2013).

94. Sarah Barmak, "The Day the Web Went Dark; U.S. Anti-Piracy Bills Spark Outrage Online," *Toronto Star,* January 21, 2012.

95. Matthew Garrahan, "President Taps 'Hollywood ATM,'" *Financial Times,* March 9, 2012.

96. Erica Orden and Peter Nicholas, "Movie Mogul's Starring Role in Raising Funds for Obama," *Wall Street Journal,* September 30, 2012.

97. Anna Palmer and Robin Bravender, "Chris Dodd's Debut with Hollywood a Flop," *Politico,* January 19, 2012.

98. Tina Daunt, "Hollywood Moguls: No 'Obama Boycott' over Piracy Stance," *Hollywood Reporter,* January 18, 2012.

99. Ryan Nakashima, "AP: Hollywood Warms to China's New Openness," Yahoo! News, April 16, 2012, http://news.yahoo.com/hollywood-warms-chinas-openness-211340104.html (accessed May 6, 2013).

100. Orden and Nicholas, "Movie Mogul's Starring Role."

101. Garrahan, "Obama Taps 'Hollywood ATM.'"

102. Robert Herbold, interview with the author.

103. Opensecrets.org, "Facebook Inc.," https://www.opensecrets.org/lobby/clientsum.php?id=D000033563 (accessed May 6, 2013).

104. "Silicon Valley is waking up to the fact that we have to be part of the process in Washington," writes John Battelle. "For too long we've treated 'government' as damage, and we've routed around it." Alex Howard, "The Week the Web Changed Washington," O'Reilly Radar, January 20, 2012, http://radar.oreilly.com/2012/01/the-week-the-web-changed-washi.html.

105. Marketwatch.com, "Google, Facebook Continue to Flood Washington with Cash for Lobbying Efforts; Consumer Watchdog Calls Record Spending Cynical Bid to Buy Influence," January 23, 2013.

106. John Allison, interview with the author.

107. Saki Knafo, "Joe Biden Talks Violent Video Games with Industry Reps in Wake of Newtown Shooting," *Huffington Post,* January 11, 2013.

108. Eric Lichtblau, "Makers of Violent Video Games Marshal Support to Fend Off Regulation," *New York Times,* January 12, 2013.

109. Jeffrey Grubb, "Obama: 'Congress Should Fund Research into the Effects Violent Video Games Have on Young Minds,'" VentureBeat, January 16, 2013, http://venturebeat.com/2013/01/16/obama-congress-should-fund-research-into-the-effects-violent-video-games-have-on-young-minds (accessed May 6, 2013).

110. Opensecrets.org, "Entertainment Software Assn," https://www.opensecrets.org/lobby/clientsum.php?id=D000025695 (accessed May 6, 2013).

6. SLUSH FUNDS

1. FBI.gov, "Famous Cases and Criminals: Al Capone," http://www.fbi.gov/about-us/history/famous-cases/al-capone.

2. *Encyclopaedia Brittanica,* "Meyer Lansky," http://www.britannica.com/EB-checked/topic/330022/Meyer-Lansky.

3. Ken Silverstein, "Beltway Bacchanal: Congress Lives High on the Contributor's Dime," *Harper's* (March 2008).

4. Halimah Abdullah, "Whitfield Spent $24,000 from Leadership PAC at Beverly Hills Hotel," *Lexington Herald-Leader,* October 4, 2009.

5. Brody Mullins and Brad Haynes, "Some PACs Run After Politicians Drop Out," *Wall Street Journal,* May 6, 2009.

6. Aaron Blake, "Rep. Joe Kennedy III Launches Political Action Committee," *Washington Post,* April 12, 2013.

7. GenYPack, "Congressman Aaron Schock," http://genypac.com/about/congress-man-aaron-schock.

8. Marcus Stern and Jennifer LaFleur, "*Leadership PACs:* Let the Good Times Roll," *Pro Publica,* September 26, 2009.

9. Ibid.

10. Janie Lorber, "Being in Congress Has Perks," *Roll Call,* October 18, 2011.

11. Corbin Hiar, "*Congressional Perks:* Lawmakers' Most Surprising Benefits," Center for Public Integrity, November 23, 2011, http://www.publicintegrity.org/2011/11/23/7495/congressional-perks-lawmakers-most-surprising-benefits.

12. Stern and LaFleur, "Leadership PACs: Let the Good Times Roll."

13. Federal Election Commission (FEC), "Candidate and Committee Viewer: Republican Majority Fund," http://www.fec.gov/fecviewer/CandidateCommitteeDetail.do.

14. Federal Election Commission (FEC), "Candidate and Committee Viewer: America Forward Leadership PAC," http://www.fec.gov/fecviewer/CandidateCommitteeDetail.do.

15. Federal Election Commission (FEC), "Candidate and Committee Viewer: Rely on Your Beliefs Fund," http://www.fec.gov/fecviewer/CandidateCommitteeDetail.do.

16. Ibid.

17. Jonathan Tamari, "Andrews' Wife Vetted Use of Campaign Funds on Trip," *Philadelphia Inquirer,* September 12, 2012.

18. U.S. House of Representatives, Office of Congressional Ethics, "Report," Review 11-3260, p. 15; and Tamari, "Andrews' Wife Vetted Use of Campaign Funds on Trip."

19. House Office of Congressional Ethics, "Report," p. 27.

20. Federal Election Commission (FEC), "Candidate and Committee Viewer: Americans Nationwide Dedicated to Electing Republicans," http://www.fec.gov/fecviewer/CandidateCommitteeDetail.do.

21. Ibid.

22. House Committee on Appropriations, "Full Committee Members," http://appropriations.house.gov/about/members.

23. Federal Election Commission (FEC), "Candidate and Committee Viewer: Toward Tomorrow," http://www.fec.gov/fecviewer/CandidateCommitteeDetail.do.

24. Federal Election Commission (FEC), "Candidate and Committee Viewer: Impact PAC," http://www.fec.gov/fecviewer/CandidateCommitteeDetail.do.

25. Federal Election Commission (FEC), "Candidate and Committee Viewer: Heartland PAC," http://www.fec.gov/fecviewer/CandidateCommitteeDetail.do.

26. Stern and LaFleur, "Leadership PACs: Let the Good Times Roll."

27. Luke Rosiak and Glenn Thrush, "Rangel's Son Got Campaign Cash," *Politico*, December 4, 2008.

28. Federal Election Commission (FEC), "Candidate and Committee Viewer: Democratic Future," http://www.fec.gov/fecviewer/CandidateCommitteeDetail.do; Josh Israel, Aaron Mehta, and Gabriel Debenedetti, "Political Inaction Committees: How Political Action Committees Are Spending Your Donations," Center for Public Integrity, October 5, 2010, http://www.publicintegrity.org/2010/10/05/2460/political-inaction-committees-how-political-action-committees-are-spending-your.

29. Rachel Leven, "FEC to Congress: Expand Ban on Personal Use of Political Committee Funds," *The Hill*, May 12, 2012.

7. TRUST ME: YOU'RE GONNA NEED TO PAY ME

1. "Too Big Not to Fail," *The Economist*, February 18, 2012.

2. Ibid.

3. "Over-regulated America," *The Economist*, February 18, 2012.

4. "Too Big Not to Fail," *The Economist*.

5. Ibid.

6. Amanda Becker, "Multitudes of Lobbyists Weigh in on Dodd-Frank Act," *Washington Post*, November 22, 2010.

7. U.S. Department of the Treasury, "Financial Stability Oversight Council," http://www.treasury.gov/initiatives/fsoc/Pages/home.aspx; Cornell University Law School, Legal Information Institute, "Dodd-Frank: Title X — Bureau of Consumer Financial Protection," http://www.law.cornell.edu/wex/dodd-frank_title_x.

8. Alan Siegel and Irene Etzkorn, *Simple: Conquering the Crisis of Complexity* (New York: Twelve, 2013), p. 22.

9. See Anthony Giles Heyes, "Expert Advice and Regulatory Complexity," *Journal of Regulatory Economics* 24, no. 2 (2003): 120; and Anthony Heyes, "Revolving

Doors and Regulatory Complexity, or, Another Reason Why American Regulation Is So Darn'd Difficult," http://www.soc.uoc.gr/calendar/2000EAERE/papers/Pdf2/H4-Heyes.pdf.

10. George LeMieux, interview with the author.

11. Promontory, "Careers," http://www.promontory.com/OurCareers.aspx.

12. Ben Protess and Jessica Silver-Greenberg, "Former Regulators Find a Home with a Powerful Firm," *New York Times*, April 10, 2013.

13. Tim Carney, "Dodd-Frank's Winners: Revolving-Door Regulators," *Washington Examiner*, July 24, 2011.

14. Hogan Lovells, "Senior Counsel to U.S. House Committee on Financial Services Rejoins Hogan Lovells" (press release), March 7, 2011, http://www.hoganlovells.com/newsmedia/newspubs/detail.aspx?news=1836.

15. George LeMieux, interview with the author.

16. Robert Wenzel, "The Completely Disgusting Government/Crony Capitalism Revolving Door," *Economic Policy Journal* (December 27, 2012).

17. "We're about to receive legislation that could better be entitled 'The Lawyers' and Lobbyists' Full Employment Act.'" Harvey Pitt, "The Ugly Truth About Financial-Regulatory Reform," *The Daily Beast*, July 13, 2010.

18. Cass Sunstein, *Simpler: The Future of Government* (New York: Simon & Schuster, 2013) pp. 12, 35.

19. Silverglate, *Three Felonies a Day*, p. xxxvi.

20. John Allison, interview with the author.

21. Joel A. Mintz, *Enforcement at the EPA: High Stakes and Hard Choices* (Austin: University of Texas Press, 1995).

22. Anthony Heyes, "Revolving Doors and Regulatory Complexity," Discussion Papers in Economics 99/1, Royal Holloway University of London, Department of Economics, February 2000.

23. John Hofmeister, interview with the author.

24. Christine Simmons, "New Rules Create Jobs for Attorneys at Hedge Funds," *New York Law Journal* (December 28, 2012).

25. Senator Ron Johnson, interview with the author.

26. John Cochrane, "Three Kinds of Regulation," The Grumpy Economist, January 2, 2012, http://johnhcochrane.blogspot.com/2012/01/three-kinds-of-regulation.html.

27. Richard Williams, "Regulatory Overload," Mercatus Center, George Mason University, February 8, 2012, http://mercatus.org/publication/regulatory-overload-0.

28. Murphy & McGonigle, "Murphy & McGonigle Professionals," http://www.murphymcgonigle.com/Staff/?id=24.

29. "Former Senior SEC Official Joins Murphy & McGonigle," PR Newswire, February 22, 2011, http://www.bizjournals.com/prnewswire/press_releases/2011/02/22/PH51642.

30. Financial Industry Regulatory Authority, "FINRA Leadership," http://www.finra.org/AboutFINRA/Leadership/P127206.

31. Securities and Exchange Commission, "Robert Colby, Deputy Director of Trading and Markets Division, to Leave SEC After 27 Years of Service" (press release), February 2, 2009.

32. Cooley LLP, "SEC Commissioner Roel C. Campos Joins Cooley" (press release and announcements), August 23, 2007.

33. Skadden, Arps, Slate, Meagher & Flom LLP & Affiliates, "Brian V. Breheny," http://www.skadden.com/professionals/brian-v-breheny (accessed May 9, 2013); and "SEC Deputy Director Brian V. Breheny Joins Skadden as Partner," October 4, 2010, http://www.skadden.com/news-events/sec-deputy-director-brian-v-breheny-joins-skadden-partner (accessed May 9, 2013).

34. Silverglate, Three Felonies a Day, p. 46. See chapter 2 of Silverglate's book for examples.

35. Thomas Scully, interview with the author.

36. Peter H. Stone and Louis Jacobson, "Former Medicare Chief Soldiers on in Wake of Ethics Investigation," Government Executive, April 9, 2004.

37. Congressman Bruce Braley (website), "Braley Renews Push to Streamline Regulations, Hold Government Accountable," April 15, 2013, http://braley.house.gov/press-release/braley-renews-push-streamline-regulations-hold-government-accountable.

38. Glenn Greenwald, "Obamacare Architect Leaves White House for Pharmaceutical Industry Job," The Guardian, December 5, 2012.

39. See Daschle's account in Getting It Done: How Obama and Congress Finally Broke the Stalemate to Make Way for Health Care Reform (New York: St. Martin's Press/ Thomas Dunne Books, 2010).

40. Chris Frates, "Lobbyists Call Bluff on 'Daschle Exemption,'" Politico, July 26, 2010.

41. Opensecrets.org, "Myers, John," http://www.opensecrets.org/lobby/lobbyist.php?id=Y0000045287L.

42. Timothy P. Carney, "Top Obama Health Aide Cashes Out After Health 'Reform,'" Washington Examiner, May 29, 2011.

43. Ibid.

44. Timothy P. Carney, "Obamacare Improves Another Life: Bill's Architect Cashes Out to Pharma Giant," Washington Examiner, December 6, 2012.

45. Patrick Dixon, "Energy Use Consulting — Boom Industry," GlobalChange.com, http://www.globalchange.com/energy-use-consulting-boom-industry.htm.

46. Tanina Rostain, "The Emergence of 'Law Consultants,'" Fordham Law Review 75 (2006): 1410.

47. Alice Ramey, "Going 'Green': Environmental Jobs for Scientists and Engineers," Occupational Outlook Quarterly (Summer 2009): 5.

48. Nebraska Department of Environmental Quality, "What Every Nebraska Busi-

ness Should Know About Environmental Permits" (fact sheets), http://www.deq. state.ne.us/Publica.nsf/Pages/EAD007.

49. Gregg LaBar, "Mandating Safety Programs," *Occupational Hazards* (February 1998).

50. Joe Nocera, "The Foreclosure Fiasco," *New York Times*, January 14, 2013; Alan Zibel and Dan Fitzpatrick, "Scant Relief in Foreclosure Payouts," *Wall Street Journal*, April 9, 2013.

51. Jeff Horwitz and Kate Berry, "Foreclosure Reviews: Exorbitant for Banks, Gold Mines for Consultants," *American Banker*, November 1, 2012.

52. Ibid.; Nocera, "The Foreclosure Fiasco"; Zibel and Fitzpatrick, "Scant Relief in Foreclosure Payouts."

53. Joe Costanzo, "Charges Brought in Payoff Case; Ex-Regulator over Envirocare Is Accused," *Deseret News*, March 25, 1999.

54. Eric Helland and Michael Sykuta, "Deregulation and Board Composition: Evidence on the Value of the Revolving Door," CORI Working Paper 01-01, University of Missouri–Columbia, Contracting and Organizations Research Institute, January 2001, p. 12.

55. Michael J. Licari, "Bureaucratic Discretion and Regulatory Success Without Enforcement," in *Politics, Policy, and Organizations: Essays on the Scientific Study of Bureaucracy,* ed. George Krause and Kenneth J. Meier (Ann Arbor: University of Michigan Press).

56. Siegel and Etzkorn, *Simple,* pp. 11, 4–5.

57. Michael J. Waggoner, "The House Erred: A Carbon Tax Is Better Than Cap and Trade," Legal Studies Research Paper Series, Working Paper 09-18, *Tax Analysis* (October 15, 2009): 1261.

58. Ibid., p. 1262.

59. Siegel and Etzkorn, *Simple,* p. 42.

60. Ibid., p. 197.

61. Heyes, "Revolving Doors and Regulatory Complexity."

8. PROTECTION FOR A PRICE: WHAT ABOUT A WASHINGTON CORRUPT PRACTICES ACT?

1. Ronald J. Ostrow, "Bribery, Intimidation Reported Among Duties of Mafia Lawyers," *Los Angeles Times,* January 30, 1986.

2. Silverglate, *Three Felonies a Day,* p. xxv.

3. Ibid., p. xxxvi.

4. Fulmer and Knill, "Political Contributions and the Severity of Government Enforcement," pp. 1, 16.

5. Ibid., 20.

6. Maria Correia, "Political Connections, SEC Enforcement, and Accounting Qual-

ity," Working Paper 61, Stanford University Rock Center for Corporate Governance, August 1, 2012.

7. Frank Yuy and Xiaoyun Yu, "Corporate Lobbying and Fraud Detection," *Journal of Financial Quantitative Analysis* 46 (2011): 1865–91.

8. Sanford C. Gordon, "Assessing Partisan Bias in Federal Public Corruption Prosecutions," *American Political Science Review* 103, no. 4 (November 2009): 534–54.

9. Marilyn Young, Michael Reksulak, and William F. Shughart II, "The Political Economy of the IRS," *Economics and Politics* 13, no. 2 (July 2001): 201.

10. Matthew Mosk, "IRS Suspicion Widens: GOP Donors Question Audits," ABC News, May 15, 2013, http://abcnews.go.com/Blotter/irs-suspicion-widens-gop-donors-question-audits/story?id=19184358#.UZumepUeZG4.

11. Opensecrets.org, "Barack Obama's Bundlers," http://www.opensecrets.org/pres12/bundlers.php?id=N00009638.

12. Claire Heininger, "Corzine Profile Rises in Obama Camp," NJ.com, June 23, 2008, http://www.nj.com/news/ledger/topstories/index.ssf/2008/06/corzine_profile_in_obama_camp.html.

13. James B. Stewart, "Trustee Sees Customers Trampled at MF Global," *New York Times*, June 8, 2012.

14. Mark Melin, "The Untold Story: Legal Professor Views MF Global with Suspicion," *Opalesque Futures Intelligence*, December 13, 2012, http://www.opalesque.com/OFI1310/The_Untold_Story_Legal_Professor_Views_MF_Global310.html.

15. Paula Dwyer, "Six Reasons Why Jon Corzine Should Exit Wall Street," *Bloomberg*, April 9, 2013.

16. Bruce Bialosky, "Corzine's Crime of the Century," *National Review Online*, February 5, 2013, http://www.nationalreview.com/articles/339811/corzine-s-crime-century-bruce-bialosky.

17. Louis J. Freeh, as Chapter 11 Trustee of MF Global Holdings Ltd., et al., *Plaintiff, v. Jon S. Corzine*, Bradley I. Abelow, and Henri J. Steenkamp, Defendants, pp. 57–58.

18. Silla Brush, "Gensler Recusal Faulted in CFTC Watchdog's MF Global Report," *Businessweek*, May 22, 2013.

19. Elaine Knuth, "MF Global's Original Sin," *Futures*, November 1, 2012.

20. Ben Protess and Azam Ahmed, "MF Global Inquiry Turns to Its Primary Regulator," *New York Times*, January 5, 2012; Mark Melin, "CME Group Independent Investigation Halted," *Opalesque Futures* 45 (November 14, 2012): 19; Mark Melin, "Who Knew What and When Did They Know It? Who Gave a CFTC Lawyer His Marching Orders?" *Opalesque Futures* 45 (November 14, 2012).

21. Mark Melin, "Delay in Congressional Report on MF Global Announced," *Opalesque Futures 45* (November 14, 2012): 11.

22. Azam Ahmed and Ben Protess, "No Criminal Case Likely in Loss at MF Global," *New York Times*, August 15, 2012.

23. Stanley Haar, *Opalesque Futures* (December 12, 2012): 20.

24. "MF Global Bankruptcy: Commodity Customer Coalition," discussion on LinkedIn (subscription and group membership required), http://www.linkedin. com/groupItem?view=&gid=4166821&type=member&item=180381682&trk=g roup_search_item_list-0-b-cmr&goback=.fps_PBCK_lisa+timmermann_*1_*1 _*1_*1_*1_*2_*1_Y_*1_*1_*1_false_1_R_*1_*51_*1_*51_true_*2_*2_*2_*2_*2 _*2_*2_*2_*2_*2_*2_*2_*2_*2_*2_*2_*2_*2_*2_*2.npv_150142457_*1_*1_ NAME*4SEARCH_HBWz_*1_en*4US_*1_*1_*1_7328f4d9*5526a*54785*58966 *526ee346fb534*50_1_6_ps_*1_*1_*1_*1_*1_*1_*1_*1_*1_*1_*1_*1_*1_*1_*1_* 1_*1_*1_*1_*1.gna_4166821.

25. U.S. Commodity Futures Trading Commission, "Release: PR6626-13," June 27, 2013.

26. Kaja Whitehouse, "Corzine off the crook," *New York Post,* July 7, 2013.

27. *Encyclopaedia Britannica,* "Tanaka Kakuei," http://www.britannica.com/EB-checked/topic/582189/Tanaka-Kakuei.

28. Dickinson Wright PLLC, "Foreign Corrupt Practices Act: A Compliance Road-map," http://www.worldcompliance.com/Libraries/WhitePapers/FCPA_Compli-ance_Roadmap_White_paper.sflb.ashx.

29. Mike Koehler, "The Facade of FCPA Enforcement," *Georgetown Journal of International Law* 41 (2010): 150–51.

30. Lawrence J. Trautman and Kara Altenbaumer-Price, "The Foreign Corrupt Practices Act: Minefield for Directors," *Virginia Law and Business Review* 6, no. 1 (Spring 2011).

31. Professor Mike Koehler, "Examining Enforcement of the Foreign Corrupt Practices Act," prepared statement before the Subcommittee on Crime and Drugs of the Senate Committee on the Judiciary, November 30, 2010.

32. Mike Koehler, "The Foreign Corrupt Practices Act in the Ultimate Year of Its Decade of Resurgence," *Indiana Law Review* 43, no. 389 (2010): 389.

33. Mike Koehler, "Lanny Breuer and Foreign Corrupt Practices Act Enforcement," *Bloomberg BNA White Collar Crime Report* 8 *(March 22, 2013),* p. 204, http://papers.ssrn.com/sol3/papers.cfm?abstract_id=2238156.

34. U.S. Department of Justice (DOJ), "Lanny A. Breuer, Assistant Attorney General, Criminal Division, Prepared Keynote Address to the Tenth Annual Pharmaceutical Regulatory and Compliance Congress and Best Practices Forum," November 12, 2009, http://www.justice.gov/criminal/pr/speeches-testimony/documents/11-12-09breuer-pharmaspeech.pdf.

35. Illustration source: Securities and Exchange Commission, "SEC Enforcement Actions: FCPA Cases," www.sec.gov/spotlight/fcpa/fcpa-cases.shtml and http:// www. justice.gov/criminal/fraud/fcpa/cases/2013.html.

36. Covington & Burling LLP, "Foreign Corrupt Practices Act," http://www.cov. com/offices/office.aspx?office=61&OfficeSpecialty=a596d0f4-4dde-428f-ba11-65cb429c9917.

37. Trautman and Altenbaumer-Price, "The Foreign Corrupt Practices Act: Minefield for Directors," p. 158.

38. DOJ, "Lanny A. Breuer . . . Prepared Keynote Address . . .," November 12, 2009.

39. U.S. Department of Justice, "Assistant Attorney General Lanny A. Breuer Speaks at the 24th National Conference on the Foreign Corrupt Practices Act," November 16, 2010, http://www.justice.gov/criminal/pr/speeches/2010/crm-speech-101116.html.

40. Barbara Black, "The SEC and the Foreign Corrupt Practices Act: Fighting Global Corruption Is Not Part of the SEC's Mission," *Ohio State Law Journal* 73, no. 5 (2012): 1114.

41. Matthew C. Turk, "A Political Economy Approach to Reforming the Foreign Corrupt Practices Act," *Northwestern Journal of International Law and Business* 33, no. 2 (2013): 340.

42. Amy Deen Westbrook, "Enthusiastic Enforcement, Informal Legislation: The Unruly Expansion of the Foreign Corrupt Practices Act," *Georgia Law Review* 45 (Winter 2011): 489, 494.

43. Trautman and Altenbaumer-Price, "The Foreign Corrupt Practices Act: Minefield for Directors," p. 160.

44. Lanny Breuer, speech delivered at the annual meeting of the Washington Metropolitan Area Corporate Counsel, January 26, 2011, quoted in Jessica Tillipman, "A House of Cards Falls: Why 'Too Big to Debar' Is All Slogan and Little Substance," Public Law and Legal Theory Paper 2012-8, George Washington University Law School, January 13, 2012, p. 54.

45. Mike Koehler, "The FCPA, Foreign Agents, and Lessons from the Halliburton Enforcement Action," *Ohio Northern University Law Review* 36, no. 2 (2010): 468.

46. Thomas McSorley, "Foreign Corrupt Practices Act," *American Criminal Law Review* 48 (Spring 2011): 749.

47. Mike Koehler, "Big, Bold, and Bizarre: The Foreign Corrupt Practices Act Enters a New Era," *University of Toledo Law Review* 43 (Fall 2011): 123.

48. Koehler, "Lanny Breuer and Foreign Corrupt Practices Act Enforcement."

49. Koehler, "Big, Bold, and Bizarre," p. 123.

50. Joe Palazzalo, "An FCPA Compliance Defense? No Way, Breuer Says," *Wall Street Journal*, April 1, 2011.

51. Westbrook, "Enthusiastic Enforcement, Informal Legislation," p. 497.

52. Koehler, "The Facade of FCPA Enforcement," p. 998.

53. U.S. Department of Justice, "Remarks by Lanny A. Breuer, Assistant Attorney General for the Criminal Division, at the American Bar Association National Institute on White Collar Crime," February 25, 2010, http://www.justice.gov/criminal/pr/speeches-testimony/2010/02-25-10aag-AmericanBarAssociation.pdf; Westbrook, "Enthusiastic Enforcement, Informal Legislation," pp. 530–31.

54. See Trautman and Altenbaumer-Price, "The Foreign Corrupt Practices Act: Minefield for Directors," p. 159; and Amy Deen Westbrook, "Double Trouble:

Collateral Shareholder Litigation Following Foreign Corrupt Practices Act Investigations," *Ohio State Law Journal* 73, no. 5 (2012): 1223.

55. Latham & Watkins LLP, "Understanding the FCPA Enforcement Trends in the Aerospace and Defense Industry: A Launch Pad to Effective Management of Anticorruption Risks," April 2013.

56. Tillipman, "A House of Cards Falls," p. 53.

57. Bruce Hinchey, "Punishing the Penitent: Disproportionate Fines in Recent FCPA Enforcements and Suggested Improvements," *Public Contract Law Journal* 40 (2011): 393, 54.

58. Mike Koehler, "Revisiting a Foreign Corrupt Practices Act Compliance Defense," *Wisconsin Law Review* 609 (2012): 646–47.

59. U.S. Department of Justice Criminal Division and Securities and U.S. Exchange Commission Enforcement Division, *A Resource Guide to the U.S. Foreign Corrupt Practices Act,* November 14, 2012, http://www.sec.gov/spotlight/fcpa/fcpa-resource-guide.pdf.

60. Turk, "A Political Economy Approach to Reforming the Foreign Corrupt Practices Act."

61. Covington & Burling LLP, "Steven E. Fagell," http://www.cov.com/sfagell.

62. Covington & Burling LLP, "White Collar Defense & Investigations: Anti-Corruption," http://www.cov.com/practice/white_collar_and_investigations/anti_corruption.

63. All from Koehler, "Big, Bold, and Bizarre," p. 126.

64. Nathan Vardi, "The Bribery Racket," *Forbes,* June 7, 2010.

65. See Thomas O. Gorman and William P. McGrath Jr., "The New Era of FCPA Enforcement: Moving Toward a New Era of Compliance," *Securities Regulation Law Journal* (Winter 2012): 342.

66. "Former Chief of DOJ Fraud Unit Discusses Healthcare and FCPA Enforcement," Metropolitan Corporate Counsel, October 2012.

67. Mike Koehler, "Foreign Corrupt Practices Act Enforcement as Seen Through Wal-Mart's Potential Exposure," *Bloomberg BNA White Collar Crime Report,* September 21, 2012, p. 7.

68. Black, "The SEC and the Foreign Corrupt Practices Act," p. 1111.

69. Opensecrets.org, "Oil & Gas: Long-Term Contribution Trends," http://www.opensecrets.org/industries/totals.php?cycle=2012&ind=E01.

70. Michael Gilbert and Joshua W. B. Richards, "The SEC's Investigation of the FCPA Violations and Sovereign Wealth Funds," *The Hedge Fund Law Report* (February 3, 2011); Association of Corporate Counsel, "Industry-wide Sweep Launched into Possible Violation of FCPA by U.S. Bank and Private Equity Firms," *Lexology* (January 26, 2011).

71. "Financiers Switch to GOP," *Wall Street Journal,* April 26, 2011.

72. Opensecrets.org, "Hedge Funds: Long-Term Contribution Trends," http://www.opensecrets.org/industries/totals.php?cycle=2012&ind=F2700.

73. Ashley Southall, "Obama Vows to Push Immigration Changes," *New York Times*, October 25, 2010.

74. Stephen Gandel, "Not Just Wal-Mart: Dozens of U.S. Companies Face Bribery Suspicions," CNNMoney, April 26, 2012, http://finance.fortune.cnn.com/2012/04/26/walmart-bribery-investigations.

75. Emily Jane Fox, "Adelson's Company 'Likely' Violated Bribery Law," CNNMoney, March 3, 2013, http://money.cnn.com/2013/03/03/news/companies/sands-casino-adelson-corruption/index.html.

76. Russ Choma, "Bentonville's Influence in Washington," Opensecrets.org, May 2, 2012, http://www.opensecrets.org/news/2012/05/bentonvilles-influence-in-washingto.html.

77. Walmart, "Jim C. Walton," http://corporate.walmart.com/our-story/leadership/board-of-directors/jim-walton.

78. Gandel, "Not Just Wal-Mart."

79. Clare O'Connor, "40 Behind-the-Scenes Billionaires Funding the 2012 Election," *Forbes*, March 22, 2012.

80. Sara Sun Beale, "Rethinking the Identity and Role of United States Attorneys," *Ohio State Journal of Criminal Law* 6 (2009): 371–372.

81. Silverglate, *Three Felonies a Day*, p. 267.

82. Ben Protess, "DealBook: Once More Through the Revolving Door for Justice's Breuer," *New York Times*, March 28, 2013 .

83. Covington & Burling LLP, "Lanny A. Breuer," http://www.cov.com/lbreuer.

84. "Lanny Breuer Back to Covington," *Corporate Crime Reporter*, March 28, 2013; Protess, "Once More Through the Revolving Door for Justice's Breuer"; and Koehler, "Lanny Breuer and Foreign Corrupt Practices Act Enforcement."

85. Turk, "A Political Economy Approach to Reforming the Foreign Corrupt Practices Act," p. 350.

86. Covington & Burling LLP, "International: Anti-Corruption," http://www.cov.com/practice/international/anti_corruption.

87. Paul Hastings, "Paul Hastings Adds Assistant Chief of Department of Justice's Foreign Corrupt Practices Act Unit in Washington, D.C.," March 11, 2013, http://www.paulhastings.com/news/details/?id=a7a72f26-8aa5-6986-8b86-ff-00008cffc3.

88. "Friday Roundup," FCPA Professor Blog, March 15, 2013, and "Former FCPA Prosecutor Heads to Paul Hastings," The BLT: The Blog of *Legal Times*, March 11, 2013.

9. IT'S A FAMILY AFFAIR

1. Mark Preston, "Reid to Enlist K Street," *Roll Call*, January 24, 2005.

2. Elsa Walsh, "Minority Retort: How a Pro-Gun, Anti-Abortion Nevadan Leads the Senate's Democrats," *The New Yorker*, August 8, 2005.

3. This account of Reid's early years is drawn from Harry Reid, *The Good Fight: Hard Lessons from Searchlight to Washington* (New York: Berkley Publishing Group, 2008).

4. Walsh, "Minority Retort."

5. Reid, *The Good Fight,* 271–72.

6. Ibid., pp. 247.

7. Ibid., pp. 257–63.

8. Ibid., pp. 260–62.

9. Walsh, "Minority Retort."

10. David McGrath Schwartz, "Harry Reid Talks Softly, but Carries a Big Stick," *Las Vegas Sun,* August 31, 2011.

11. Harry Reid, "If We Can Beat Mob, We Can Fight DeLay-Style Politics," *Houston Chronicle,* January 13, 2006.

12. Karoun Demirjian, "Top 10 Nevada Land Swaps Stalled in Congress," *Las Vegas Sun,* February 28, 2013.

13. Harry Reid, "The Changing Role of Government: A Federal Perspective," *GW Policy Perspectives,* May 13, 2013.

14. Chuck Neubauer and Richard T. Cooper, "Desert Connections," *Los Angeles Times,* August 20, 2006.

15. Chuck Neubauer and Richard T. Cooper, "The Senator's Sons; in Nevada, the Name to Know Is Reid," *Los Angeles Times,* June 23, 2003.

16. Ibid.

17. Josh Harkinson, "Gold Member," *Mother Jones* (March–April 2009).

18. MapLight, "U.S. Congress — Find Contributions: Legislator, Harry Reid; Contributor, Barrick; Election Cycle, 2002, 2004, 2006, 2008, 2010, 2012" (accessed April 29, 2013).

19. Schwartz, "Harry Reid Talks Softly, but Carries a Big Stick."

20. Ibid.

21. Alan Snel, "Arena Doomed Without NBA, Developer Says," *Las Vegas Review-Journal,* February 5, 2013; and Jon Ralston, "Lawyers Say Harry Reid's Son Used Majority Leader as Leverage to Settle Henderson Case," Ralstonflash.com, March 16, 2013. Ralston is a longtime newspaper reporter in Las Vegas.

22. Cited in Ira Stoll, "Brownstein, Hyatt's Stimulus Boast," FutureOfCapitalism.com, June 15, 2010, http://www.futureofcapitalism.com/2010/06/brownstein-hyatts-stimulus-boast.

23. Brownstein Hyatt Farber Schreck, "Josh M. Reid," http://web.archive.org/web/20110213081843/http://www.bhfs.com/People/jreid.

24. Jane Ann Morrison, "No Matter What He Does, Josh Reid Can't Shake Father's Shadow," *Las Vegas Review Journal,* December 1, 2011.

25. Michael Lyle, "Josh Reid Starts as Henderson's New City Attorney," *Las Vegas Review Journal,* January 3, 2012.

26. FindTheData, "Compare Individual Political Contributions," http://fec-individuals.findthedata.org/search/cmte_id/C00496893.

27. Opensecrets.org, "De-Ling Zhou," http://www.opensecrets.org/usearch/?q=De-Ling+Zhou&searchButt_clean.x=0&searchButt_clean.y=0&cx=01067790746295 5562473%3Anlldkv0jvam&cof=FORID%3All.

28. Marcus Stern, "U.S. Senator Reid, Son Combine for China Firm's Desert Plant," *Reuters*, August 31, 2012.

29. Ibid.

30. Federal Election Commission, "AO 2003-10 Solicitation of Nonfederal Funds by a Relative of a Federal Candidate" (FEC record), August 2003, p. 6.

31. Federal Election Commission (FEC), "Candidate and Committee Viewer: Friends of Harry Reid," http://www.fec.gov/fecviewer/CandidateCommitteeDetail.do.

32. Federal Election Commission (FEC), "Candidate and Committee Viewer: Reid Majority Fund," http://www.fec.gov/fecviewer/CandidateCommitteeDetail.do.

33. Federal Election Commission (FEC), "Candidate and Committee Viewer: Reid Victory Fund," http://www.fec.gov/fecviewer/CandidateCommitteeDetail.do.

34. Federal Election Commission (FEC), "Candidate and Committee Viewer: Searchlight Leadership Fund," http://www.fec.gov/fecviewer/CandidateCommitteeDetail.do.

35. Ibid.

36. Jon Ralston, "Rory Reid's Gubernatorial Campaign Circumvented Contribution Limits, Created 91 Shell PACs to Infuse $750,000 into Campaign," *Las Vegas Sun*, March 4, 2011.

37. Jon Ralston, "Rory Reid's House of Cards Crumbles," *Las Vegas Sun*, March 6, 2011.

38. Jon Ralston, "Who Funded Rory Reid's PAC—California Bigwig, Vegas Cab Magnate, Unions, Gamers," *Las Vegas Sun*, March 4, 2011.

39. FEC, "New Statement of Organization (Form 1) filers," http://www.fec.gov/press/press2011/new_form1dt.shtml.

40. Reid Searchlight Fund, "Statement of Organization," http://images.nictusa.com/pdf/918/13031051918/13031051918.pdf#navpanes=0.

41. Searchlight Lake Tahoe Victory Fund, "Statement of Organization," http://images.nictusa.com/pdf/708/13031060708/13031060708.pdf#navpanes=0.

42. See Chris Anderson's LinkedIn profile at: http://www.linkedin.com/pub/chris-anderson/1a/bb5/42a.

43. Roseann Moring, "Blunt Headed to the Senate," *Springfield News-Leader*, November 3, 2010.

44. Shailagh Murray and Thomas B. Edsall, "Pursuing a Fast Track to Party Leadership," *Washington Post*, October 1, 2005.

45. Thomas B. Edsall, "House Majority Whip Exerts Influence by Way of K Street," *Washington Post*, May 17, 2005.

46. "Four Million Reasons Why Roy Blunt Isn't the Consummate Washington Insider," FiredUpMissouri.com, http://www.firedupmissouri.com/content/four-million-reasons-why-roy-blunt-shouldnt-isnt-consummate-washington-insider.

47. John B. Judis, "Tom DeLay's Ties to Roy Blunt," *The New Republic,* October 27, 2005. The author has confirmed these cash movements on FEC records and financial disclosures.

48. Paul Sloca, "Youngest Blunt Makes Mark as Capitol Lobbyist," *Southeast Missourian,* March 10, 2003, http://m.semissourian.com/story/103696.html.

49. Sam Dealey, "Rep. Blunt's Son Aided by Donors from Out-of-State," *The Hill,* July 9, 2003.

50. Citizens for Responsibility and Ethics in Washington (CREW), "Beyond DeLay: The Twenty Most Corrupt Members of Congress (and Five to Watch)," http://www.citizensforethics.org/page/-/PDFs/Reports/CREW_Beyond_Delay_Report_20060920.pdf?nocdn=1.

51. Bill Bell Jr., "Parties in Missouri Use Loophole to Fill Pockets of Candidates," *St. Louis Post Dispatch,* August 21, 2000.

52. Associated Press, "Follow the Money: DeLay's Campaign Finances," Fox News, October 5, 2005, http://www.foxnews.com/story/0,2933,171368,00.html.

53. Sloca, "Youngest Blunt Makes Mark as Capitol Lobbyist."

54. Robert Kaiser, *So Damn Much Money: The Triumph of Lobbying and the Corrosion of American Government* (New York: Alfred A. Knopf, 2009).

55. Terry Ganey, "Brother's Lobbying Won't Sway Decisions, Blunt Says," *St. Louis Post Dispatch,* November 24, 2004.

56. Jim Snyder, "Former Missouri Gov. Matt Blunt Joins Cassidy," *The Hill,* February 3, 2009.

57. Opensecrets.org, "Blunt, Abigail P.," http://www.opensecrets.org/lobby/lobbyist.php?id=Y0000031637L&year=2003.

58. David D. Kirkpatrick, "Post Comes with Renewed Scrutiny of Record," *New York Times,* September 30, 2005; "Family Traditions," *St. Louis Post Dispatch,* April 27, 2005.

59. Citizens for Responsibility and Ethics in Washington (CREW), "CREW Reveals Newest Majority Leader — Rep. Blunt — One of the Most Unethical Members of Congress," September 29, 2005, http://www.citizensforethics.org/index.php/press/entry/crew-reveals-new-majority-leader-one-of-the-most-unethical-representatives.

60. John Gizzi, "Politics 2003: Week of January 27," Human Events, January 27, 2003, http://www.humanevents.com/2003/01/27/politics-2003brweek-of-january-27.

61. Associated Press, "Blunt Says Lobbyist Brother Won't Try to Influence Executive Branch," *Southeast Missourian,* November 25, 2004, http://www.semissourian.com/story/151016.html.

62. Christopher Tritto, "Blunt Force: Capitol Connections Fuel GOP Dynasty," *St. Louis Business Journal,* January 30, 2006.

63. Ibid.

64. Kit Wagar, "Missouri OKs Law That Thwarts Discount Brokers," *Kansas City Star*, July 24, 2005.

65. David Martin, "Laundry Rooms," *Kansas City Pitch*, February 16, 2006, http://www.pitch.com/kansascity/laundry-rooms/Content?oid=2181024.

66. Ibid.

67. Associated Press, "Blunt's Brother Involved in Ethanol Business Plan," KWMU, June 5, 2006; David A. Lieb, "Mo. Treasurer: Conflicts Bar Aid for Ethanol Plant," *USA Today*, September 25, 2008; and National Institute on Money in State Politics, "Blunt, Andrew B.," http://www.followthemoney.org/database/lobbyist. phtml?l=27667.

68. David A. Lieb (Associated Press), "Documents Reveal Missouri License Records Fee Increase Set to Pay for Computer System," *Southeast Missourian*, May 22, 2008, http://www.semissourian.com/story/1406919.html.

69. Associated Press, "Lawmakers Balk at Driver's License Records Fee Increase," *Southeast Missourian*, May 7, 2008, http://www.semissourian.com/story/1400583. html.

70. Missouri Ethics Commission, "Lobbyist Search: Reichard; Year, 2007," http://www.moethics.mo.gov/EthicsWeb/Lobbying/Lob_SearchLob.aspx; Tritto, "Blunt Force."

71. National Institute on Money in State Politics, "Blunt, Andrew B."

72. Missouri Governor's Office, "Blunt Announces New Resource to Help Missourians Find the Lowest Price for Their Prescription Medicine," January 10, 2007, http://web.archive.org/web/20070208102909/http://www.gov.mo.gov/press/ DSSPricePosting011007.htm.

73. Keegan Hamilton, "Libertarians Shun Chief Wana Dubie," *Riverfront Times*, January 30, 2008.

74. Glen Justice, "For Lobbyist, a Seat of Power Came with a Plate," *New York Times*, July 6, 2005.

75. James Ridgeway, "Sticky Fingers," *Village Voice*, January 18, 2006.

76. John H. Fund, "Blunt Instruments," *American Spectator*, March 2006.

77. Mary Curtius and Richard Simon, "Not the Majority Leader They Expected," *Los Angeles Times*, February 3, 2006.

78. Bill Lambrecht, "Carnahan Barely Bests Blunt in Fundraising for Missouri Senate Race," *St. Louis Post Dispatch*, April 26, 2010.

79. Cassidy & Associates, "Andy Blunt," http://www.cassidy.com/team/77.

80. Opensecrets.org, "Expenditures: Representative Roy Blunt, 2009–2010," http://www.opensecrets.org/politicians/expend.php?cycle=2010&cid=N00005195& type=I.

81. National Institute on Money in State Politics, "Blunt, Andrew B."

82. Jake Wagman, "Former Governor Blunt to Head Auto Lobbying Group," *Political*

Fix, February 2, 2011; "Standing Committees of the 112th Senate" (Washington, D.C.: U.S. Government Printing Office), p. 343.

83. Dan Margolies, "Hiring of Amy Blunt Adds to Law Firm's Clout," *Kansas City Star*, August 15, 2006.

84. Ibid.

85. Carl Hulse and Philip Shenon, "DeLay Denounces Report on Payments to His Family," *New York Times*, April 7, 2005.

10. CONCLUSION: PROTECTION FOR THE REST OF US

1. Jonathan Martin and Carrie Budoff Brown, "Feds: Blagojevich 'Has Taken Us to a Truly New Low,'" *Politico*, December 9, 2008.

2. Bob Secter and Jeff Coen, "Jesse Jackson Jr. Knew of $1 Million Offer for Senate Seat, Prosecutors Say," *Chicago Tribune*, July 7, 2010.

3. Thomas G. Donlan, "Business as Usual," *Barron's*, December 15, 2008.

4. Sarah Ostman, "Blagojevich Speaks on Possible Gag Order, Patti's Hair," *Chicago Sun-Times*, June 21, 2010.

5. John Kass, "Blagojevich Fishes for Excuse, Hooks a Keeper," *Chicago Tribune*, March 18, 2002.

6. J. Gregory Sidak, "Review Essay: The Petty Larceny of the Police Power," *California Law Review* 86 (1998): 663.

7. Donlan, "Business as Usual."

8. Sheryl Gay Stolberg, "Lobbying Bill Passes Narrowly in the House," *New York Times*, May 4, 2006.

9. Quoted in Currinder, *Money in the House*, p. 286.

10. Wendy Kaminer, "To Democrats, Free Speech Makes a Racket," *Wall Street Journal*, May 9, 2000.

11. Quoted in Jessica A. Levinson, "Timing Is Everything: A New Model for Countering Corruption Without Silencing Speech in Elections," *St. Louis University Law Journal* 55 (2011): 853.

12. *Buckley v. Valeo*, 424 U.S. 1, 30.

13. The Rules of the Florida House of Representatives, August 9, 2011.

14. Kate Ackley, "Maxing Out? A Five-Day-a-Week Congress May Mean a Full Calendar of Fundraisers," *Roll Call*, January 8, 2007.

15. Quoted in Currinder, *Money in the House*, p. 286.

16. Jessica A. Levinson, "Timing Is Everything: A New Model for Countering Corruption Without Silencing Speech in Elections," *St. Louis University Law Journal* 55 (2011): 853–85, 874, http://slu.edu/Documents/law/Law%20Journal/Archives/Levinson_Article.pdf.

17. Ibid., p. 880.

18. Quoted in Marian Currinder, *Money in the House*, p. 296.

19. Quoted in ibid., p. 252.
20. Brian Baird, "We Need to Read the Bills," *Washington Post,* November 26, 2004.
21. Ian Talley, "Need for Speed (Read) to Pass Climate Bill," *Wall Street Journal,* May 20, 2009.
22. Pete Kasperowicz, "Rand Paul Puts Forward Measure That Would Force the Senate to Read Bills," *The Hill,* July 2, 2012.

APPENDIX 1

1. Data was obtained from NRCC office in March of 2013. List does not include information for the following members: Dana Rohrbach, Don Young, Jim Sensenbrenner, Jeff Fortenberry, Jim Bridenstine, Justin Amash, Mark Sanford, Marlin Stutzman, Paul Broun, Raul Labrador, Rodney Alexander, Shelley Capito, Steve Stockman, Steven Palazzo, Tim Huelskamp, Tom Graves, and Walter Jones.
2. Data was obtained from DCCC office in 2013.

APPENDIX 2

1. Source: http://www.opensecrets.org/pacs/industry.php?txt=Q03&cycle=2012&view=R

INDEX

ACKNOWLEDGMENTS

This book would not have happened without the dedicated work of Rick White, David Healy, Jr., Sally Jo Roorda, Seamus Bruner, and Wynton Hall. My sincere thanks also goes to Stuart Christmas, Michelle Chandler, Eric Eggers, Peggy Sukhia, Jay Woodham, Tony Mock, Brian Baugus, Bryan Trochessett, Jerome Hudson, Zach Huffman, Mary Francis Dunlap, Blaine Cherry, Joshua Eller, and Sandy Schulz. Thanks also to the board of the Government Accountability Institute who made this possible: Chairman Stephen K. Bannon, Vice Chairman Rebekah Mercer, Ron Robinson, Owen Smith, and Hunter Lewis. Thanks, too, to John Raisian of the Hoover Institution for his friendship and support.

Bruce Nichols of Houghton is not only a superb editor but also a man of keen insight and wisdom. Thanks, Bruce, for another great ride together. And my agent, Glen Hartley, never ceases to amaze me in his ability to keep a project focused. The same goes for Lynn Chu.

A special appreciation goes to my children, Jack and Hannah, who have inspired me with their grace and character during difficult times. I love you both very much.

The author alone is the responsible for the contents of this book.